Church of England, Book of Common Prayer

The Latin Prayer Book of Charles II

an account of the Liturgia of Dean Durel, together with a reprint and translation of

the catechism therein contained, with collations, annotations and appendices

Church of England, Book of Common Prayer

The Latin Prayer Book of Charles II
an account of the Liturgia of Dean Durel, together with a reprint and translation of the catechism therein contained, with collations, annotations and appendices

ISBN/EAN: 9783337186555

Printed in Europe, USA, Canada, Australia, Japan

Cover: Foto ©Lupo / pixelio.de

More available books at **www.hansebooks.com**

THE LATIN PRAYER BOOK OF CHARLES II;

OR,

An Account of the Liturgia of Dean Durel,

TOGETHER WITH A

REPRINT AND TRANSLATION

OF THE

CATECHISM

THEREIN CONTAINED, WITH COLLATIONS, ANNOTATIONS, AND APPENDICES.

BY

CHARLES MARSHALL, M.A.,
Chaplain to the Lord Mayor of London, 1849-50;

AND

WILLIAM W. MARSHALL, B.A.,
Late Scholar of Hertford College, Oxford; and of the Inner Temple.

Oxford:
JAMES THORNTON, HIGH STREET.
—
1882.

PUBLISHED BY
JAMES THORNTON, OXFORD.

LONDON: *SIMPKIN, MARSHALL, AND CO.*

TO THE

Very Reverend Arthur Penrhyn Stanley, D.D.,

DEAN OF WESTMINSTER;

DEAN OF THE ORDER OF THE BATH; DEPUTY CLERK OF THE
QUEEN'S CLOSET, CHAPEL ROYAL, ST. JAMES'S; HONORARY CHAPLAIN IN
ORDINARY TO HER MAJESTY THE QUEEN; CHAPLAIN TO
H.R.H. THE PRINCE OF WALES, ETC., ETC.

IN humbly presenting this work to your hands, allow us to explain that the origin of our selection, for its dedication, of one occupying so notable a position in the Church of England as yourself is in the interesting historical fact, that the Convocation of Canterbury committed to two of your illustrious predecessors in the Deanery of Westminster, Bishop Earle and Archbishop Dolben (with others), the translation of the Revised Liturgy of 1661 into the Latin language. Moreover our choice is confirmed by public repute to the effect that than yourself no one more intelligently appreciates the excellency and the reasonableness of the Christian Religion considered in itself, and in its Divine design for the great purposes of bringing men off from the love of sin to the love of God; no one more highly values the Protestant principles, viz., that in investigating the Christian Religion the judgment of sense and reason is not to be renounced, and that men are not equally bound to believe the greatest repugnances to sense and reason with the most Fundamental Verities of the Christian Faith; and no one is more deeply sensible of the disastrous consequences of marring the beauty of the most excellent religion in the world by sacerdotal errors and superstitions; these consequences being the discouragement of the faith of those who honour the Christian Religion in its primitive purity and apostolical simplicity, and the hindrance of those, who are offended by a corrupted Christianity, from belief in any Religion. May the various talents with which God has entrusted you be long employed in defence and furtherance of pure and undefiled Religion.

Your faithful servants,
CHAS. MARSHALL, M.A.
WM. W. MARSHALL, B.A.

[*Since our work was first placed in the Publisher's hands, the Dean has passed to his rest. But in remembrance of his kind acceptance of this Dedication, expressed in a letter of Feb. 18th of this year (1881), we feel unable to change or withdraw it. We therefore leave the Dedication in its original form, merely adding this note to account for its appearance, and to signify our deep regret at his lamented death.*]

PREFACE.

"PREFACES, and passages, and excusations, and other speeches of reference to the person," writes Bacon, "are great wastes of time; and though they seem to proceed of modesty, they are bravery." We shall endeavour therefore to set forth the purpose and scope of our work in the briefest language.

We have been led to the present undertaking by a desire to attract more attention to the Latin Prayer Book of 1670, and we desired this for two reasons. Firstly, on account of the remarkable scarcity of the Book itself; even in many notable Libraries, including those of Trinity Coll., Camb., of Westminster Abbey, of Exeter, Ely, Carlisle, Bangor, and other cathedrals, of Chetham College, Manchester, and of Althorpe House, etc., we are informed that no copy is to be found. Secondly, because Durel's *Liturgia* shows what the Revisers understood to be meant by the words which they retained and the words which they inserted; it shows the thought of the time as expressed by a contemporary and an authorized exponent.

Our work will, we anticipate, be accepted by Evangelicals at large, on account of the Protestantism of Durel's Translation and its accordance with the theological opinions of the English Reformers and of the leading English divines for nearly a century after the

Reformation, and with the universally received divinity of Churchmen throughout the reigns of Elizabeth and James; and because Dean Durel simply trod "the old paths" in which the Reformers and their immediate successors walked.

Nor, we trust, will this volume prove unacceptable to the searcher after truth in the ranks of the High Church party. For Durel was a Caroline Divine, and Dr. Pusey, the confessed champion of conservative Catholicity, has stated that the times of the Caroline divines form the "golden period of English Theology."

In the notes on the Catechism, no pains have been spared to make the quotations accurate and precise, in order that they may prove of service for purposes both of study and reference. They contain all the Catechism of Queen Elizabeth's Latin Version, with the chief differences of the translator's predecessor Aless, and of his successor Whitaker; all the Catechism of Vautrollier, as the representative of the three unauthorized Elizabethan Prayer Books; practically (except one passage) all the Small Catechism of Dean Nowell, which is especially important as the immediate forerunner of that of 1604; together with frequent quotations from Nowell's Large and Middle Catechisms, and from the Welsh Prayer Book of 1664, the Greek Prayer Books of Whitaker, Petley, and Duport, the Latin versions of Parsell and of Harwood, and the modern Latin Prayer Books of Parker, Bagster, and Messrs. Bright and Medd.

The translation of the Catechism purports to be as literal as the English will admit, and all words not represented in the original are in brackets, with the exception of the indefinite article. In scriptural quotations the forms "thou," "thee," and "thy" are retained; elsewhere the words "you" and "your" are substituted, as more in accordance with modern usage. In the Catechism of our English Prayer Book the two are confused.

In conclusion, we must express our great obligations to the Rev. Sydney Thelwall, B.A., Vicar of West Leigh, whose assistance has been of the highest value in the preparation of our notes, and especially with regard to the collation of Duport and of Bagster; to the Rev. J. Harrison, D.D., Vicar of Fenwick, who has given us permission to use a portion of one of his very important works; to the Rev. Dr. Osborn, President of the Wesleyan Conference, who has given us valuable information in reference to the Letters of Orders of John Wesley; to the Rev. R. K. Bateson, B.D., Queen's Coll., Camb., in whose Library is a copy of Durel's *Liturgia* dated 1685, to which we have had access; to the Rev. J. O. Brook, Incumbent of Worthington, who lent us a copy of the same date; to the Rev. H. Parry, B.A., Vicar of Llanvair-is-gaer, Diocesan Inspector of Schools, the Rev. W. Glanffryd Thomas, Vicar Choral of St. Asaph's Cathedral, the Rev. J. Pryce, M.A., Rector of Trefdraeth, and the Rev. T. J. Jones, B.A., Vicar of Llanvair Caereinion, who have given us much information about Welsh Prayer Books and other matters connected with the Principality; and to all others who have aided us with their knowledge, judgment, or research.

Should our work tend in some small degree to the solution of the question propounded long ago by Pilate—*What is truth?*—we shall rest content; for our labour will not have been in vain.

CONTENTS.

PART I.

HISTORICAL.

CHAPTER I.

	PAGE
LIFE OF DEAN DUREL	1

CHAPTER II.

HISTORY OF THE LATIN TRANSLATION OF THE REVISED PRAYER BOOK 11

CHAPTER III.

AUTHORITY OF DEAN DUREL'S LATIN PRAYER BOOK 21

    APPENDIX A.—AN ACCOUNT OF DUREL'S ORDINATION ... 29

    APPENDIX B.—ON THE AUTHORIZED VERSION OF THE BIBLE 29

PART II.

CRITICAL AND EXEGETICAL.

CHAPTER I.

EDITIONS OF THE "LITURGIA" AND OTHER VERSIONS ... 33

CHAPTER II.

MEANING OF THE TERM "PRIEST" 46

CHAPTER III.

	PAGE
MEANING OF THE EXPRESSION "ALMS AND OBLATIONS"	61
APPENDIX C.—COPY OF A BRIEF	81
ADDENDA	81

PART III.

THE CATECHISM.

REPRINT, TRANSLATION, AND ANNOTATIONS	85
APPENDIX D.—ARCHBISHOP LEIGHTON'S CATECHISM	189
APPENDIX E.—ON DR. OVERALL'S OPINION OF THE LORD'S SUPPER	190
APPENDIX F.—ON AUGUSTINE'S USE OF THE WORD "SACRAMENT"	193
APPENDIX G.—ANALYTICAL TABLE OF THE SACRAMENTS	194
APPENDIX H.—ON THE USE OF THE ADVERB "GENERALLY" AND COGNATE WORDS	195
APPENDIX I.—ON "GENERALLY NECESSARY"	197

INDEX	199
VOCABULA	204

PART I.
HISTORICAL.

CHAPTER I.

LIFE OF DEAN DUREL.

"The love which a king oweth to a weal public should not be restrained to any one particular; yet that his more special favour do reflect upon some worthy ones is somewhat necessary, because there are few of that capacity."—BACON.

JOHN DUREL, the future translator of the Prayer Book, was born at St. Helier in Jersey. He entered Merton College, Oxford, in 1640, at the age of fifteen, and resided in St. Alban's Hall adjoining. In 1642, when Oxford was garrisoned for the king, he retired to France, and two years later took his degree of Master of Arts in the Sylvanian College at Caen in Normandy; subsequently he studied theology at Saumur under Moses Amyraldus. Having returned to his native place, he was expelled thence together with his countryman, M. le Couteur. He then proceeded to Paris, where he received episcopal ordination, about the year 1651, from the Bishop of Galloway, in the chapel of Sir Richard Browne, his majesty's resident in France.[1] Soon after this he resided at St. Malo and received two invitations, neither of which he was able to accept. The first was from the members of the Reformed Church at Caen, who wished him to become one of their ministers; the second from the landgrave of Hesse, who, on the recommendation of the ministers of Paris, asked him in kindly terms to proceed to his highness's court,

Life of Durel.

Residence in France.

Ordination at Paris.

---

[1] See Appendix A for an account of this ordination.

and preach there in the French language. He became, however, chaplain to the Duke de la Force, father of the Princess of Turein.

We next hear of Durel in connection with the French Chapel of the Savoy. A brief account of the origin of that chapel is necessary to estimate the importance of his connection with it. About the year 1642, the Duke of Soubize finding it troublesome, through his infirmities, to go to the Walloon Church in the city from his residence, which was near the court at Whitehall, had a French sermon preached before him in his house every Sunday. This proved so convenient for the French residing in that neighbourhood that at his death a French church was set up near the Strand. The city church felt much aggrieved at this, and upon the king's restoration addressed to him a petition that the French congregation at Westminster might be forbidden to assemble. The latter presented a petition on their part to the contrary effect. In reply to these memorials, the king broke up the congregation at Westminster, but set up a new church under the immediate jurisdiction of the Bishop of London, "wherein divine service should be performed in French according to the book of common prayer by law established, his majesty providing one minister," etc. "By virtue of the said grant the liturgy of the church of England was first read in French in the Fr. ch. at Westm. assembled by the king's special favour in the chappel of the Savoy in the Strand, on Sunday 14 July 1661, and the same day in the morning our author Durel (who had the chief hand in setting up this church according to this new model) did preach, and in the afternoon Le Couteur, then dean of Jersey."[1] In the following year, 1662, Durel's French translation of the Prayer Book, of which we shall have occasion to speak more fully hereafter, received the sanction of a royal ordinance.

The Savoy Chapel.

Established by the king.

Durel appointed to preach.

His French Prayer Book.

The next year saw the commencement of a series of promotions

[1] See Wood's "Athenæ Oxonienses" (edited by Bliss), vol. iv. col. 28. London, 1820.

and honours which were showered with no sparing hand upon Durel. He was by this time chaplain in ordinary to Charles the Second, and was appointed prebendary of North Aulton in the church of Salisbury. In the February following (1664) he was made prebendary of Windsor, and also about that time of Durham, and had a rich donative conferred upon him. At the close of 1669 he was made Doctor of Divinity, as a member of Merton College, "by virtue of the chancellor's letters read in a full convocation." It is interesting to note the high opinion entertained with regard to him by the chancellor. We are informed, says Wood, that "his fame was so well known to them (the academians) especially for the great pains he had taken in the church, that he could hardly propose any thing to them in his behalf, in which they would not be willing to prevent[1] him;" and further, "of his parts and learning they were better judges than himself, but had not so much experience of his loyalty, fidelity and service to his majesty as himself," etc. In 1677 he was, by royal authority, made Dean of Windsor and of Wolverhampton, and was also presented to the valuable living of Witney, partly through the influence of the king. On the ninth of November in the same year, as we find in the Ashmolean MSS., Dr. Durel was sworn Registrar of the Garter. He died on the 8th of June, 1683. Had he lived, Wood thinks he would certainly have been promoted to a bishopric.

Durel, chaplain to Charles II.

Prebendary of Salisbury, Windsor, and Durham.

Degree of D.D.

Chancellor's letter.

Dean of Windsor.

Benefice, Witney.

Registrar of Garter.

In religious principles Durel was what is called a "good Churchman," with hardly more sympathy for Dissent than for Papacy. On the one hand we have the testimony (quoted by Wood) of Father Simon, priest of the congregation of the oratory, who calls him "a learned English Protestant," and his works amply prove his claim to that title. On the other, he

His religious views.

---

[1] For this use of the word "prevent" (prae-venio, "to go before," "anticipate"), cf. "Prevent us, O Lord, in all our doings, with thy most gracious favour," in the Communion Service.

HISTORICAL.

was in no way a Puritan in his views. With reference to Charles II., Mr. Green writes in his "History of the English People:" "In heart, whether the story of his renunciation of Protestantism during his exile be true or no, he had long ceased to be a Protestant. Whatever religious feeling he had was on the side of Catholicism; he encouraged conversions among his courtiers, and the last act of his life was to seek formal admission into the Roman Church."[1] If this be so, Charles II. would not be the prince to have a Puritan for his chaplain and trusted favourite. Nor would a reputed Puritan be receiving an important commission, like that for the translation of the Liturgy into French, only two months after that memorable St. Bartholomew's Day, when "nearly two thousand rectors and vicars, or about a fifth of the English clergy, were driven from their parishes as Nonconformists."[2] We see from this that he was what in those days was considered a High Churchman. If more evidence in support of this is needed, we have the testimony of his sermon, "The Liturgy of the Church of England asserted" (1661–2), which was preached in French on the 14th of July, 1661, the occasion of the opening of the Savoy chapel, and in which he vindicates many things in the newly revised liturgy which had been censured by the Nonconformists; and again of his more elaborate work, "Sanctæ Ecclesiæ Anglicanæ adversus iniquas atque inverecundas Schismaticorum Criminationes Vindiciæ," etc. (London, 1669), the reply to which was entitled, in the reprint of 1676, "The Nonconformists vindicated from the abuses put upon them by Mr. Durel and Mr. Scrivner." He is described by Wood as "the judicious and laborious advocate for the Church of England both in word and deed:"[3] and we must remember that Wood's testimony is that of a cotemporary. "He was," says the same authority, "a person of unbyassed and fixed principles, untainted and steady loyalty, as constantly adhering to the sinking

Protestant, but not Puritan.

No sympathy with Dissent.

Wood's opinion.

---

[1] "History of the English People." By John Richard Green, M.A., Honorary Fellow of Jesus' College, Oxford. Vol. iii. p. 344. London, 1879.
[2] Ibid. p. 361. [3] "Fasti," vol. ii. col. 317. Ed. 1820.

cause and interest of his sovereign in the worst of times; who dar'd with an unshaken and undaunted resolution to stand up and maintain the honour and dignity of the English church, when she was in her lowest and deplorable condition. He was very well vers'd also in all the controversies on foot between the church and the disciplinarian party; the justness and reasonableness of the established constitution of the former, no one of late years hath more plainly manifested, or with greater learning more successfully defended against its most zealous modern oppugners than he hath done, as by his works following is manifest."[1]

Such was the character of the man wisely selected by the reigning monarch for the task of the necessary translations into French and Latin of the newly revised Prayer Book. Probably no better instrument for the work could have been found. We have seen that he was a staunch and thorough Churchman, of unbiassed principles and steady loyalty, and a sound scholar, especially in the matter of theological controversy.

The French translation was the first published. Probably the necessity for it was the more urgent. There were in the realm certain churches connected with the Establishment using the French language, as in the Savoy, and in the islands of Jersey and Guernsey. For these, of course, a French Prayer Book was absolutely necessary. We have seen, for example, that the liturgy of the Church of England was read in French in the new Savoy chapel in July, 1661. This was the year before the final revision of the English Prayer Book, after the completion of which in 1662 Durel's French version immediately appeared. It was directly sanctioned by a royal ordinance. Charles R. commands that this version, so soon as printed with the approbation of one of the chaplains of the Bishop of London, be adopted in all churches and chapels of the realm using the French language, and conforming to the Church of England; and forbids the use of any other besides. This order was given at White-

Durel's French Prayer Book.

Its authority.

---

[1] "Athenæ," vol. iv. col. 89. Lond. 1820.

hall, the 6th of October, 1662. The necessary testimonial from the Bishop's chaplain is appended in Latin on the same page: "I have perused this French Version of the English Liturgy by Mr. John Durel, and certify that I have found it in accordance with the English Original throughout. Geor. Stradling, S.T.P. domestic Chaplain to the Reverend Father in Christ Gilbert[1] Bishop of London."

Its Title. This is dated April the 6th, 1663. The title of the book is "LA LITURGIE. *C'est à dire,* Le formulaire des Prieres Publiques, de l'Administration des Sacremens, *Et des autres* CEREMONIES & *Coûtumes de l'Eglise, selon l'usage de l'Eglise* Anglicane: AVEC LE PSEAUTIER, ou les Pseaumes de David, *Pontuez selon qu'ils doivent estre, ou chantez, ou leus dans les* EGLISES.[2]

There are two things which remain to be noticed with regard to this French Prayer Book. First, the fact that the signature of this same George Stradling, "Cleri Dioeces. Landavensis Procurator," occurs among the names of those who attested the unanimous consent of the Lower House of Convocation to the alterations in the English Prayer Book. Secondly, the dates are important: *Date of first use.* the revised English Prayer Book was approved by the king in council on February the 24th, 1662. The king's mandate for the French version was given on October the 6th of the same year, and the book began actually to be used in the Savoy chapel before the close of the year. The shortness of the time intervening between the publication of these two versions might alone lead us to expect that Durel was not able to devote that care and study to his French translation which he did give to his later Latin version, and would doubtless cheerfully have bestowed upon the French Liturgy also, if the urgency of the case had not demanded an extreme rapidity of execution. This expectation is unfortunately somewhat justified. In parts the new version is careful and exact, but in other parts it is hardly more than a reprint of a former version, entitled

---

[1] See Appendix D.
[2] The imprint of the copy in the Bodleian Library which we have inspected is, "A LONDRES Pour *Robert Scott,* & se vend chez *Geo. Wells & Sam. Carr* dans le Cymitiere de St. *Paul* 1678."

"LA LITURGIE ANGLOISE. OU LE LIVRE DES PRIERES PUBLIQUES, de l'Administration des Sacremens, & autres Ordres & Ceremonies de l'Eglise d'Angleterre. Nouvellement traduit en François par l'Ordonnance de sa Majesté de la Grande Bretaigne."[1] This retention of the words of the earlier version we regard as very unfortunate, insomuch as such portions of the book cannot furnish us with so conclusive a proof of the views held at the time of the last revision of the English Book as we should have derived from an entirely new translation. An example of the mistakes which may result from taking previously existing materials is given by Mr. Clay ("*Liturg. Services of Q. Elizabeth.*" Parker Society. 1847. Pref. xxxii.), who shows how the misprint of "postridie" for "pridie," "ouer night," in the Second Rubric before the Communion of the Sick, originated in Aless's version of 1551, and was perpetuated by Haddon and his followers throughout the reign of Elizabeth.

Earlier version, partly copied by Durel.

By the "Act for the Uniformity of Publick Prayers," etc., 14 Carol. II., two other translations of the Prayer Book were required, one into the Welsh, the other into the Latin tongue. We are tempted to digress here from the main thread of our subject to consider for a moment the former of these versions. We do so for two reasons. In the first place, because it gives an instance of the care of Charles II. for the welfare of all his subjects; and affords a proof of a praiseworthy desire on the monarch's part to perpetuate, by a provision for its liturgy, the ancient Cymric tongue, which has well been termed the only living link uniting Cæsar and Agricola with ourselves: just as further on in the Act an English Prayer Book is ordered also to be placed in the churches for the promotion of the knowledge of the English language, which would tend to increase the external intercourse, commerce, and prosperity

Welsh and Latin Prayer Books required by Act of Uniformity.

The Welsh Prayer Book.

---

[1] The imprint of the copy in the Bodleian Library which we have inspected is, "A LONDRES, *par* IEHAN BILL, Imprimeur du Roy. M.DC.XVI. Avec privilege de sa Majesté." In the above transcript "u" and "v" have occasionally been changed, as "Nouvellement" for "Nouuellement."

of the Principality. And secondly, because we shall have occasion to refer to the Welsh version in our notes on the Catechism and elsewhere, and shall, we fear, be compelled to point out that such care was not always taken by its authors as we might have desired and expected; in fact, they compiled largely from the book in use before the revision, and did not translate "truly and exactly" from the Revised English Prayer Book, as the Act of Uniformity ordered them to do; nor can we plead for them shortness of time and pressing necessity, as we did in the case of Durel's French Prayer Book, for the Act gave them three years for the completion of their task.

In 1546 William Salesbury published the first Welsh Book ever printed: it contained the Alphabet, Calendar, Creed, Lord's Prayer, and Ten Commandments. In 1551 he followed it up with the translation of the Epistles and Gospels for the year, and in 1567 a joint translation of the Prayer Book was issued by William Salesbury and Bishop Richard Davies at their own expense. This was in the same year in which their translation of the New Testament was published. It is said that Queen Elizabeth gave William Salesbury a patent for seven years for printing in Welsh the Bible, Common Prayer, and Administration of the Sacraments. There is, however, no authority in the Act of Uniformity of 1 Eliz. for a Welsh translation of the Prayer Book, though it is ordered that the Book of Common Prayer shall be used by "all, and singular ministers in any Cathedral, or Parish-Church, or other place within the Realm of *England*, *Wales*, and the Marches of the same, or other of the Queens dominions,"[1] etc.

<small>History of it.</small>

In the Act of Uniformity of Charles II., however, due provision for such a translation is made; the clause referring to it runs as follows:—"Provided always, and be it Enacted by the Authority aforesaid, That the Bishops of *Hereford, Saint Davids, Asaph, Bangor,* and *Landaff* and their Successours shall take such order among themselves, for the

<small>14 Car. II. Provision for Welsh Prayer Book.</small>

[1] See next note.

souls health, of the Flocks committed to their Charge within *Wales*, That the Book hereunto annexed be truly and exactly Translated into the *Brittish* or *Welsh* tongue, and that the same so Translated and being by them, or any three of them at the least viewed, perused, and allowed, be Imprinted to such number at least, so that one of the said Books so translated and Imprinted, may be had for every Cathedral, Collegiate, and Parish-Church, and Chappel of Ease in the said respective Dioceses and places in *Wales*, where the *Welsh* is commonly spoken or used before the first day of *May*, One thousand six hundred sixty-five ; " [1] etc.

This Act also, as we have said, necessitated the preparation of a new Latin version. The clause referring to the use of the Latin Prayer Book runs as follows : " Provided always, That it shall and may be lawfull to use the Morning and Evening Prayer, and all other Prayers and Service pre- scribed in and by the said Book, in the Chappels or other Publick places of the respective Colledges and Halls in both the Universities, in the Colledges of *Westminster*, *Winchester*, and *Eaton*, and in the Convocations of the Clergies of either Province in Latine ; Any thing in this Act contained to the contrary notwith- standing." *(Latin translation required by 14 Car. II.)*

This Latin version Dr. Durel published in 1670. In succeeding chapters we shall have to speak more fully of the circumstances attending its preparation and publication, of its character and value, and of the impress of authority which it bears. We shall see the labour and the length of time devoted to the work, and the assist- ance Durel enjoyed from other learned and prominent men of his day. We shall see that, as a result of this, his Latin version differs some- what from his French translation in being deliberate and mature, and expresses in careful and studied language the opinions of himself and his colleagues, or rather, we should say, the opinions of the Established Church of his day. In short, we shall find that, as Mr.

---

[1] These quotations from the Acts of Uniformity are taken from the Book of Common Prayer, " Printed by John Field, Printer to the University of Cambridge, 1662." The copy inspected is at the Bodleian Library.

Blunt remarks, "Dean Durel's Latin Version is a most excellent one, whether it is viewed as to scholarship, theology or loyalty to the Church of England."[1]

[1] "The Annotated Book of Common Prayer," p. 586. App. IV. Rev. J. S. Blunt, M.A., F.S.A. Rivingtons, 1866.

CHAPTER II.

HISTORY OF THE LATIN TRANSLATION OF THE REVISED PRAYER BOOK.

"The genuine sense, intelligibly told,
Shows a translator both discreet and bold."—ROSCOMMON.

IN his first edition of 1670 Dr. Durel calls himself the "Editor" not the Translator of the Latin Prayer Book. The chief reason for his adoption of this title appears to be that the translation was not originally committed to his care, but that he was appointed to carry on and complete the work of previous translators, who for various causes had been compelled to relinquish the task. In the account in Latin of the Sessions of Convocation we find as follows:—"Session LXXX Saturday April 26, between the hours of 8. and 10. in the forenoon of the same day, etc. And a debate having been held and made among them concerning a translation of the book of public prayers into the Latin tongue, the lord bishop of London,[1] etc. from and with the consent of his brethren, etc. committed the care of the same translation to the reverends John Earle Dean of the Blessed Peter Westm' and John Peirson professors respectively of sacred theology. And this having been done and said the lord, etc. continued, etc. according to the schedule, etc.[2]"

[margin: Dean Durel the Editor. Appointment by Convocation of Earle and Peirson for preparing Latin Version.]

This was in 1662, two months after the approval of the English Book by the king in council, and sixteen days after the Act of Uniformity, which necessitated a Latin translation, had passed the House of Lords. We see, therefore that Convocation lost no time

---
[1] This was Gilbert Sheldon, who was raised to the Primacy in the next year. See App. D.
[2] See Cardwell's Synod. ii. 671.

in preparing to carry out the requirements of the Bill, but provided for compliance with its provisions while it was still only in progress.

Of John Earle, Durel's predecessor in the chaplaincy to the king, we shall have occasion to speak hereafter; but as Peirson soon retired from the work of translation it will be more convenient to review his life in this place. John Peirson (or Pearson),

John Peirson. then, was born at Snoring about the year 1612. He was educated at Eton and Cambridge, taking his M.A. and entering holy orders in 1639. He was made prebendary of Netherhaven in the church of Sarum, and in 1640 was appointed

Prebendary of Sarum. chaplain to Lord keeper Finch, by whom he was presented to Torrington, in Suffolk. During the civil wars he was chaplain to Lord Goring. In 1650 he was made minister of St. Clement's East Cheap, and ten years later was presented by Juxon, bishop of London, to the rectory of St. Christopher's in the City. He was created D.D. at Cambridge, in pursuance of the king's letters mandatory, installed Prebendary of Ely, Archdeacon of Surrey, and before the close of 1660 made Master of Jesus College. In the next year he was appointed Margaret Professor of Divinity; and was

Commissioner for Review of Liturgy. one of the commissioners for the review of the liturgy in the conference at the Savoy, being named in the king's warrant as a coadjutor on the episcopal side. In the April of 1662 he was made Master of Trinity College, Cambridge, and in the same month, as we have seen, was appointed one of the translators of the liturgy into Latin. In the August of the same year he resigned his rectory of St. Christopher's and the prebend of Sarum; for what reasons we do not know, but it may have been from early symptoms of that loss of health and memory with which he

Retires from the work of Translation. was so grievously afflicted in the last years of his life. Whatever the reason was, however, it was probably for the same cause that he was unable to carry out the preparation and revision of the Latin Version. His labours, however, were such as met with reward; he was appointed Bishop of Chester in 1673, and held that office at his death thirteen years subsequently. Dr. Bentley says of him that "Pearson's very dross was gold;" and another writer informs us that the Nonconformists allowed he was "the first of their opponents in candour and ability." *Bishop of Chester.*

John Peirson having retired from the work at all events before the revision of the Latin translation, John Dolben was appointed by Convocation to assist Earle in his labours. The Latin account of these proceedings in Convocation is to the following effect:—"Session CXXV Wednesday May 18, between the hours of 8 and 10 in the forenoon of the same day, etc. the book of prayers drawn up in Latin being introduced, the matter was referred to the care and revision of the reverend father in Christ John by divine permission bishop of Sarum, and John Dolben S.T.P. dean of Westm'. And thereupon the said most reverend father,[1] etc. continued, etc. according to the schedule, etc.[2] " *Appointment by Convocation of Dolben to assist Earle.*

This John, bishop of Salisbury, is the John Earle called in the account of Session LXXX. Dean of Westminster. Between that time (1662) and the date of Session CXXV. in the year 1664, John Earle had been promoted, while at work on the translation, to the bishopric of Sarum. A brief narrative of his life, and also that of John Dolben, is necessary to show the position which these translators occupied with reference to their church and their king. John Earle entered at Merton College, Oxford, where Durel subsequently studied, in the year 1620.[3] In 1631 he was made proctor, and also chaplain to the Earl of Pembroke. He took the degree of D.D. in 1642, and the next year was one of the assembly of divines, and chancellor of the cathedral church of Salisbury. Some four years after the appointment of Dr. Duppa, tutor of the Prince of Wales, to the bishopric of Salisbury, Earle, then chancellor of that church, was *Earle.* *Chancellor of Sarum.*

---

[1] Gilbert Sheldon, now Archbishop of Canterbury: see the beginning of this chapter.
[2] See Cardwell's Synod, ii. 682, 683.
[3] See Wood's "Athenæ," vol. iii. col. 716, 717.

chosen to take his place as tutor and chaplain to the young
Charles. Earle, however, lost all he had for his adherence
to Charles I., and suffered in exile with his son. After
the defeat of the latter at Worcester, Earle saluted him at
Rouen upon his arrival at Normandy. He was thereupon made chaplain and clerk of the closet. After the return of Charles II., Earle
was appointed Dean of Westminster, a preferment which
seems always to have been regarded as a peculiar mark
of royal favour. In 1661 he was with Peirson one of
the coadjutors to the episcopal divines at the Savoy
Conference. He became Bishop of Worcester in the
November of 1662, shortly after his appointment to the
work of translation, and in the following year was made Bishop of
Salisbury. He retired to Oxford when the king and court
settled there owing to the plague in London and Westminster, and died at University College in the same year,
1665. On one of his works, the translation into Latin
of Hooker's "Ecclesiastical Polity," Wood remarks that
he was "the fit man to make the learned of all nations happy, in
knowing what hath been too long confin'd to the language of our
little island;" and no less was he the fit man to prepare that translation of the Prayer Book which, as Durel says in his Dedication to
the King, "is now set anew before the eyes (of the Christian world)
in a language familiar to all Men of Learning."

Tutor and Chaplain to Charles II.

Dean of Westminster.

Coadjutor at Savoy Conference.

Bishop of Sarum.

Died, 1665.

John Dolben, who was appointed by Convocation to assist Earle
after Peirson's retirement, was born in Northamptonshire in 1625.[1]
He was educated at Westminster School, and entered
Christ Church, Oxford, in 1640, the same year in which
Durel entered at Merton College: they were both of the age of
fifteen at the time of their matriculation. In the civil
wars Dolben served as an officer in the royal army at Oxford and elsewhere, and rose to the rank of major.
Returning to college on the decline of the king's affairs he took his

Dolben.

Major in royal army.

---

[1] See Wood's "Athenæ," vol. iv. col. 188.

degree in 1647 and entered into holy orders. At the Restoration he obtained a canonry of Christ Church, took his D.D., and was appointed Dean of Westminster, when Earle was promoted to the bishopric of Worcester in 1662. He received this preferment at the recommendation of his wife's uncle, Bishop Sheldon,[1] who was in great favour with the king. In 1664 he was made clerk to the closet, and in the same year was Prolocutor of the Lower House of Convocation. It was in this year that Convocation appointed him to be Earle's coadjutor in the translation of the Prayer Book, his wife's relation, then Archbishop Sheldon, presiding on the occasion. In 1666 he became Bishop of Rochester, but was allowed by the king to retain the deanery of Westminster. He was afterwards chosen almoner to his majesty, and "by virtue of the king's congé d'eslire" was elected to the archbishopric of York in 1683. He died in the year 1686, three years after his appointment. His portrait may be seen in the Hall of Christ Church, Oxford. Wood, the antiquarian, appears to have been personally acquainted with him.

Dean of Westminster.

Prolocutor of Lower House of Convocation.

Bishop of Rochester. 1666.

Archbishop of York.

The reason why Convocation paid so much attention to the Latin translation of the revised Prayer Book is easy to be seen. Partly, no doubt, it was because such a version was required by the Act of Uniformity for the use of the Universities and the chief public schools; for the use, that is to say, of the future theologians, politicians, and legislators of the kingdom. But besides this it was the custom of the time to have important writings in a duplicate form, one copy in English, the other in Latin. So we have the titles of Acts of Parliament in Latin up to Charles II. So also at an earlier date, in the reign of Elizabeth, we have the two copies of the Articles, in English and in Latin, both apparently of equal authority and yet differing somewhat in their phraseology. Without

Reasons for a Latin Version.

Duplicate form of State and Church documents.

---

[1] Donor of the Sheldonian Theatre, Oxford, which was built 1664-9, from designs by Sir Christopher Wren. See Appendix D.

wishing to place the Latin Prayer Book of Charles II. upon precisely the same footing as the Latin copy of the Articles, we may very well conceive that it was not intended to be a mere translation, but to be a safeguard against such misconstruction as a living language is ever subject to by reason of the fluctuation in the meaning of its terms.

Mr. Blunt writes of Dean Durel's version, "The Psalms, Canticles, Epistles, and Gospels, are all printed from the ancient Salisbury Use; and the expressions of the latter are often followed, and even retained, in the Prayers, although most of these have been re-translated from the English."[1] A careful examination of the Sarum book amply confirms Mr. Blunt's statement, and we may add that many of the expressions in Durel's version appear to be taken from the authorized Latin version of Queen Elizabeth (1560), and the later Latin Prayer Book of 1574. Yet, in spite of this, most of the Prayers were, as Mr. Blunt remarks, "re-translated from the English," and the same may be said as truly of the Catechism. The translators seem to have endeavoured "to keep the mean between the two extremes," to use the words of the Preface to the English Prayer Book; on the one hand, they re-translated wherever such a course was necessary or advisable with a view to a clear expression of the intention of the revisers; on the other, they followed the injunctions of Charles II. to the commissioners at the Savoy Conference by avoiding as much as possible all unnecessary alterations of the Forms and Liturgy wherewith the people were altogether acquainted. As regards the following of the Sarum Use, that is easily accounted for: Peirson was a prebendary in that church, Earle was first chancellor and then bishop of Sarum, and Durel also held a prebend there.

Character of Dean Durel's version.

Partly followed Sarum Use, etc.

The most part was re-translated.

It remains now to examine the circumstances under which Durel resumed the work of translation, which Earle and Dolben were for various reasons unable to complete. In 1662 Durel succeeded

[1] "The Annotated Book of Common Prayer," p. 586. Appendix iv. Rivingtons, 1866.

Earle as chaplain to the king. In 1665, on the 26th of April, the great Plague of London broke out. In consequence of its ravages the king, queen, and court left the city and Westminster: they went to Salisbury on July the 27th, and thence to Oxford; Earle, then bishop of Salisbury, also proceeding thither. Here the Parliament met on the 9th of October; and here, on the 17th of November, Dr. Earle died. As the work of translation was first committed to Earle when he was chaplain to the king, it appears probable that at his death his papers relating to the translation were handed over to his successor in the chaplaincy; just as his successor in the deanery of Westminster took Peirson's place upon his retirement. Earle's colleague, Dolben, appears to have had no connection with the translation, at all events after his appointment to the bishopric of Rochester, in the November of 1666, and had, so far as we can discover, no part in the final preparation of the version which Durel undertook for his royal master. Probably one reason for his retirement was that, as his acquaintance Wood says, he was not a man of great learning; he "had much of his [Archbishop Williams'] boldness and confidence in him, but little of his learning."[1] However this may be, in the January of 1667 Durel was left alone in the work. There is a letter from him to Archbishop Sancroft among the Tanner MSS. in the Bodleian Library, which we have examined and copied. It reads as follows:—

Durel's resumption of the translation.

Death of Earle.

Retirement of Dolben.

Submission of a Latin Liturgy to Archbishop Sancroft.

"Reverend Sir

"I send you here as much as I have found of the latin liturgie amongst my papers; I thought I had some sheets more, and I am sure I had two copies, but I find but this one (which therefore I pray, be pleased carefully to preserve) the other having been lost, at the removing of my books when the city was burnt. I send you withal some sheets of my Vindiciæ, which I beseech you to peruse and to

---

[1] "Athenæ," vol. iv. col. 869.

amend at your leasure (?). I shall waite upon you, after the 30. of January with the other papers you have perused already;

"Your most humble
"and most obliged
"servant

"Jan. the 25th 1666   "John Durel."

It will be observed that Durel dates this letter 1666; the Bodleian Catalogue dates it 166⅚: the reason for this is that in Durel's time the new year began on the 25th of March, not on the 1st of January.

We may conjecture in passing that the sheets of the Latin Prayer Book here mentioned were Dolben's copy. Earle died, as we have seen, in the November of 1665; the portion of the trans-

This copy probably Dolben's. lation which he had finished would be handed to Durel; Durel being engaged at this time upon his Vindiciæ, which appeared the year before his Latin version of the Prayer Book, would at the moment place this copy prepared by Earle on one side. In the September of the following year the Fire of London occurred, and it was probably this copy that was lost in the removal of Durel's books. The other copy, which he forwarded to Dr. Sancroft, would then be that which Dolben had sent him, some two months later, on his appointment to his bishopric. This explanation is, of course, conjectural, but there can be little doubt that the two copies were those of Earle and Dolben. Durel would hardly call his own work "the latin liturgie," but "my latin liturgie," as he says further on in the letter, "my Vindiciæ;" nor, again, would he be likely to have two copies of his own MS., nor to have forgotten in so short a time how many sheets he had, that is to say, how far he had proceeded in the work of translation. The Latin Liturgy which he sent was therefore, in all probability, Earle and Dolben's version.[1]

---

[1] Lord Selborne ("Liturg. of the Eng. Church," p. 73) writing of the Latin Prayer Book, "edited" in 1670 by John Durel, and "dedicated to the King, as if translated by public authority," gives the following as a reason for believing that Durel's "may be the same Latin translation which was made under the direction of Convocation, as recorded in its Acts of 26 April, 1662, and 18 May, 1664":— that "it can hardly be supposed, that a version made under such auspices would have been entirely

This Latin Liturgy, then, was submitted to Archbishop Sancroft to receive his criticism and elicit his suggestions, before Durel commenced his completion and final revision for the press. No more valuable assistance could be conceived; for, as we shall have occasion to observe hereafter, it was Dr. Sancroft who prepared, from Bishop Cosin's copy, now in the Cosin Library at Durham, that copy of the English Prayer Book, with suggestions for its alteration, which was produced in Convocation in November, 1661. Archbishop Sancroft appears to have helped Durel on other occasions with his works. For we find in the Bodleian Library, among the Tanner MSS., two other letters from Durel to him. In the first (Feb. 25, 166⅔) Durel says, "I am exceedingly beholding both to your worthy self and to the worthy judge of the Prerogative (whom I will thank by a letter, etc.), for the trouble you have been pleased to take about my papers, and for the rectifying of my mistakes. . . . But here is yet more work for both of you in the inclosed paper which you may peruse more leisurely." The second is dated from Windsor, Feb. 18, 166⅔, and encloses a chapter for perusal.

Value of this submission to Dr. Sancroft.

Sancroft's friendship for Durel.

We must, however, remark in conclusion that, though Durel owed much to his predecessors in the work, to the Sarum Missal, and the Elizabethan versions, yet it must not be supposed that his own contributions to the translation were so small as to justify the application to him of the title of "Editor," which he so modestly assumes. His cotemporary, Dr. Barlow, who was appointed Librarian of the Bodleian in 1652, and in 1675 was made Bishop of Lincoln, had a very different opinion of the merit of his work. In a copy of Durel's Latin Prayer Book of 1670, in the Bodleian Library, we find Dr. Barlow's motto, αἰὲν ἀριστεύειν, on the title-page, and this inscrip-

Durel's share in the translation.

Dr. Barlow's opinion.

---

suppressed, and the work of a private translator preferred." On "dedicated" Lord Selborne notes: "The Dedication (signed 'J. D. Editor') says, praestantissimam hanc Liturgiam . . . redditam voluisti; unde merito Augustissimo Nomini Tuo nuncupatur haec Latina illius Versio." He also refers to Gibson's "Syn. Angl.," pp. 230, 239. See also Daniel's "Codex Liturgicus," vol. iii. p. 318: "Melius librum interpretati sunt 1662 John Earle, Decanus Westmonasteriensis, atque J. Pearson." (Cf. the commencement of the present chapter.)

tion lower down in Dr. Barlow's handwriting :—"Lib : Tho : Barlow ex dono J. Durelli S. Theol : Doctoris hujus Liturgiæ Interpretis :" "Thomas Barlow's Book presented by John Durel Doctor of Sacred Theology and Interpreter of this Liturgy."

He calls Durel "In-terpres." What the word "interpreter" meant in those days we see in the Dedication to Lord Vaux, Baron of Harroden, which is prefixed to "The Life of the Apostle St. Paul .... now Englished by a Person of Honour :" London, 1653. This work is

Meaning of this term. in the Bodleian Library, and is bound up with Dr. Sancroft's "Modern Policies." The dedicator there writes, "In lieu of Translator, I might beg leave to say Interpreter; for, You have not onely given us in English the things signified in the French, which is the duty of a Translator, but you have rendered the very mentall conception of the Author, which, in Aristotles stile, is the office of an Interpreter." Dr. Barlow's selection of this word to describe Durel in relation to his Latin version shows both how accurately he apprehended the meaning of the term "In-

Position of Durel's version with reference to the Prayer Book. terpres," and how fully he understood the position which that version was intended to occupy with reference to the English Prayer Book. We shall frequently have occasion to remark, in our notes on the Catechism, how Durel often neglects literal translation in order to bring out more clearly, by a periphrasis, the actual meaning and intention of the compilers of our revised English Prayer Book. His version is not, and was not meant to be, a slavish translation of the English book, but its object was to render "the very mentall conception" of the last revisers of the Liturgy into a language which was, as Durel says, familiar to all men of learning throughout the world.

CHAPTER III.

AUTHORITY OF DEAN DUREL'S LATIN PRAYER BOOK.

"That king that holds not religion the best reason of state, is void of all piety and justice, the supporters of a king."—BACON.

BEFORE concluding the historical portion of our subject we must consider the further authority given to the Latin Prayer Book after Dr. Durel's resumption of the work. We have seen that the translation of the revised Prayer Book was originally committed by Convocation to Earle and Peirson, and subsequently to Earle and Dolben; that, after the death of Earle and the retirement of Dolben, Dr. Durel resumed their work; and that in his completion of the translation he enjoyed the advice and counsel of Archbishop Sancroft. Two more points remain to be noticed. Firstly, the dedication of Durel's Latin version to the king, and the stamp of authority which is thereby placed upon it; and, secondly, the series of promotions, only stopped by death, which were conferred upon him as a reward for his labours and his loyalty to Church and Crown. *[margin: Recapitulation.]* *[margin: Further authority of Durel's Liturgia.]*

The part of the Dedication to the King, in the Latin Prayer Book of 1670, which refers to the book itself, reads, when translated into English, as follows:— *[margin: The Dedication to the King.]*

"To the Most Serene and Most Mighty Monarch
  CHARLES II.,
    BY THE GRACE OF GOD,
  King of *Great Britain, France & Ireland;*
    DEFENDER OF THE FAITH.

"Sire, Most August and Most Gracious of Kings . . . . *Through him* (God) *do Kings rule; through him alone have you recovered your lost kingdoms; so that none of all the Kings can be called King* BY THE GRACE OF GOD *with better right than your Majesty. Accordingly it behoved to honour with a solemn*[1] *rite as the author of them all, that*

---

[1] Or perhaps "yearly," referring to the "special office" mentioned below.

HISTORICAL

Most Good and Most Great God, who has heaped such benefits upon you, as with a hand shown from Heaven, & to reverence him with a grateful heart. That thing in truth . . . . has been fulfilled by your Majesty, in the Restitution of the Public Worship of the Deity, to wit, in the bringing back to its old estate of that Sacred Liturgy (with the addition also of a special Eucharistic Office for Your Majesty's happy return to Your people) which men devoted to Religion among us in the time of our Ancestors, Reformers, Holy Martyrs and Confessors of Christ, formerly rendered exact according to the rule of the Divine Word and of the early Piety of Christians; . . . . Whether in truth it be of such a kind, that it ought or could rightly be rejected & blotted out of remembrance by persons professing the Christian religion let the Christian world judge, before whose eyes it is now set anew in a language [1] *Familiar to all Men of Learning. To me at least there is no doubt but that, if all the Churches which profess that Christ is the Redeemer of the human race, should agree upon one and the same Form of Sacred Liturgy (which thing must be hoped for) this of ours would prevail by many votes over all the rest which are in use in the various Churches, so that thenceforth it alone would everywhere obtain, ... May God, to whose glory this most excellent Liturgy of the Holy Church of England in spite of the snarling of Schismatics, You, Most Serene King, have wished to be translated*[2] *(whence deservedly is this Latin Version of that other [i.e., the English Liturgy] dedicated to Your Most August Name) hear the Prayers. . . . Which things are heartily prayed for your Majesty by,*

"Sire, Most August and Most Gracious of Kings,

"of your Subjects and Servants,

"the Most Humble and

"Most Obedient,

"J. D. Editor."

---

[1] Idiomate: the word "idiom" even in the English of this time meant "language," as in "The Life of the Apostle St. Paul." Lond. 1653.

[2] The Latin is "redditam." This might be simply "restored"; but (1) "hæc" (this) is generally used by Durel for the Latin, and "illa" (that) for the English version; and (2) the words he uses for "restored" above are neither of them "redditam:" "*Restituto Publico Numinis Cultus, Sacra nempe illâ Liturgiâ postliminio reductâ.*" For this use of "reddere" in a contemporary writer, see "England's *sole and Soveraign way of being saved*," a preface to which is written by Dr. Manton of the Savoy Conference: "LXX. reddiderunt verbo ἐπιζητεῖν." See Lord Selborne, p. 19 above.

We must also note that the book is printed by Roger Norton, King's Printer (Regius Typographus), and sold by Sam. Mearne, King's Bookseller (Regius Bibliopola); just as Queen Elizabeth's "Liber Precum Publicarum," etc., was issued "per nostrum Typographum." *The Imprint.*

It is necessary, therefore, to stop for a moment and examine briefly the question of the Royal Supremacy. We may conveniently discuss it under four heads: the nature of the authority which it conferred; examples of the use of that authority; the growth of the English Liturgy under its fostering care; and, lastly, its application to the Latin Prayer Book of Durel. *The Royal Supremacy.*

It must be borne in mind that Papal supremacy, or authority legislative, judicial, and executive, had been exercised for some centuries over the Churches of England, Scotland, and Ireland, as branches and integral parts of the Western or Latin Church. This foreign supremacy was abolished by the legislatures of the three kingdoms in the sixteenth century. Henry VIII. was acknowledged as Supreme Head of the Church by the clergy in 1528. This Royal Supremacy was confirmed by Parliament in 1534. Supreme ecclesiastical authority, vested in the reigning sovereign, is enacted by the statute of 26 Henry VIII. in the following clear and precise terms: *Ecclesiastical supremacy transferred from the Pope to the King.*

26 Hen. VIII.

"That the king our sovereign lord, his heirs and successors, kings of this realm, shall be taken, accepted, and reputed the only supreme head in earth of the Church of England, and shall have and enjoy, annexed to the imperial crown of this realm, as well the style and title thereof, as all honors, dignities, pre-eminences, jurisdictions, privileges, authorities, immunities, profits, and commodities to the said dignity of the supreme head of the same Church belonging and appertaining;—And shall have power from time to time to visit, repress, redress, reform, order, correct, restrain, and amend all such errors, heresies, abuses, offences, contempts, and enormities, whatsoever they be, which, by any manner of spiritual authority or jurisdiction, may lawfully be reformed, repressed, ordered, *Nature of Royal Supremacy.*

redressed, corrected, restrained, or amended, most to the pleasure of Almighty God, the increase of virtue in Christ's religion, and for the conservation of the peace, unity, and tranquillity of this realm ;—any usage, custom, foreign laws, foreign authority, prescription, or any other thing to the contrary notwithstanding."

In harmony with this statute we have such documents as the "Renuntiatio *Papæ*, et Recognitio *Regis* in Caput Ecclesiæ per Custodem et Collegium (omn. anim. in Oxonia),"[1] where the reigning prince is acknowledged "tanquam supremum Caput Ecclesiæ Anglicanæ." And Dr. Burn tells us that "after the abolition of the papal power there was no branch of sovereignty with which the princes of this realm, for above a century after the Reformation, were more delighted than that of being the supreme head of the Church," etc. (" Eccles. Law," tit. "Supremacy ").

_{"Renuntiatio Papæ, et Recognitio Regis."}

_{Burn.}

So, too, at the very time when Durel's book was in course of preparation, Bishop Stillingfleet refers in these words to the supremacy of Charles II. as king. It was, he says, for the Church of England's great honour that "as she gradually regained her *light* so it was with the *influence* of *Supreme Authority*." "Nothing doth more argue the excellent constitution of our *Church* than that therein the purity of a *Christian Doctrine* is joined with the most hearty acknowledgement of your *Majesty's Power* and *Supremacy*." This, " one of the richest *Jewels* of it," was then (1665) adorning the "*Imperial Crown*."

_{Stillingfleet.}

Such was the nature of the Royal Supremacy in matters ecclesiastical. A few instances of its previous employment will suffice, though exercises of sovereignty of a similar kind to the issuing of the Latin translation of the Prayer Book by the authority of Charles II. occur again and again in the history of the Church. For example, in 1536, Burnet tells us, that "Cranmer looked on the putting of the Bible in the people's hands as the most effectual means for pro-

_{Example of use of supremacy.}

_{The Bible as promoting Reformation.}

---

[1] In the Bodleian Library.

moting the Reformation; and therefore moved that the king might give order for it." "At court it was said that nothing would make the difference between the Pope's power and the King's Supremacy appear more eminently than if the one gave the people the free use of the Word of God; whereas the other had kept them in darkness and ruled them by a blind obedience." "The king gave order for setting about this with all possible haste; and within three years the impression of it was finished." <small>King's order.</small>

Other injunctions with reference to the English translation of the Bible were issued in the reigns of Henry VIII. and Edward VI., until in 1604, by virtue of the Royal Supremacy, James I. commissioned fifty-four learned men of the Universities and other places to make a new and more faithful translation of the Bible according to rules which he himself prescribed. This translation was published in 1611. It is the one now in use. Since that time there has been no authorized translation of any part of the sacred volume into the English language. On the title-page it is said to be, "By his Majesty's special command." In the Dedication to the King by the translators, the sovereign is acknowledged as "the principal Mover and Author of the work." Through the wide world it is recognized as the "Authorized Version;"[1] and Durel's translation of the Prayer Book has precisely the same sanction in the authority which it derived from the Supreme Head of the Church of England. <small>Other royal injunctions. Order of James I. Authorized Version.</small>

We may next remark the growth of our English Liturgy under royal patronage and protection. Under the Papal Supremacy the services were performed in Latin. Under the Regal Supremacy the English Prayer Book has been brought to its present state. In 1535 came out Marshall's Primer. Two years later appeared "The Godly and Pious Institution of a Christian Man," which was republished, with corrections, in 1540 and 1543. In <small>Growth of English Liturgy under Royal Supremacy. The Primers.</small>

[1] See App. B, p. 29.

1539 this was followed by Bishop Hilsey's Primer, which was "to teach the people that the king was the supreme head immediately under God of the spiritualty and temporalty of the Church of England."[1] In 1545 came out "The Primer set forth by the King's Majesty, and his Clergy, to be taught, learned, and read; and none other to be used throughout all his dominions." In 1547, the first year of the reign of Edward VI., Archbishop Cranmer, Bishop Ridley, and several other bishops and divines were commissioned by the king in council to compile a liturgy in the English language, free from the erroneous doctrines by which the Latin liturgies of the Church while unreformed had been distinguished.

First and Second Prayer Books of Ed. VI. The first Prayer Book of Edward VI. was accordingly published in 1549. His second Prayer Book followed in 1552. Upon the accession of Elizabeth, several learned divines, headed by Archbishop Parker, were appointed to make another review of King Edward's Liturgies. Her English Prayer Book was published in 1559, the "Litany and Suffrages" having appeared in the previous year.[2] In 1560 followed her Latin Prayer Book, of which Haddon is supposed to have been the editor.

Prayer Book of Queen Elizabeth.

After the Conference at Hampton Court, in the first year of James I., between the king, with Archbishop Whitgift and other bishops and divines, and the Puritans, a few further alterations were introduced. This brings us to the time of Charles II. and of Durel; when, as we find in the Preface to the English Prayer Book, "great importunities were used to His Sacred Majesty, that the said Book might be revised, and such Alterations therein and Additions thereunto made, as should be thought requisite for the ease of tender Consciences: whereunto His Majesty, out of his pious inclination to give satisfaction (so far as could be reasonably expected) to all his subjects of what persuasion soever, did graci-

Prayer Book of James I.

Prayer Book of Charles II. Extract from Preface.

---

[1] Proctor, "Common Prayer," p. 16.
[2] Clay, "Lit. Services, Queen Elizabeth," p. 1. Parker Society, 1847.

ously condescend." As a result and proof of his acquiescence, Charles II. issued a commission to empower twelve bishops, among whom was Bishop Cosin, Durel's friend and patron, and the same number of Presbyterian divines to consult together upon other and further alterations. Among the coadjutors on the Episcopal side were Dr. Earle, dean of Westminster, and Dr. Peirson, who were afterwards connected with the translation of the Prayer Book into Latin. Archbishop Sancroft also, to whose criticism Durel submitted the Latin version, was officially connected with many of the suggestions and improvements adopted in the English book. The king's commission gave the above-mentioned bishops and divines the power to "compare the Common Prayer Book with the most ancient Liturgies that had been used in the Church in the most primitive and purest times;" and required them "to avoid as much as possible all unnecessary alterations of the Forms and Liturgy wherewith the people were altogether acquainted and had so long received in the Church of England." Subsequently, as the result of this regal power and motion, the Liturgy was brought by those whose services the king employed for the purpose to that state in which it now stands; the Royal Supremacy being exercised to secure accuracy in the publication. By that supremacy also the Psalmody of the Church of England was allowed and controlled from the Reformation.

Royal Commission for Savoy Conference.

Cosin.

Earle and Peirson.

Sancroft.

Terms of Commission.

Returning now to the Latin Prayer Book, we see that the allowance for its use sprang from the Parliament, and the provision for its preparation from the King. As in the case of the Bible in the vulgar tongue, and of the Liturgy in the vulgar tongue, so by regal authority, sanction, and care Durel prepared for the use of the Church his Latin translation of the Book of Common Prayer; and consistently and loyally, in a tone similar to that adopted by the last translators of the Bible, he dedicated his work to the Sovereign of the Realm, the Supreme Head of the Church of England.

Connection of the supremacy with the Latin Prayer Book.

Were it necessary to determine more exactly the position which
Dr. Durel occupied towards the "Liturgia," we should
Dr. Durel's position. say that he represented the King, as Earle, Peirson, and
Dolben represented the Convocation; and the post thus
assigned to him was similar to that held by the reviser or revisers of
the Articles in Queen Elizabeth's time, who accomplished the final
review under her orders, and who, as it is supposed, introduced by
her royal command the first clause of the Article entitled, "Of the
Authority of the Church."

We must now proceed briefly to notice the approval which Durel's
labours obtained in the eyes of the king, and the rewards
Durel's promotion by royal favour after the preparation of his Liturgia. which were conferred by the royal hand upon him. At
the close of 1669, as he was putting the last touches to
his translation, the Chancellor of Oxford speaks, as we
have seen, in high terms of Durel's "loyalty, fidelity, and
service to his majesty." The king did not prove himself
unmindful of or ungrateful for his services. On the contrary, in
1677 Durel was appointed by regal authority to the deanery of
Windsor, and of Wolverhampton; and, partly through the king's
influence, to the rich living of Witney, near Oxford. And, moreover,
we have the opinion of his cotemporary Wood that, had his career
not been cut short by death, it would have been crowned with preferment to a bishopric. This shows conclusively that, for the
thirteen years intervening between the publication of his Latin Prayer
Book and his decease, his version was considered a good and sound
translation by the Supreme Head, and by others who occupied
positions of high authority in the English Church.

APPENDIX A.

An Account of Durel's Ordination.

On Trinity Sunday, June 12, 1650, he (Dr. Thomas Sydserff, Bishop of Galloway)[1] ordained in the chapel of King Charles II.'s ambassador—Sir Richard Browne—at Paris, as deacons and priests, Durell and Brerint (afterwards Deans of Windsor and Durham), on which occasion the sermon was preached by Dr. Cosin, then dean of Peterborough. Evelyn, in his Diary, having been present there, states that "the Bishop of Galloway officiated with great gravity, after a pious and learned exhortation declaring the weight and dignity of their functions, especially now in a time of the poor Church of England's affliction.

"He magnified the sublimity of the calling from the object, viz., the salvation of men's souls, and the glory of God; producing many human instances of the transitoriness and vanity of all other dignities, and that of all the Roman conquerors," &c.

"He then proceeded to the ordination. They were presented by the Dean in their surplices, before the altar, the Bishop sitting in a chair at one side; and so were made both Deacons and Priests at the same time, in regard to the necessity of the times, there being so few Bishops left in England, and consequently danger of a failure of both functions. Lastly they proceeded to the Communion."

APPENDIX B.

On the Authorized Version of the Bible.

It appears to be the fashion in the present day to question the authority of the "Authorized Version." Even Dean Perowne is reported to have said as follows at the annual meeting of the Peterborough Auxiliary of the British and Foreign Bible Society on April 11, 1881:—"They sat for seven years, and in 1611 they gave us not a new Bible, but simply a revision of the old Bishops' Bible, which is the one published by 'authority to be read in churches.' It has no authority whatever. It superseded the Bishops' Bible simply because the people liked it better. It had no authority from the Crown or Convocation or Parliament. On what ground it was said to be authorized I don't know" (Bible Society's *Monthly Reporter*).

Now, under the Pope's Supremacy the Bible was not allowed, and the vulgar tongue was prohibited in religious worship; under the King's Supremacy the

---

[1] Died Bishop of Orkney in 1663; the last of the Episcopal succession of 1610 as concerns Scotland.

sovereign power was exercised again and again, until that exercise culminated, so far as the Scriptures were concerned, in the Authorized Version of 1611.

Let us look at the evidence. First, we have these statements in the Translators' Preface to the Authorized Version, original edition of 1611 :—

"And what can the King command to bee done, that will bring him more true honour then this? and wherein could they that haue beene set a worke, approue their dutie to the King, yea, their obedience to God, and loue to his Saints more, then by yeelding their seruice, and all that is within them, for the furnishing of the worke? . . . yet euen hereupon did his Maiestie beginne to bethinke himselfe of the good that might ensue by a new translation, and presently after gaue order for this Translation which is now presented vnto thee."

This testimony is very important, because as clerics the translators allow the supreme authority to the King in his right to order the translation.

The translators also say in their Preface that the king was led to think about the advantage of a new translation and to order it owing to the Puritans, who said "they could not with good conscience subscribe to the Communion booke, since it maintained the Bible as it was there translated, which was as they said, a most corrupted translation." So that the Authorized Version was not a revision of the Bishops' Bible, but a new translation caused by the dissatisfaction of the Puritans with the Bishops' Bible.

The question whether it was a new translation or a revision is settled by the translators in their preface in another part. They say, "If you aske what they had before them, truely it was the *Hebrew* text of the Olde Testament, the *Greeke* of the New." After quoting Augustine and Hierome, they say, "If trueth be to be tried by these tongues, then whence should a Translation be made, but out of them?" So they set these tongues before them, they tell us, to translate, "being the tongues wherein God was pleased to speake to his Church by his Prophets and Apostles."

They went over their work again; they took, they say, "twise seuen times seuentie two dayes and more" for the work; they consulted the translators or commentators, Chaldee, Hebrew, Syrian, Greek, Latin, Spanish, French, Italian, and Dutch.

So that two things are clear; first, that the originator and authorizer of the work was the King; and secondly, that it was a new Translation.

So Laud's Visitation Articles, in 1622 and 1628, require a Bible "of the latest edition" to be provided.

And we see the opinion of the work which obtained half a century after the work was finished by the remarkable fact that the Puritan divines at the Savoy Conference, when they urged that the Epistles and Gospels in the Prayer Book should be taken from the version of A.D. 1611, spoke of it as "the new translation allowed by authority" (Cardwell's "Conferences," p. 307).

PART II.
CRITICAL AND EXEGETICAL.

CHAPTER I.

EDITIONS OF THE "LITURGIA," AND OTHER VERSIONS.

"Of translations, the better I acknowledge that which cometh nearer to the very letter of the very original verity."—HOOKER.

THE first edition of Durel's Latin Prayer Book was published in 1670, and the book is now of no ordinary rarity. A copy of the title-page forms the frontispiece of this work: without professing to be a facsimile, it is a close and exact imitation. The Prayer Book is excellently printed, and we find "i" and "j," and "u" and "v," according to the modern mode of use. It will bear favourable comparison with any book of the seventeenth century that we have seen, almost the only difference from modern type being the ancient form of "s." The type of the Catechism is similar to that of our reprint. We have examined copies of this edition in the Bodleian Library at Oxford (from which copy the text of the Catechism is taken), the University Library at Cambridge, the British Museum, and the Cathedral Library at Norwich. Unfortunately the Catechism is torn out of the Norwich copy. The removal of valuable testimony which bears upon religious controversy is, sad to say, not uncommon;[1] and impartial students of truth cannot be too grateful for a Library

Scarcity of Durel's "Liturgia:" title of Ed. 1670.

Copies collated.

Mutilation.

---

[1] *E.g.* From a letter of Alfricus, archbishop of Canterbury (end of tenth century), in Bennett College Library, the following important passage opposed to Transubstantiation has been erased. Fortunately, it remains in another copy:—"Non fit tamen hoc sacrificium corpus ejus in quo passus est pro nobis, nec sanguis ejus quem pro nobis effudit: sed spiritualiter corpus ejus efficitur et sanguis" (L. xii. 156). "Yet this sacrifice does not become his body in which he suffered for us, nor his blood which he shed for us: but is spiritually made his body and blood."

like that in the British Museum, where such unremitted diligence is displayed in the collection and preservation of documentary evidence. It is interesting to observe that the former owner of this Norwich copy has filled in the initials subscribing the dedication thus—J*oän* D*urell:* this owner was evidently a cotemporary, as the MS. date is 1673, three years after the publication of the book. The Bodleian
<small>Bodleian copy.</small> copy is especially interesting, as it was presented by Dr. Durel himself to Dr. Barlow, and this fact is recorded on the title-page in the handwriting of the latter (see Part I. ch. 2, p. 19).

With regard to the title itself it should be noted that in all previous Latin Prayer Books we find "Publicarum," not "Communium,"
<small>"Communium" in title.</small> whereas Durel's word "Communium" is retained even by Harwood, and so up to a comparatively late date. In the title of the Act of Uniformity, 1 Eliz., we have "Common Prayer," and in the title of the Act of Uniformity, 14 Car. II., "Publick Prayers"; but in the body of that Act "Common Prayers." Upon perusing both Acts it appears that "Publick Prayers" had come to mean, not "Open Prayers," which was a general term for any prayers "*for other to come unto, or hear, either in Common Churches, or private Chappels,*" etc., but the ordinary services of Morning and Evening Prayer. That the term did not include all the services of the Church is seen from the title of 14 Car. II., "*Publick Prayers, and Administration of Sacraments, and other Rites and Ceremonies;*" so that it was practically equivalent to "Common Prayer," in the sense of "Gyffredin" in the title of the Welsh Book, that is, "Ordinary Prayer" as opposed to the special services. But
<small>Not same as "Publicarum."</small> such is not the use of the Latin word "Publicarum," at all events in the title of Queen Elizabeth's Latin Prayer Book, for there we have, "Liber Precum PVBLICARVM, SEV ministerij Ecclesiasticę administrationis Sacramentorum, aliorūq'; rituū," etc.; which shows that "Publicarum" included even the administration of the Sacraments. When therefore Durel had to translate *The Book of Common Prayer, And* [not *or*] *Administration*

of *the Sacraments and other Rites*, etc., he could not say, " Precum Publicarum," which would have included all the rest, but was obliged to use the expression " Precum Communium," which was a term of limited import.

The same precision of language and freedom from undue copying of previous Prayer Books is very noteworthy in Durel. His is not a revised, but a new version; a translation, not a compilation; and not only a translation, but an interpretation. Many marks of independence will be pointed out in the notes on the Catechism, but one may be mentioned here: in our English Book, at the end of *The Order how the Psalter is appointed to be read*, there is a note that "the Psalter followeth the Division of the Hebrews, and the Translation of the great English Bible," etc.; at this place in Durel's " Liturgia " the following note is added:—"* *Hoc intelligitur de Psalterio in Editione Anglicana Liturgiæ; Nam in hac Latina Editione, sequuti sumus Vulgatam Latinorum Versionem, quemadmodum in Epistolis & Evangelis;*" *i.e.*, "This is understood of the Psalter in the English Edition of the Liturgy; For in this Latin Edition, we have followed [note, not "sequutus sum," in the singular; it is difficult to say whether " we " may refer to the king, or to Durel and the other translators] the Latin Vulgate Version, just as in the Epistles and Gospels."

Precision of Durel's version.
A new translation.
Special order for Psalter.

There is a smaller edition published at the same Sam Mearne's, King's Bookseller, and dated MDCLXXX.: a copy is in the British Museum, where we have seen it, and collated it on the most important passages. In this and subsequent editions the Dedication is omitted.

Ed. 1680.

The next copy we have fully collated is that of 1685. There is one in the Bodleian Library, and we have also had access to two in private hands.[1] It has, verbatim, the same title as the first edition of 1670, with changes in the formation of letters,

Ed. 1685.

---

[1] One of the latter, very kindly lent to us by the Rev. J. O. Brook, has a frontispiece representing Charles II.; but we are inclined to doubt whether this belongs to the book, or has been bound up in mistake: this copy originally belonged to William Pitt. The other has no frontispiece.

it being, like the edition of 1680, a smaller book. The imprint is different: "*LONDINI*, Apud CAR. MEARNE, Bibliopolam Regium ad Insignia Regia prope Charing-Cross. MDCLXXXV." The copy in the Bodleian has a frontispiece of an angel bringing from heaven a scroll, with LITURGIA ECCLESIÆ ANGLICANÆ inscribed upon it; underneath is, "*Apud Carolum Mearne Bibliopolam Regium ad Insignia Regia prope Charing Crosse 1685.*" It will be noticed that the King's Bookseller was still one of the family of Mearne.

We also have in our own library a copy of the edition of 1687. The frontispiece is precisely the same as that of 1685, and bears, in fact, the same date, "*1685.*" The title-page is printed from the same type, excepting the imprint, "*LONDINI*, Apud *Henricum Bonwick*, ad insigne Leonis rubri in Cœmeterio D. *Pauli*. MDCLXXXVII;" and the whole book is word by word and letter by letter the same, even to the binder's marks, except that Carolus is changed to Jacobus, and there is the requisite alteration in the prayer for the Royal Family. The death of Charles II. and the accession of James II. rendered the reprint of the Latin Prayer Book necessary; but upon comparing the edition of 1687 with that of 1685, we find sufficient proof that the form of 1685 was not broken up, and that the edition of 1687 was printed from that form. All the misprints of 1685 are retained in that of 1687, though these are, indeed, wonderfully few.

Ed. 1687.

The title-page of the edition of 1696 is the same verbatim, except the imprint, which runs: "*LONDINI*, Excudebat *E. Jones*, Impensis *A. Swall* & *T. Childe*, ad insigne Monocerotis in Cœmeterio D. Pauli, MDCXCVI." It has the same engraving for a frontispiece as the editions of 1685 and 1687, but it is now said to be, "*Impensis* Abelis Swall," etc., and is dated "MDCXCVI." A copy of this edition we have inspected in the Bodleian. We have also seen another edition of the same date in the British Museum, but with a different imprint; in place of "ad insigne . . . MDCXCVI" is "& Prostant apud *Jacobum Knapton* ad insigne Coronæ in Cœmeterio

Ed. 1696.

Another Ed. 1696.

D. Pauli MDCXCVI." Both these books have many of the same binder's marks as Eds. 1685 and 1687, but there are some corrections made in misprints.

There is also a copy of the edition of 1703 in the Bodleian, which we have collated. It is almost literatim the same as that of 1696 so far as the latter edition went, but this edition contains the prayers used by Convocation, and the Thirty-nine Articles. Accordingly there is this addition made to the Title: "Huic Editioni Precum Formula accessit, quae, durante Comitiorum Ecclesiasticorum Consessu, utriq; Domui Convocationis usui esse solet ; Triginta Novem Ecclesiæ *Anglicanæ* Articulis insuper adjectis." The imprint is: "LONDINI, Excudebat *E. Jones*, Impensis *D. Brown, T. Benskin, J. Walthoe*, & *F. Coggan*, MDCCIII." There is a new frontispiece to this edition, connecting it with the royal power : it is a representation of Queen Anne kneeling before a table, on which is a copy of "*Liturgia Ecclesiæ Anglicana*" (as we are told by an inscription on the wall immediately above). Underneath is, "*Anna D. G. Angliæ Scotiæ Franciæ et Hiberniæ Regina Fidei defens.* &c." {Ed. 1703.}

The number of editions required is some indication of the demand for Durel's Latin Prayer Books which obtained among his cotemporaries. There were at least seven editions published within thirty-four years (1670 to 1703), and it is remarkable that copies are so exceedingly scarce as they are at the present time. {Number of Editions, and demand for the "Liturgia."}

Up to this date there is practically no change in the "Liturgia" through its various editions, with the exception of the addition of the Convocation Prayers, etc. But we find in the Bodleian another Prayer Book, dated 1713, by Tho. Parsell, with many changes, though it is founded upon Durel's. It has the same title to "Ceremoniarum." It then continues thus: "IN ECCLESIA ANGLICANA receptus : Itémque Forma & Modus Creandi Ordinandi & Consecrandi EPISCOPOS, PRESBYTEROS, & DIACONOS. *Epistolæ, Evangelia,* & *Psalmi* Inseruntur juxta *SEBASTIANI* {Parsell's Prayer Book, Ed. 1713.}

CASTELLIONIS Versionem. Editio altera priori longè emendatior. *LONDINI:* Apud *R.* & *J. Bonwicke, J.* & *B. Sprint, Benj. Tooke, M. Atkins, T. Varnam* & *J. Osborne.* MDCCXIII." The frontispiece represents a congregation at prayer, with the minister and the clerk at their desks. Under the engraving is, " Agite, veneremur supplices, flexis ante Dominum Creatorem nostrum genibus. PSAL. xcv. 6." The book is dedicated to "D^{no} *Gulielmo Dawes,*" bishop of Chester, showing that it is no longer a reprint of the authorized version of Durel, but a private work.

Ed. 1716. The edition of 1716 has the same title and frontispiece, but we have "*B. Tooke*" for *Benj. Tooke, M. Atkins* has dropped out, and the date is "1716:" there are also differences in the form of letters.

Parsell's (Typis G. Bowyer) Ed. 1733. There is another edition in the Bodleian with the same frontispiece, and the same title with different form of letters; but in place of "Editio altera," etc, we have "Editio quinta prioribus longè emendatior," and the imprint is, "*LONDINI,* Typis G. BOWYER, Impensis J. J. & P. KNAPTON, J. & J. BONWICKE, J. OSBORN & T. LONGMAN, B. MOTTE, S. BIRT, T. WARD & E. WICKSTED. MDCCXXXIII."

Ed. 1744. The next edition in the Bodleian is 1744. The frontispiece is again the same, and the title-page also is precisely the same as the edition of 1733, with the alteration of "sexto" for "quinta," and a fresh imprint: "*LONDINI,* Typis *G. Bowyer,* Impensis J. & J. BONWICKE, R. WARE, J. & P. KNAPTON, S. BIRT, T. LONGMAN, C. HITCH, T. OSBORN, & E. WICKSTED. MDCCXLIV."

Harwood's Prayer Book, Ed. 1785. The next Prayer Book which need be remarked is the "Liturgia, seu Liber Precum Communium," etc., by Edwardus Harwood S. T. P., who (according to the title-page) "Hanc editionem recensuit et a mendis compluribus repurgavit." It is printed in London, "Impensis Gulielmi Bent," who is called in Harwood's Preface, "Meus amicus summus." This Prayer Book of Harwood is largely a revised version of Parsell's book. The edition which he followed was evidently one of the later ones, as many words occur in the Catechism according to the Eds. of 1733 and 1744, where the language had been altered from that of 1713; *e.g.*, "adeptos," not "adepturos;" "collata," not "collocata," etc. With an edition of 1785 in private hands we have compared the reprint of 1840.

Before leaving the Latin Prayer Books, we may notice three modern versions. First, that published by Messrs. S. Bagster and Sons. In the preface to the first edition of 1821 in the Chetham Library, Manchester, this version is said to be "nearly a reprint of the Edition which was first published by *W. Bowyer*, in 1720, with some alterations and additions by the present Editor, sometimes taken from the Translation by Mr. Thomas Parsel, the 4th edition of which was published in 1727." The Catechism, however, appears to be very much nearer Durel's version than Parsell's, if Parsell's editions of 1713, 1716, 1733 (G. Bowyer) and 1744 (ditto), which we have collated, may be taken as any indication. These editions are all very different from Durel's, being almost precisely the same as Harwood's version. Most, if not all, of the differences from Durel, in the Catechism of Bagster's edition, are given in our notes on the Catechism, and it will be seen that they are not numerous, though important. This is the case even in ed. 1866, from which (after a collation with ed. 1834) our quotations are given, unless the contrary is stated; and the ed. of 1821 (as we find by a collation made since most of our notes were written) is precisely the same as ed. 1866 in the readings of the Catechism, with the exception, however, of one most important passage,[1] which was subsequently altered from Durel's words to the reading of Parsell's earlier editions.

Modern Prayer Books.
(1) Bagster's Edition.

Secondly, we find an excellent Latin Prayer Book, "Liber Precum Publicarum," etc. Londini: Impensis Joannis Gulielmi Parker, MDCCCXLVIII. This is founded chiefly, if not wholly, on the authorized Latin versions of Queen Elizabeth and of Charles II. (Durel's), and these two books are acknowledged in the preface.

(2) J. W. Parker's "Liber Precum."

---

[1] See note on "quod nobis datur" in Catechism.

Lastly, there is the "Liber Precum Publicarum Ecclesiæ Anglicanæ," by the Revs. W. Bright, M.A., and P. G. Medd, M.A. Rivington. The copy in our possession [*Editio Altera*] is dated 1869. In the preface it is stated that the "Liber Precum Publicarum" of 1560 has not been neglected; no on the other hand, did the authors think proper to follow it throughout, " quippe qui nec publicam Ecclesiæ auctoritatem præ se ferret' (upon which we must remark that it was at all events the very book specifically ordered by Queen Elizabeth, the supreme head of the English Church, to be used in the colleges of Cambridge, etc.); and further, "nec, novis postea recensionibus factis, cum hodierno Libro satis consentiret." This last is a valid reason for not following Queen Elizabeth's book, but it is no reason for not following throughout (as the authors do in part) Durel's "Liturgia," which is the only Latin version cotemporary with the Last Review, and therefore the only one of value in showing what the revisers thought was meant by the words which they retained and the words they introduced. Whatever value such a work as the "Liber Precum Publicarum" of Messrs. Bright and Medd may have as showing the opinions of two learned men in the nineteenth century, it can have no value in showing the doctrines held in the seventeenth century. To the student of the period of the seventeenth century the only safe guide among Latin Prayer Books is Durel's "Liturgia," published at the very time, with the royal authority, and after careful preparation by an intimate friend of the principal revisers.

<small>(3) Messrs. Bright and Medd's version.</small>

<small>Value of Durel's "Liturgia," as distinguished from modern versions.</small>

Turning now to the earlier Latin Prayer Books which are quoted in the notes on the Catechism, the version of Aless (in the Bodleian) has this title: "ORDINATIO ECCLESIÆ, SEV MINISTERII ECCLESIASTICI, IN FLORENTIS-simo Regno Angliæ, conscripta sermone patrio, & in Latinam linguam bona fide conuersa, & ad consolationem Ecclesiarum Christi, ubicunque locorum ac gentium, his tristissimis temporibus, EDITA,

<small>Earlier versions. Aless.</small>

AB ALEXANDRO ALESIO SCOTO SACRÆ THEOLOGIÆ DOCTORE. LIPSIÆ IN OFFICINA VVOLFGANGI GVNTERI. Anno M.D.LI." The Catechism in Queen Elizabeth's book is almost verbatim the same as the one in Aless's version; but, as Queen Elizabeth's book has the stamp of the royal authority, it has been thought better to quote from it, pointing out at the same time any remarkable divergencies from Aless.

The copy of Queen Elizabeth's Latin Prayer Book, which has been used in this work, is in the Bodleian Library. It is generally supposed to have been prepared by Walter Haddon. Its title is: "Liber Precum PVBLICARVM, SEV ministerij Ecclesiasticę administrationis Sacramentorum, alioruq'; rituū & cęremoniarum in Ecclesia Anglicana. *Cum prilegio Regiæ Maiestatis.*" The mandate of Elizabeth, dated the 6th of April in the second year of her reign, is prefixed, and at the end of the book is: "*Excusum Londini apud Reginaldum Wolfium, Regiæ Maiest. in Latinis typographum. Cum priuilegio Regiæ Maiestatis.*" The readings of this copy have been collated with another in the Library of Sion College, London, of which the senior of the present authors was formerly a Fellow. The date is 1560.

<small>Latin Prayer Book of Queen Elizabeth.</small>

For an account of Whitaker's Prayer Book, which followed this in the Latin, see below among the Greek Prayer Books. <small>Whitaker.</small>

The Latin Prayer Book of 1574, quoted in the notes, is in the Bodleian Library. Mr. Clay writes: "since Prayer Books in Latin published during her [*i.e.*, Elizabeth's] reign have been often confounded with her own, a short account of them appears indispensable. They bear the names of Wolf, Vautrollier, and Jackson, as the printers; and in the case of the last two, 'per assignationem Francisci Floræ.' Wolf, in 1571, (or rather in 1572, for the Psalter has both dates,) sent out what we may rightly deem the earliest version into Latin of the whole Prayer Book. Herbert's Ames, p. 611. This the other printers carefully followed, and the copies (octavo) more commonly met with, though still very rare, are one in 1574 by Vautrollier and

<small>Wolf, Vautrollier, and Jackson.</small>

another in 1594 by Jackson." ("Liturgies, etc., set forth in the Reign of Queen Elizabeth." Parker Society. M.DCCC.XLVII.)

Vautrollier. The title of Vautrollier's book from "LIBER" to "Anglicana" is the same as that of Queen Elizabeth's, with some differences in the form of letters. The design of the title-page is totally different. After "Anglicana" the imprint runs as follows: "*EXCVSVM LONDINI, PER ASSIGNATIONEM* Francisci Floræ. CVM PRIVILEGIO Regiæ Maiestatis." At the end of the book we have "*LONDINI* Excudebat Thomas Vautrollerius. 1574."

Jackson. With this book we have carefully collated the Catechism in a Prayer Book printed by Jackson, which is also in the Bodleian Library. The title is still the same with again differences in the formation of letters, etc. After "*Anglicana*" is added the imprint, "Excusum Londini, per assignationem Francisci Floræ. CVM PRIVILEGIO Regiæ Maiestatis. 1594." At the end of the book there is "*LONDINI* Excudebat Ioan. Iacksonus. 1594."

There is also a Latin version of the Prayer Book in "DOCTRINA, ET POLITIA ECCLESIÆ ANGLICANÆ, etc. LONDINI, Apud JOANNEM BILLIUM. 1617. Cum Priuilegio." This book *Mockett.* was by Mockett, but as it was immediately proscribed and burnt, it has not been thought necessary to quote its readings in the notes on the Catechism except upon one passage.

Coming to the Greek Prayer Books, the first version to be especially noticed is that by Elias Petley: "ΛΕΙΤΟΥΡΓΙΑ ΒΡΕΤ-
Greek Prayer ΤΑΝΙΚΗ, etc. LIBER PRECVM PVBLICARVM
Books. Ac Celebrationis Sacramentorum reliquorumq; Rituum
Petley, & Cæremoniarum in Ecclesiâ nostrâ *Anglicanâ*, in
Ed. 1638. studiosæ juventutis gratiam nunc primùm græcè editus. *Operâ & Studio* ELIÆ PETILI *Presbyteri*. *LONDINI* Typis *Tho. CotesI* pro *Richardo Whitakero* ad insignia Regia in Cœmeterio D. *Pauli*, MDCXXXVIII." It is dedicated to William (Laud), archbishop of Canterbury. There is a copy in the Bodleian.

This appears to be the first version of the *whole* book after the additions of 1604, but William Whitaker had long before brought out a Latin and Greek Prayer Book, which he dedicated to his uncle, Dean Nowell. The title of the copy collated by us in the Bodleian is, " *LIBER PRECVM* Publicarum Ecclesiæ Anglicanæ, in iuuentutis Græcarum literarum studiosæ gratiam, latinè græcéq ; editus. Βίβλος κ. τ. λ. *LONDINI Anno Domini* MDLXIX." At the end is "Excusum Londini apud Reginaldum Wolfium," etc. In his preface or dedication Whitaker says, "*Exemplar autem Latinum* etc. *quod sequutus sum, regia ante annos aliquot authoritate impressum fuit, eo nimirum consilio, vt forma publicarum in Ecclesia nostra precum exteris etiam gentibus manifesta fieret. Quamuis verò alicubi ab Anglicano libro Latinus, quem ego sum sequutus, primo aspectu differre videatur, & aliud quiddam sonare, nihil tamen est aliud, quàm quòd alter altero aliquando contractior aut fusior sit, quodq' ; ille paucis contineat, idem hic pluribus exprimat verbis.*" This forms a good comment on the virtue of the Royal Authority, and on the reason for its exercise with regard to the Latin Prayer Book, and an excellent defence of the Elizabethan version against the attacks that have been made upon it on the ground of loose translation.

<small>Whitaker, Ed. 1569.</small>

<small>Remarks upon Queen Elizabeth's Latin Prayer Book.</small>

We come now to the better-known version of Duport. The title of this work is " ΒΙΒΛΟΣ ΤΗΣ ΔΗΜΟΣΙΑΣ *ΕΥΧΗΣ* καὶ Τελέσεως ΜΥΣΤΗΡΙΩΝ, κ. τ. λ. Ἐν τῇ ΚΑΝΤΑΒΡΙΓΙΑ, Ἐξ τυπώθη παρ' ΙΩΑΝΝΟΥ ΦΙΕΛΔΟΥ, τοῦ τῆς Ἀκαδημίας Τυπογράφου. Ἔτει ἀπὸ τῆς Θεογονίας ͵αχξε (*i.e.*, 1665)." As Petley's version is dedicated to William (Laud), archbishop of Canterbury, so Duport also dedicates his work to Gilbert (Sheldon), archbishop of Canterbury. Duport is largely indebted to Petley throughout the book, and numerous instances of this will be seen in the notes on the Catechism. The copy quoted in those notes is in the Bodleian, and we have collated it with a copy dated 1818 in private hands.

<small>Duport, Ed. 1665.</small>

For an account of the Welsh Prayer Books quoted, see note on "quod nobis datur" in the Catechism.

<small>Welsh Prayer Books.</small>

Before concluding this chapter a few words must be said upon the editions of Dean Nowell's Catechisms, which are quoted in the notes. For the Large Catechism we have used the excellent reprint (1853) of the Parker Society. The title is "CATECHISMVS, siue prima Institutio, Disci-PLINA QVE PIETATIS Christianæ, Latinè explicata." The original was printed "Londini, IN OFFICINA REGIN-ALDI Wolfij, Regiæ Maiest. in Latinis Typographi." The date is 1570.

Nowell's Catechisms.

Large Catechism.

Norton's translation is quoted from the same book. The title is, "A CATECHISME, or first Instruction and Learning of Christian Religion." It has the same date.

The copy of the Middle Catechism which we quote is in the Bodleian. The title runs: "ΧΡΙΣΤΙΑΝΙΣΜΟΥ ΣΤΟΙΧΕΙ-ΩΣΙΣ, κ.τ.λ. CHRISTIAnæ pietatis prima institutio, ad vsum scholarum Græcè & Latinè scripta." The imprint is, "LONDINI, Apud Ioannem Dayum. An. 1575. Cum gratia & Priuilegio." This Norton also translated.

Middle Catechism.

The most important, however, is the Small Catechism. Its title runs as follows, in Ed. 1633:—"CATECHISMVS PARVVS pueris primum qui ediscatur, proponendus in Scholis Latinè & Græcè. Excudebat Aug. Matth. pro Societate Bibliopolarum Londinensium. Anno 1633." It is dedicated to "Reverendissimis in Christo Patribus ac Dominis Matthæo [i.e., Parker], Archiepiscopo Cantuariensi, Edmundo (i.e., Grindal) Archiepiscopo Eboracensi, Edwino (i.e., Sandys), Episcopo Londinensi, alijsq; reverendis Patribus, Episcopis Ecclesiæ *Anglicanæ vigilentissimis fidelissimisque Pastoribus," by "A. N." Of the Greek version, he says, "Eundem hunc Catechismum Gulielmus Witacherus, cognatus meus meo rogatu Græce etiam reddidit," etc.

Small Catechism. Ed. 1633.

A copy of this edition is in the Bodleian, and as it is somewhat better printed we have quoted from it, except in the portion upon the Sacraments. There, to insure greater accuracy, we give the readings of the edition of 1584 in the Bod-

Ed. 1584.

leian, giving also the variations of 1633. The title-page of this edition is much the same as that of 1633; it has, however, a different border, "*pueris primùm qui*" in italics, "*dus in Scholis Latinè*" in italics, "& Græce" not in italics, and the imprint is "LONDINI. *Apud Ioannem Dayum.* Anno 1584. *Cum gratia & Priuilegio, Regiæ Maiestatis.*" Copies of this Small Catechism are exceedingly rare, as are also copies of Norton's translation of it. On account of this scarceness, and also because this Small Catechism was the immediate forerunner of the Catechism as we now have it in our Prayer Books, it has been thought advisable to give the readings of the Latin throughout the notes; the only exceptions to this are that the Creed, Commandments, and Lord's Prayer are quoted from the Large Catechism, with the variations of the Small added, and that the long expansion of the answer on our duty to our neighbour is omitted. With these exceptions the Latin of the Small Catechism is given at length in the notes.

Scarcity of Small Catechism. Its value.

Quoted throughout, with few exceptions.

Upon the importance and authority of these Catechisms it is sufficient to quote the memoir (p. vii.) in the Parker Society's reprint of the Large Catechism : " We may judge of the high estimation in which these works were held, when we learn from the various injunctions, &c. put forth at that time by public authorities, that no Catechisms were allowed to be used by clergymen and schoolmasters, except one or other of Nowell's."[1]

Authority of Nowell's Catechisms.

[1] The references given are: Cardwell, "Synodalia," i. 128; Grindal's "Remains," pp. 142, 152.

CHAPTER II.

MEANING OF THE TERM "PRIEST."

ὁ δὲ, διὰ τὸ μένειν αὐτὸν εἰς τὸν αἰῶνα, ἀπαράβατον ἔχει τὴν ἱερωσύνην.
Heb. vii. 24.

PROBABLY no better instance can be found of the value of Durel's "Liturgia," in determining the use and meaning of terms at the last revision, than that supplied by the word "priest," or "presbyter." There has of late years been much discussion as to the value of the term "priest," in our present Prayer Book. Does it mean a sacrificer, or does it simply mean a minister of the Second Order in the Church, in other words a Presbyter? This is of great importance; for if there is no sacrificer, there is no sacrifice; whereas, if the Church does admit a sacrificer, she opens a door for "the sacrifices of masses," which, in her Thirty-first Article, she denounces as "blasphemous fables, and dangerous deceits."

Reasons for this chapter.

Monsignor Capel once wrote: "My contention is that in the English Communion priest means minister, not sacrificer; altar is reduced to communion-table, and offering sacrifice to ministering communion; and that, consequently, Anglican consecrators do not impart sacrificial power, nor do Anglican 'ordinandi' purpose receiving it." This is a very accurate statement of the case. We shall show by the evidence of Durel's Latin Prayer Book, supported by early history, by ecclesiastical documents, and by the opinions of divines of the sixteenth and seventeenth centuries, that "priest" was retained in the revised Prayer Book, not in the sense of sacrificer, but of presbyter. There is a wide difference between

Monsignor Capel.

Durel and history show Priest stood simply for Presbyter.

the two. The Presbyter is a Minister of the Second Order, and the difference between a Minister and a Sacrificer is this: the former represents God to the people, the latter represents the people to God; the former declares God's message, the latter offers a human service; the former is the ambassador of the King, the latter is ordained for the people.

In Durel's Latin Prayer Book we have a form of the word "presbyter" once in the title-page; seventeen times in the Act of Uniformity, 14 Car ii., where as a generic term "Clerus" is used; ninety-six times in the Liturgy, etc.; twenty-eight times in the Form and Manner of Making, Ordaining, etc.; and eighteen times in the Forms of Prayer for the Fifth of November, etc.; one hundred and sixty times in all. Whereas the Second Order in the Church is not once denoted by the term "sacerdos." This is the same in all editions, and in Ed. 1703, where the Form of Prayer used in Convocation is added, we still have "presbyter" in that Form. *Presbyter 160 times in Durel's "Liturgia."*

The reasons of Durel's preference for the term "presbyter" are twofold. First, that it is an unequivocal word. There can be no sacrificial connotation attaching to it: whereas the word "sacerdos" does convey to most ears a sacrificial notion. No such idea was involved in the old English "preost" or "priest." Wm. Nicholls, D.D. (born 1664), speaks of the sacrificial connotation of "priest" as having arisen from the English Bible, and as not existing in the French word, *prêtre*. He writes as follows: "*Ordering of Priests.*] Our *English* Word *Priest* comes immediately from the *French* Word *Prestre* or Prêtre, which is but a Contraction of Presbyter, or Πρισβύτερος, and in its proper Signification does denote no more than Elder. But there seems to be an abuse of the Word crept into our Language, and that of considerable Standing; *viz.* to use the Word only for a Sacrificer. For, according to our common way of speaking, whenever the Word Priest is named, People have presently a Notion of Sacrifice, which was never intended by the first Imposi- *Durel's first reason for use of Presbyter. It (like Priest originally) has no sacrificial implication. Dr. Nicholls.*

tion of the Word. But that, which has made this Mistake among us incurable, is our *English* Translation of the Bible, which constantly translates *Cohen*, Priest; whereas it signifies Sacrificer, and ought so to be translated. And this the *French* Translation does; for tho' the *French* have the Word Prêtre in use among them, yet they always chose to translate *Cohen*, *Sacrificateur*. The Compilers of the *Scotch* Liturgy, taking Notice of the common Interpretation which is put upon this Word, and the Inconveniences which attended it, chose to use the Original Word Presbyter, instead of Priest, throughout that whole Common-Prayer-Book. The Title which is given in Scripture to this Order, is Πρεσβύτεροι, *Acts* xiv. 23. xv. 2. 1 *Tim.* v. 1. and Διάκονοι Εὐαγγελίου, *Eph.* iii. 7. Θεοῦ, 2 *Cor.* vi. 4. Χριστοῦ, *Col.* i. 7. but are never called Ἱερεῖς (*sic*) which is the proper Word to signify Sacrificators, or such Priests who offered Sacrifice. The ἱεράτευμα ἅγιον, *the holy Priesthood*, 1 Pet. ii. 5, and the βασίλειον ἱεράτευμα, *the Royal Priesthood*, 1 Pet. ii. 9. are spoken of the Laiety as well as Clergy ('A Supplement to the Commentary on the Book of Common-Prayer.' Lond. MDCCXI.)."

Priest retained in its pure sense. The word "priest," then, which the revisers retained, had originally no sacrificial connotation, and Durel *Durel has Presbyter even at Consecration of Elements, etc.* shows that they retained the word in its pure and early sense by employing everywhere, even in the crucial instances of the Consecration of the Elements, the Absolution, etc., the unequivocal and plain term "presbtery."[1]

Durel's second reason. Presbyter the correct word in early times. The next reason for Durel's use of the word "presbyter" to translate "priest" is that "presbyter" was from the earliest times the correct word for denoting a minister of the Second Order. We do not mean to say that the English "priest" and French *prêtre* are connected etymologically

---

[1] It is interesting to compare Durel upon another point connected with this. It has been asserted that "discreet" in the first exhortation at the Communion means "discrete," "set apart," such as a licensed confessor. But Durel solves this by giving us "ad me accedat aut alium prudentem ac doctum verbi Dei Ministrum adeat;" "prudentem" cannot mean "set apart." For the use of "discreet," cf. Archbishop Whitgift (1530-1603); "Honest, discreet, quiet, and godly learned men will not be withdrawn by you."

with the Greek Πρεσβύτερος. Such may be the case, and the opinion has gained much ground from a misapplication of Milton's line, in his "Ode on the New Forcers of Conscience under the Long Parliament:"— *Derivation of Priest.*

"New Presbyter is but Old Priest, writ large."

But this derivation appears at least doubtful.[1] However it is certain that no better word could be found in Latin to represent Priest than Presbyter. Or rather we should say that Presbyter is the original and correct word, and that Priest in English simply represents the older Presbyter. This we shall see from the following considerations. *"Priest" represents older "presbyter."*

The word Presbyter, as applied to this order of ministers, dates from the earliest times. Even in the New Testament we find the Greek Πρεσβύτεροι, as Dr. Nicholls shows, applied to them; whereas ἱερεύς is never used of the Christian minister: the word "priest" occurs thirty times in the New Testament; it is used nineteen times of the Levitical priest, and also of Christ and Melchisedec, and of the whole body of Christians (*e.g.*, Rev. i. 6; v. 10; xx. 6); but not once for the Christian Minister. *The term in the New Testament.*

---

[1] Milton's line refers to the substitution of Presbyter for Priest by the Scotch Church, and not to the supposed derivation of Priest from Presbyter. We venture here to suggest a new derivation which seems more in accordance with the rules of philology. The French *être* is of course from the old French *estre*, which again is the Latin *esse*. If, then, F. *être* = O. F. *estre* = L. *esse*, then F. *prêtre* should = O. F. *prestre* = L. *presse*. The O. F. is *prestre*, but *presse* must be for *prae-esse*, *i.e.*, *prae-esse* (*cf.* F. *present*, L. *praesent—*," in the participle of the same verb). For instances of infinitives used for substantives in French, a use which obtained even in the Latin of the best age, compare *avoir*, *faire*, and even *être* itself. The only difficulty, then, is the double vowel *prae-esse*, as we do not find *prae-estre*; but probably such was the form in very old French, as the old English *preost*, and the later *preest* (Pecock's "Repressor," *circa* 1449), *priestes* (pl.) and *priest* (Latimer's "Ploughers," 1549), *priestis* (pl. Lyndesay's "Monarche," 1552), *Preist* (ibid.), and our modern *priest* all point to a double vowel in the original word, though the shorter forms *prest* and *preste* do occasionally occur. If this derivation be true, the Priest is simply the President, and it is remarkable that the word *prae-esse* is used to describe one of the functions of a Sacerdos in a mediæval ordinal quoted by Mr. Proctor ("Common Prayer," p. 443): "Sacerdotem oportet offerre, benedicere, praeesse, praedicare, conficere, et baptizare." So, earlier still, Justin Martyr (died A.D. 165) writes in "Apol. 2 ad Anton. Pium Imperat.," quoted by Bishop Cowper in "Seven Dayes Conference," 1623: "*Die qui Solis dicitur, omnes qui in oppidis vel agris morantur, unum in locum conveniunt, commentaria que Apostolorum, vel Prophetarum scripta leguntur, quamdiu hora patitur; deinde ubi is qui legit destitit, is qui praeest admonet*, ... *Quibus copiæ suppetunt*, etc. (see this passage quoted in next chapter p. 62); *quodq; colligitur, apud eum qui praeest re onitur.*" Cf. also *praesint* in Art. XXVI., "Of the Unworthiness of Ministers."

Turning to the Fathers,[1] we find that Ignatius (who died not later than 112 A.D.), in his epistle to the Magnesians, Sect. 2, mentions Damas as bishop, Bassus and Apollonius as presbyters, and Sotian as a deacon; again, in his epistle to the Philadelphians, Sect. 7: "Attend to the bishop, to the presbytery, and to the deacons;" and in his epistle to the Trallians, Sect. 2, he writes: "Be ye subject . . . to the presbyters, as to the Apostles of Jesus Christ." In the second century Irenæus was first presbyter, then bishop of Lyons; and Dionysius first presbyter, then bishop of Rome. Again, Tertullian (about the close of the second century) writes: "When your captains, that is to say, the deacons, presbyters, and bishops, fly, who shall teach the laity that they must be constant?" (De Fuga in Pers.) And "The high priest, who is the bishop, has the chief right in administering it, then the presbyters and deacons, but not without the authority of the bishop." (De Baptism. Cap. 17.) Then Optatus (fourth century) writes: "To what purpose should I mention deacons, who are in the third, or presbyters, in the second degree, of priesthood, etc. (Lib. i.)?" At the end of this fourth century Aerius, an Arian, maintained that there ought to be no order higher than that of Presbyters. Lastly, Jerome, who was ordained presbyter at Antioch in 378 A.D., wrote as follows (De Eccles. Script.): "Till through instinct of the devil there grew in the church factions, and among the people it began to be professed, I am of Paul, I am of Apollos, I am of Cephas, churches were governed by the common advice of presbyters; but when every one began to reckon those whom himself had baptized his own, and not Christ's, it was decreed in the whole world, that one chosen out of the presbyters should be placed over the rest, to whom all care of the church should belong, and so the seeds

In the Fathers.
Ignatius.
Irenæus and Dionysius.
Tertullian.
Optatus.
Aerius.
Jerome.
Jerome here speaks of apostolical times.

---

[1] These quotations are from the "Elements of Christian Theology," by G. Tomline, D.D., F.R.S., Lord Bishop of Winchester. Thirteenth Edition, 1837.

of schism be removed." Jerome is here speaking of apostolical times, as in the same book he tells how, in accordance with this, James, Timothy, Titus, and Polycarp were appointed bishops.

In pursuance of this usage of apostolical and primitive times, we find the Latin "Presbyter," as denoting the Second Order, at a very early age of the Church in England. In the Latin Life of "the Venerable Bede," who was born about 673 A.D., we find "Sacris autem a Joanne Beverlacio Episcopo sanctissimo, a quo in bonis literis fuerat eruditus, annum trigesimum agens, initiatus atque inauguratus fuit hinc presbyter appellatus." Again, in an early Ordinal quoted by Mr. Proctor ("Common Prayer," p. 444), the consecration runs thus: "Deus sanctificationum omnium auctor, cujus vera consecratio, plenaque benedictio est, tu, Domine, super hos famulos tuos, quos presbyterii honore dedicamus, munus tuæ benedictionis effunde:" etc. And in an Ordinal of the eleventh century, given in a note on the same page, we have "Vis presbyterii gradum in nomine Domini accipere?" (The latter is quoted from Martene, "Eccl. Rit." ii. 146.) So that in very early times the Second Order of Ministers was conferred with the title of "presbyter."[1]

Presbyter in Early English Church.

Bede a Presbyter.

Early Ordinals.

About the time of the last revision, indeed, presbyter was not only the correct Latin word, but was considered the better term even in English. Archbishop Whitgift (died 1604) considered that "priest" was but a contraction of "presbyter," and meant nothing more than Presbyter. Hooker[2] held similar views. The latter was a man almost universally honoured by English Churchmen; the former was the great opponent of the Puritan party in his day. Again, when Archbishop Laud, whose tendencies to Romanism were undoubted,

About last review, presbyter thought better English word than priest.

Whitgift and Hooker.

Laud, and the Scotch Prayer Book.

---

[1] Cf. its use in the Romish Church; *e.g.*, Decree of Sacred Congregation at Rome: "Amisso vel ablato Breviario, non tenetur Presbyter Officio." "The Frauds of Romish Monks and Priests," 1704.

[2] See Hooker, Bk. V., ch. 78, secs. 2, 3.

drew up a Prayer Book for the Church of Scotland at the request of Charles I. in 1637, even he thought proper to use the word "presbyter," not "priest," from beginning to end. And in the later Scotch Communion Office of 1765 the term "presbyter" is used in the Rubrics. Again, Dr. Todd, of Trinity College, Dublin, states with regard to the Prayer Book of 1608 (in Stephen's "Book of Common Prayer," Introd. p. xxix., Eccl. Hist. Soc. 1849), that the word "priest" does not occur in any part of Archbishop Daniell's Irish version of the Prayer Book of King James I., but that it is everywhere throughout the Rubrics translated by the word "minister." See also Dr. Nicholls, quoted above. And lastly, in the attempted Revision of the English Book in 1689, it was suggested to read, "The Minister that consecrates ought always to be an Archbishop, Bishop, or Presbyter," and "Ordination of Priests, *i.e.*, Presbyters" (Proctor's "Com. Prayer," pp. 150, 157).

Irish Prayer Book.

Attempted Revision of 1689.

The fact is, that there is no Order of "Sacerdotes" in the Reformed Church of England;[1] the Second Order is that of Presbyteri. This we see not only from Durel's "Liturgia," where we find "presbyter" throughout and the "Forma & Modus Ordinandi Presbyteros," but also from the Articles, from Testimonials, Letters of Orders, Orders in Council, and from other documentary evidence.

No order of "Sacerdotes" in Reformed Church.

Presbyteri only in Second Order.

Commencing with the Thirty-nine Articles (1571), we must first observe that those who "Sacramentorum administrationi præsint" are included under the general heading "*Ministrorum*" in Art. XXVI., and are not called Sacerdotes. Secondly, that in Art. XXXI. we have the word "sacerdotem" for "priest;"—"the sacrifices of Masses, in the which it was commonly said, that the Priest did offer Christ for the quick and the dead, to have remission of pain

Evidence of the Thirty-nine Articles.

Art. XXVI.

Art. XXXI.

---

[1] Cf. Nowell's "Large Catech." where he says, "*M.* What manner of priest (*Lat.* sacerdos) is Christ? *S.* The greatest and an everlasting priest, which alone is able to appear before God, only able to make the sacrifice which God will allow and accept, and only able to appease the wrath of God." (Norton's Transl.)

or guilt, were blasphemous fables and dangerous deceits." Here "Priest" clearly refers to the "priest" or "sacerdos" of the old unreformed Church. Thirdly, in Art. XXXII. we have "Episcopis, presbyteris, et diaconis," etc. But, in the title, for "*Of the Marriage of Priests*" the Latin has "*De conjugio Sacerdotum.*" It has been asserted that this proves the authors of the Articles to have considered the priests of the English Reformed Church to be Sacerdotes. Such, however, is not the case. An able writer in a periodical a short time ago proved the worthlessness of the assertion by reducing the case to a dilemma. Either the word "Sacerdotum" refers to the persons mentioned in the Article, or it does not. If it does refer to them, it must refer to all alike, deacons as well as bishops and priests; and so can mean no more than "Episcoporum et Ministrorum" in the heading of Art. XXXVI., and can in no way denote the functions of a sacrificing priest. Indeed, it is not improbable that in the ancient Church "sacerdos" was a generic term of wide import, comprehending deacons. This Bingham shows in his "Antiquities," Bk. II., ch. xix., sec. 15. "Sacerdos," from "sacer," was then no more than one in holy orders. Besides, in Rom. xv. 16, St. Paul speaks of sacerdotally-ministering the gospel; in other words, leading men by the ministry of the gospel to present themselves a living sacrifice unto the Lord; thus, and in assisting the people to offer up the sacrifice of prayer and praise, it has been said that bishops, presbyters, and deacons alike might, in a certain sense, be termed "sacerdotes." To turn, however, to the other horn of the dilemma. If "Sacerdotum" does not refer to those mentioned in the Article, it must refer to the Romish clergy. And this is the most reasonable explanation. The writer mentioned above says: "In the Romish Church there were certain erroneous views concerning '*Opera supererogationis*,' '*Purgatorium*,' '*Connubium Sacerdotum*,' &c. 'The old order changeth,' and our reformers held it their duty to enter a protest against such doctrines. Accordingly, we have the Fourteenth Article, '*De Operibus Supererogationis*,' the Twenty-

Art. XXXII.

second, '*De Purgatorio*,' and the Thirty-second, '*De Conjugio Sacerdotum*.' In each of these three titles the words used apply to the Romish Church and its errors; and, as in the Reformed Church, there were to be no works of supererogation, for '*non possunt sine arrogantiâ et impietate prædicari;*' and no doctrine of Purgatory, for '*res est futilis, inaniter conficta;*' so there were to be no 'sacerdotes,' and no restrictions of celibacy placed upon the new clergy, the '*Episcopis, presbyteris, et diaconis.*'" To this excellent argument nothing need be added. Lastly, in Art. XXXVI., "*Of the Consecration of Bishops and Ministers*," "*De Episcoporum et Ministrorum consecratione*," the words of the Article are, "de ordinatione Presbyterorum et Diaconorum," but not a word of "sacerdotes." So that there is no recognition of an Order of Sacerdotes in the Reformed Church in the Thirty-nine Articles.[1]

Art. XXXVI.

Only Order of Presbyters in Thirty-nine Articles as regards Reformed Church.

The ancient form of *Testimonium* also recognizes the Second Order as "Presbyteratus." As an example, see one given among the "Forms of Divers Instruments," etc., in the Appendix to the "Liber Valorum," by John Ecton, Receiver of the Tenths of the Clergy. Lond. 1728: "*Omnibus Christi Fidelibus, ad quos Præsentes Literæ pervenerint, salutem & debitam reverentiam. Cum pium & officiosum sit Testimonium Veritati perhibere, cumque* Johannes Smith A.B. *Literas nostras Testimonales de Vita sua laudabili, Morumque* Probitate *concedi sibi petierit; nos tam honestæ ejus Petitioni volentes obsecundare, testamur prædictum* Johannem Smith *per tres annos proximè elapsos nobis personaliter cognitum, piè, sobriè, & honestè vitam suam instituisse, studiis suis*

Evidence of Form of Testimonium.

---

[1] See also "Memoir of Robert Daly, D.D., Bishop of Cashel," p. 441, n. Lond.: J. Nisbet & Co., 1875: "In the later edition of the Articles of 1553, we have—'Episcopis, presbyteris, et diaconis non est mandatum est (ut ?) cœlibatum voveant.' In the MS. of Convocation, 1562: 'Episcopis, presbyteris, et diaconis, nullo mandato divino preceptum est ut aut cœlibatum voveant aut a matrimonio abstineant.'—See Library T. C. D. I had some early editions of Articles, which I sold with other scarce books; among them one in Latin, in which the words were, 'Episcopi, presbyteres, et diaconi.' There is a later edition of these Articles in Latin, printed in Oxford 1636, and there is this title of one of the Articles: 'Libellus de consecratione archiepiscoporum et episcoporum, et de ordinatione presbyterorum et diaconorum.' They are the Articles of the London Synod of 1562."

sedulò operam navasse, nec quicquam (quantum scimus) unquàm tenuisse, scripsisse, vel docuisse, nisi quod Ecclesia Anglicana approbet & tueatur; eumque insuper censemus dignum qui ad Sacri Presbyteratûs Ordinem (si iis quorum interest ita videbitur) promoveatur. In cujus Rei Testimonium manus nostras præsentibus apposuimus tertio die Februarii, *A.D.* 1722." Presbyteratus.

The same is the case with the Letters of Orders. Here, too, the Second Order of the Clergy is "Presbyteratus." See the Letter of Orders of John Wesley, granted by Dr. Potter, Bishop of Oxford, in 1728: "TENORE præsentium nos Johannes permissione divina Oxon. Episcopus, Notum facimus universis quod nos Episcopus antedictus die Dominico (viz.) Vicesimo secundo die mensis Septembris, Anno Domini Millesimo Septingentesimo Vicesimo octavo in Ecclesia Cathedrali Christi Oxon. Sacros Ordines Dei Omnipotentis præsidio celebrantes; Dilectum nobis in Christo Johannem Wesley, Artis Magistrum, e Coll. Lincoln, Oxon. Socium —— ad Sacrum Presbyteratus Ordinem juxta morem et ritus Ecclesiæ Anglicanæ admisimus et promovimus ipsumqe (sic) in Presbyterum tunc et ibidem rite et Canonice Ordinavimus. Datum sub Sigillo nostro Episcopali in præmissorum fidem ac testimonium die mensis Annoque Domini supra expressis et nostræ Consecrationis Anno decimo quarto. "Jo. OXON."[1] Letters of Orders.
John Wesley.
Presbyteratus.
Presbyterum.

Lastly, Law Forms may be adduced to show that "presbyter," not "sacerdos," is the correct term for the Order of Priest in the Reformed Church: and these have the more weight as legal forms mostly follow precedent even in phraseology. For example, in the appeal of Bishop Wilson (Sodor and Man) and his clergy, all the law forms in London have "presbyter" for the Second Order of Clergy; *e.g.*, Orders in Council, July 19th, 1722, and August 7th, 1722; Petitions to Council; Report of Attorney-General and Solicitor-General to the Law Forms.
Order in Council, etc.

---

[1] Quoted from "The Works of the Rev. John Wesley," vol. i. Lond. 1809. Since writing the above, the Rev. Dr. Osborn, President of the Wesleyan Conference, has very kindly written to inform us that Wesley's Letters of Orders are preserved in the Library of the College at Headingly, near Leeds.

Report of Committee of Privy Council. King's Most Excellent Majesty, August 2nd, 1722; and the Report of Committee of Privy Council, etc., February 15th, 1722.

Decreasing use of "sacerdos" in Prayer Books before Revision. In conclusion, we purpose to show by fourteen passages how the word "sacerdos" was comparatively little used in the Prayer Book of Queen Elizabeth, was less used by Vautrollier in 1574, and was not used at all by Durel, whose verdict is final, as his "Liturgia" is the only Latin Prayer Book with any show of authority since the last revision. With regard to the use of "sacerdos" occasionally in Queen Elizabeth's reign, in many cases the word occurs in sentences taken direct from the earlier Aless, who kept the term from the ancient missals used in the unreformed Church. On the other hand, we have Reasons for the use at first. the "sacerdos" of Aless sometimes changed by Queen Elizabeth, as in the first passage quoted below from the Marriage Service. Moreover, in the Absolution and Benediction in the Communion Service, where we find "Sacerdos" opposed to "Episcopus," it is evident that "Sacerdos" is meant to express the minister of the Second Order as opposed to the bishop; it cannot mean "the sacrificer," for if the bishop were present he would probably himself take that part of the service to which a sacrificial character is wrongly assigned, and would himself be the "sacerdos" in that sense.

To proceed, then, to our passages:

(I.) Morning and Evening Prayer. "Absolutio per Ministrum solum pronuncianda" (Q. Eliz. 1560). Ditto, in Vautrollier, 1574, who however has the Rubrics in Italics.

Absolution in Morning Prayer.

"*The Absolution, or Remission of sins, to be pronounced by the Priest alone, standing; the people still kneeling*" (E.V. 1662, our present version).[1] "*Absolutio seu peccatorum remissio à Presbytero*

---

[1] In the Prayer Book of 1634, in which Dr. Sancroft copied Bishop Cosin's notes for Convocation, we find, "The absolution or remission of sinnes to be pronounced by the Minister alone. (*standing, & all the People still kneeling*)." The part in italics and in brackets is in MS. This shows that the revisers attached no great importance to the insertion of "priest" instead of

tantùm, eoque stante, plebe autem genua flectente, pronuncianda" (Durel's "Liturgia," 1670). "*Absolutio, sive Remissio Peccatorum, a Sacerdote solo pronuntianda, ipso stante; populo, ut antea, genuflexo*" (Messrs. Bright and Medd's "Liber Precum Publicarum," 1869).

(II.) Communion Service. Before Prayer for Church Militant (the so-called Prayer of Oblation). "*Post hæc minister dicet*" (Q. Eliz.). Ditto, Vautrollier. "*After which done, the Priest shall say*" (E.V.). "*Quibus peractis dicat Presbyter*" (Durel). "*Quo facto Sacerdos dicat*" (Messrs. Bright and Medd). <small>Communion Service.</small>

(III.) Ditto. The Absolution. "*Deinde eriget se Sacerdos*," etc. (Q. Eliz.). "*Deinde eriget se Sacerdos, (aut Episcopus, si adsit)*" etc. (Vautr). "*Then shall the Priest (or the Bishop, being present,) stand up*," etc. (E.V.). "*Tum Presbyter (aut Episcopus si adsit) eriget se*," etc. (Durel). "*Deinde Sacerdos, (aut Episcopus, si adsit,) se erigat*," etc. (Messrs. Bright and Medd).

(IV.) Ditto. Consecration. "*Postea Sacerdos erigens se, dicet*" (Q. Eliz.). Ditto, Vautrollier. "*When the Priest, standing before the Table*," etc. (E.V.) "*Quum Presbyter stans ante Mensam Domini*," etc. (Durel). "*Cum Sacerdos, stans ante Mensam*," etc. (Messrs. Bright and Medd).

(V.) Ditto, Benediction. "*Postremo Sacerdos uel Episcopus, si adsit*," etc. (Q. Eliz.). Ditto, Vautrollier. "*Then the Priest (or Bishop if he be present)*" etc. (E.V.). "*Postremo Presbyter (aut Episcopus si adsit)*" etc. (Durel). "*Deinde Sacerdos (sive Episcopus, si adsit)*" etc. (Messrs. Bright and Medd).

(VI.) Ditto. Second Rubric after Com. Serv. "sine convenienti

---

"minister" in this place, otherwise Bishop Cosin would have had the change made in his notes in this Prayer Book. As a matter of fact that change was not made at the revision, but between the years 1636 and 1639, and it was retained by the revisers. It has also been asserted that "*by the Priest alone*" means "and not by a Deacon;" but it is evident from the old form, "by the Minister alone," especially with Dr. Sancroft's MS. note, that it means "and not by the People." Indeed, Whitaker, in his Greek and Latin Prayer Book, dedicated to his uncle, Dean Nowell, 1569, has "Absolutio per Ministrum" etc. (as Queen Elizabeth), in the Latin; and in the Greek, Ἀπόλυσις, ἣν ὁ διάκονος μόνος ἐκφωνεῖ.

numero communicantium" (no word for Priest. Q. Eliz.). "*nisi iustus sit hominum, numerus qui cum ministro communicent,*" etc. (Vautr.). "*except there be a convenient number to communicate with the Priest*" (E.V.). "*nisi adsit communicantium numerus competens ad communicandum cum Presbytero*" (Durel). " nisi conveniens numerus adsit Communicantium cum Sacerdote" (Messrs. Bright and Medd).

(VII. and VIII.) Ditto. Fourth Rubric. "ubi multi sunt presbyteri, & Diaconi, omnes una cum Ministro." (Q. Eliz.). "*in quibus plures existant ministri ac diaconi . . . vna cum ministro*" (Vautr.). "*where there are many Priests and Deacons, they shall all receive the Communion with the Priest*" (E.V.). "*ubi sunt Presbyteri & Diaconi complures, communicabunt singuli unà cum Presbytero*" (Durel). " ubi multi sunt Presbyteri et Diaconi, omnes una cum Sacerdote" (Messrs. Bright and Medd).

(IX.) Public Baptism of Infants. " Hic Minister infantem in manus suscipiet, & nomen quæret: deinde nomine appellans, tinget illum ni (in?) aquam, sed consultè & cautè, dicens" (Q. Eliz.). "*Tunc Minister infantem in manus accipiens,*" etc. (Vautr.). "*Then the Priest shall take the Child into his hands,*" etc. (E.V.). "*Tum Presbyter Infantem in manus accipiet,*" etc. (Durel). " Deinde accipiat Sacerdos infantem in manus suas," etc. (Messrs. Bright and Medd).

<small>Public Baptism of Infants.</small>

(X.) Further on we have, " Tunc Minister, cruce signabit infantes, fronte, dicens" (Q. Eliz.). "*deinde Minister facto crucis signo in fronte infantis, dicet*" (Vautr.). "*Here the Priest shall make a Cross upon the Child's forehead*" (E.V.). "*Hic Presbyter Infantis frontem signo crucis signabit*" (Durel). " Hic Sacerdos in fronte Infantis Crucem faciat" (Messrs. Bright and Medd).

(XI.) Private Baptism of Infants. "tum baptizet eum minister (Q. Eliz.)." "*tunc Minister ad rationem publici Baptismi,*" etc. (Vautr). "*then let the Priest baptize it in the form*" etc. (E.V.). "*tunc Presbyter cum baptizet juxta formam*" etc. (Durel). " Sacerdos eum baptizet sub forma"

<small>Private Baptism.</small>

etc. (Messrs. Bright and Medd). There is, of course, no Form for *Adult Baptism* in Queen Elizabeth or Vautrollier.

(XII. and XIII.) Marriage. "Tunc uir det mulieri annulum & alia munera, aurum & argentum, & ponet super librum, cum consueto ministris debito salario, quem Minister manu tenet, ac Presbyter accepto annulo, tradet uiro, ut imponat quarto digito mulieris, dicens" (Q. Eliz.). "*& maritus annulum vxori dandum libro imponet vna cum pecunijs Ministro ac sibi seruienti debitis: & Minister*" etc. (Vautr). "*and the Man shall give unto the Woman a Ring, laying the same upon the book with the accustomed duty to the Priest and Clerk. And the Priest,*" etc. (E.V.). "*Vir autem Mulieri Annulum dabit, illum ponens super librum unà cum eo quicquid sit, quod Presbytero & Clerico jure pendi debet. Presbyter acceptum Annulum*" etc. (Durel). "vir mulieri annulum det, ponens cum super librum cum pecunia Sacerdoti et Clerico debita. Quem annulum Sacerdos" etc. (Messrs. Bright and Medd).

Marriage.

(XIV.) Ditto. "Tunc sacerdos jungens eorum dextras, dicat" (Q. Eliz.). "*His dictis, Minister eorum dexteras junget dicendo*" (Vautr). "*Then shall the Priest join their right hands together, and say*" (E.V.). "*Tum Presbyter eorum dextras junget, ac dicet*" (Durel). "Tunc Sacerdos, jungens eorum dextras, dicat" (Messrs. Bright and Medd).

It will be seen from this that in these fourteen cases, where the English Version has "Priest," Durel here (as throughout his "Liturgia") translates it by "Presbyter." And these fourteen passages contain the most important ones for testing the meaning of "Priest" at the period of revision. Messrs. Bright and Medd in these passages have a form of the word "Sacerdos" thirteen times, and of "Presbyter" once. Durel, as we have seen, does not sanction the use of "Sacerdos" at all; but even going further back to the reign of Queen Elizabeth, we find that her Prayer Book has in these passages "sacerdos" only four times, "presbyter" twice, and "minister" seven times, there being no

Durel has only "presbyter."

Messrs. Bright and Medd's Prayer Book.

Queen Elizabeth.

Vautrollier. equivalent for the word in the remaining passage; while Vautrollier's book has "sacerdos" only thrice, and "minister" the other eleven times. So that these Prayer Books have "sacerdos" in the important passages the following number of times: Queen Elizabeth four, Vautrollier three, Durel not once, Messrs. Bright and Medd thirteen times. The latter, in their preface to the reader, write as follows: "Verbum 'Priest' visum est verbo 'Presbyter' eis in locis reddere ubi de ordine eorum ageretur qui in Ministerio Christi inter Episcopos et Diaconos locum habent; ubi autem de ipsa ministerii eorum exsecutione, verbo 'Sacerdos.'" It would appear, however, a strange anomaly for persons to be ordained "Presbyteri" in order to perform the functions of "Sacerdotes." Priests must either be ordained "Sacerdotes," and perform sacerdotal functions, or be ordained "Presbyteri," and fulfil the office of presbyters. It would be an empty mockery to ordain a minister by the title of presbyter, if that title is not to be applied to him when in the execution of his ministry.

Comparison of these versions.

The re-introduction of the term "sacerdos" is historically a retrograde movement. We have in early times "sacerdos" applied to all in holy orders; under the Romish system the term acquired a sacrificial connotation; Aless followed the obsolete language of the missals somewhat freely in retaining the word; in Queen Elizabeth's book the reaction commences; the use of the term wanes in Vautrollier, and disappears in the Prayer Book of Durel. So that its revival is in opposition to all the principles of Revision and Reform. It is the awakening of a word and of a doctrine which Reformers and Revisers have striven to eradicate. Dean Durel gives us the only true word for the Second Order in the ministry, and that is Presbyter, a term born in the New Testament, cradled in the constant usage of primitive Christianity, and brought to full maturity in the best ages of the English Church.

Re-introduction of the obsolete "sacerdos."

Durel's is the only true title, "presbyter."

CHAPTER III.

MEANING OF THE EXPRESSION, "ALMS AND OBLATIONS."

"The will gives worth to the oblation, as to God's acceptance, sets the poorest giver upon the same level with the richest."—ROBERT SOUTH.

"*Eleemosynam in pauperum usus erogatam colligent, ut & alias populi oblationes in pios usus, in Amula seu lance idoneâ,*" *etc.*—Extract from Rubric after the Offertory, in Durel's "Liturgia."

"*eleemosynas atque oblationes.*"—Extract from Prayer for Church Militant, ibid.

HAVING discussed the value of the term "priest" in the light of Durel's Latin Prayer Book, we may proceed to estimate the meaning of the expression, "*accept our alms and oblations*" in the Prayer for the Church Militant. It has been a matter of controversy, especially of late years, whether the Oblation of the Elements is enjoined by the Prayer Book as we now have it—that is to say, by the revised Prayer Book of 1662. For example, Mr. Blunt writes as follows: "The substance of this rubric (*i.e.*, that of 1549, commencing, "*Then shall the minister*," etc.) is retained in that which immediately precedes the Prayer for the Church Militant, and its significance was heightened in the revision of 1661 by the introduction of the word "oblations" into that prayer. The rubric and the words of the prayer together now give to our Liturgy as complete an "Oblation of the Elements" as is found in the ancient Offices."[1] We shall show that this involves a complete misconception of the meaning of the term "oblations" in this prayer; and we are led to consider the subject at some length, both on account of its own paramount importance, and because it affords a striking illustration of the value

Reasons for this chapter.

Mr. Blunt's statement.

---

[1] "Annotated Book of Common Prayer," p. 174. Rivingtons, 1866.

of Dean Durel's translations of the Prayer Book as a whole. The student of the period of the Last Review, and the impartial inquirer into the doctrines held at that time, could have no more reliable and trustworthy evidence than that which may be obtained by collating with the English the Latin version of Durel.

The oblation of the elements was no part of the memorial ceremony of the Lord's Supper as originally instituted. Nor, indeed, was it for some time afterwards, as we gather from Justin Martyr (Apol. 2 ad Anton. Pium, Imperat.): "conclusisq; nostris precibus, panis, vinum & aquæ offeruntur, tum is qui primum locum tenet eodem modo preces, gratiarumq; actionem pro virili mittit, populusque benedicit, dicens, Amen," etc. This Bishop Cowper, 1623, translates, "our prayers being finished, bread, wine, and water are presented, and then the Preacher conceiues feruent prayer and thankesgiuing, and the people blesse God, saying, Amen;" "offeruntur" here meaning, according to Bishop Cowper, "are presented,"[1] *i.e.*, are given to the minister for use in the sacrament by the communicants who had brought them, not are offered in sacrifice by the priest. At some early period, however, in the history of Christianity it appears that part of the bread and wine so brought was offered. In those days of primitive simplicity this practice, it may be thought, meant no harm. But what means no harm often tends to harm; tendency often exists where intention is absent; and so this custom soon led on to superstition, and from superstition to idolatry. There attaches, therefore, a prime interest to the question, whether the revisers of the Prayer Book in 1662 wished to adopt and restore this idea of an oblation; whether, in fact, they intended an oblation of bread and wine, and their sanctification by being placed by the minister upon the table and offered to God, to be regarded as an integral and essential part of the commemoration service, or, indeed, any part of that service at all.

Account of oblation of elements.

---

[1] Similarly the author of the Homily translates "offeruntur" in this passage of Justin Martyr by "brought forth."

That the communicants were not intended, as in the times when the idea of an oblation originated, to bring the bread and wine, is sufficiently clear from the terms of the Rubric at the end of the Communion Service: "*The Bread and Wine for the Communion shall be provided by the Curate and the Church-wardens at the charges of the Parish.*" Great stress is, however, laid on two passages by those who hold that oblation of the elements is enjoined by the Prayer Book. The first of these is the Rubric which runs as follows: "*And when there is a Communion, the Priest shall then place upon the Table so much Bread and Wine, as he shall think sufficient.*" This is said to mean that he shall make an oblation of them; the reason alleged is that the Prayer for the Church Militant immediately follows, in which the second passage alluded to occurs: "We humbly beseech thee most mercifully [*to accept our alms and oblations, and*] to receive these our prayers, which we offer unto thy Divine Majesty." It is argued that "*alms*" refers to the Rubric on the Offertory, and "*oblations*" to that on the placing of the bread and wine; the word "*then*" in the latter Rubric meaning "at that part of the service."

Provision of elements by church-wardens in revised Prayer Book.

Position of those who hold oblation of elements.

Now even as regards the English words it is, we submit, hardly probable that so solemn an act as an oblation to Almighty God would be described in such homely and commonplace language as that of the Rubric: "*the Priest shall then place upon the Table so much Bread and Wine, as he shall think sufficient.*" Contrast with this the reverential tone of the previous Rubric relating to the offering of alms: "*the Deacons, Church-wardens, or other fit person appointed for that purpose,*" after collecting "*the Alms for the Poor, and other devotions of the people, in a decent bason*[1] *to be provided by the Parish for that purpose,*" shall "*reverently bring it to the Priest, who shall humbly present and place it upon the holy Table.*" It would appear strange that

Argument against this from the language of Rubric.

---

[1] For the use of a Bag, cf. a sermon in Lent at the church of St. Andrew of the Valley at Rome, quoted in "The Frauds of Romish Monks and Priests," Lond., 1704:—"That Monk there made me, sore against my will, put a crown into the Bag."

the terms "*reverently*" and again "*humbly present*" should be applied to an oblation of money, whereas no such expression of reverential awe was applied to the so-called oblation of the elements.

Again, does the word "*then*" imply at that part of the service im-
<small>Meaning of the word "then."</small> mediately preceding the Prayer for the Church Militant? All that the Rubric decides is that the elements shall be placed on the table "*when there is a Communion;*" that is to say, as Durel puts it, "*quoties sacra Communio celebrabitur,*" "whenever the holy Communion shall be celebrated," *then* upon each such occasion the Priest shall place, etc. In fact Duport (1665) omits "then" altogether in his Greek version: καὶ ὅτι ἡ Σύνταξις γίνεται, τοσοῦτον ἄρτον τε καὶ οἶνον, κ.τ.λ. So, too, the Welsh (1664) has no word for "then": "A phan fo Cymmun yr Offeiriad a esyd ar y Bwrdd Fara a Gwin, hyn a dybio yn ddigonol." An exactly parallel expression to that in the English Rubric is to be found in the third Rubric in the Public Baptism of Infants: "*And the Priest coming to the Font, (which is then to be filled with pure water,) and standing there, shall say,*" etc. Probably no one would assert that this means that the font should be filled on the coming of the priest to it; every one would allow that the "*then*" refers to the first words of the Rubric, "*When there are children to be baptized,*" etc.; just as does also the "*then*" in the second clause of the Rubric, "*And then the Godfathers and Godmothers, and the people with the Children, must be ready at the Font,*" etc. Other similar instances might be quoted in great abundance from the Prayer Book; two, however, will suffice for illustration. In the last Rubric but one in the Communion of the Sick we find, "*When the sick person is visited, and receiveth the holy Communion all at one time, then the Priest,*" etc.; and again in the second Rubric in the Private Baptism of Infants, "*But when need shall compel them so to do, then Baptism shall be administered on this fashion.*" Nor does the position of
<small>The position of the Rubric.</small> the Rubric necessarily imply that the elements are to be placed upon the table at that part of the service, for many of the Rubrics, and among them the very next to this, are entirely out of their proper place.

More convincing, however, than all this is the direct testimony afforded by Durel's Latin and French versions that no such thing as an oblation of the elements was intended in the words of the Prayer for the Church Militant. But we shall understand this evidence better if we review for a moment the history of alms-giving at the Lord's Supper. The oldest uninspired account of such alms-giving appears to be that given by Justin Martyr (150 A.D.): "*Quibus copiæ suppetunt, ijs (sic) si volunt, quisq. suo arbitratu quod vult largitur, quodq. colligitur, apud eum qui præest reponitur, isq. pupillis, & viduis, & ijs quos morbus aliáve causa inopes fecit, & ijs qui in vinculis sunt, & hospitibus subvenit.*"[1] "Those who have means, if they wish, give each what he wishes at his own pleasure, and what is collected is laid up at the house of him who presides, and he succours orphans, and widows, and those whom disease or other cause hath made poor, and those who are in bonds, and strangers." Passing to comparatively modern times, we find, in the First Prayer Book of Edward VI. (1549), this Rubric after the Offertory sentences: "*In the mean time, whiles the Clerks do sing the Offertory, so many as are disposed, shall offer [un]to the poor men's box every one according to his ability and charitable mind. And at the offering days appointed* [Die autem oblationum, Aless 1551] *every man and woman shall pay to the Curate the due and accustomed offerings.*"[2] The earlier form of the Prayer for the Church Militant is not placed in this book immediately after the Offertory, but is the introductory part of the Prayer of Consecration: there is no reference in it either to alms or oblations. In the Second Prayer Book of Edward VI. we have the Rubric somewhat altered. "*Then shall the Church wardens, or some other by them appointed, gather the devotion of the people, and put the same into the poor men's box: and upon the offering days appointed, every man and woman shall pay to the Curate the*

History of alms-giving at the Lord's Supper.

Justin Martyr.

First Prayer Book of Edward VI.

Offerings to poor men's box,

And to Curate.

Second Prayer Book of Edw. VI.

---

[1] Apol. 2, ad Anton. Pium Imperat., quoted by Bishop Cowper.
[2] From "The First Prayer Book of Edward VI." Parker and Co., 1877.

due and accustomed offerings." The Prayer for the Church Militant is placed in this book in its present position after the offertory, and is in much the same form. Mention is only made of "alms:"—"we humbly beseech thee most mercifully to accept our * alms, and to receive these our prayers." The reason for this was that the oblations or offerings to the Curate were considered as dues payable at fixed times. This is the same (with the exception of "almose" for "alms" in eds. 1559, and "no" for "none" in "one ed., 1552, 1559, and all afterwards") in the editions of 1559, 1604, 1607, and 1634, and in the Scotch Liturgy of 1637. In this Prayer Book of 1552 a Rubric is added at the end of the Communion in these terms: "*And note, that every Parishioner shall communicate, at the least three times in the year: of which Easter to be one: ... And yearly at Easter, every Parishioner shall reckon with his Parson, Vicar or Curate, or his, or their deputy or deputies, and pay to them or him all ecclesiastical duties, accustomably due, then and at that time to be paid.*"[1] This is the same in Elizabeth's book, 1559, and in that of James I., 1604. It is interesting to note that in this Rubric Queen Elizabeth's Latin Prayer Book gives "decimas, oblationes, ceteraque debita" as the equivalent for "*ecclesiastical duties.*" The Rubric before the Prayer for the Church Militant is "Interea ædiles seu alii, quibus illud munus assignabitur, colligent oblatam a populo eleemosynam, & in cistam ad pauperum usum reponent. Singuli item consuetas oblationes & decimas suo tempore Pastori persolvent." In the Prayer itself we have "ut clementer accipias [hæc munera, atque] has preces nostras," and in the margin, "*Si nulla largiatur eleemosyna omittitur* (hæc munera atque)."

Margin notes: Prayer for Church Militant. "Alms" only mentioned. Rubric added in 1552 on ecclesiastical duties. Queen Elizabeth's Latin Prayer Book, "decimas, oblationes, ceteraque debita." "oblatam—eleemosynam." "oblationes & decimas."

* If there be none alms given unto the poor, then shall the words of accepting our alms be left out unsaid.

We must turn now to the Scotch Liturgy of 1637. The Rubric

[1] "First Prayer Book of Edward VI." Parker and Co., 1877.

after the Offertory is as follows: "*While the presbyter distinctly pronounces some or all of these sentences for the offertory, the deacon or (if no such be present) one of the churchwardens shall receive the devotions of the people there present, in a bason provided for that purpose. And when all have offered, he shall reverently bring the said bason, with the oblations therein, and deliver it to the presbyter, who shall humbly present it before the Lord, and set it upon the holy table.*" [1] {Scotch Liturgy of 1637. "Devotions," or "oblations."} In the Prayer following, however, reference is only made, as we have seen, to alms.

We come now to the last revision of the English Prayer Book. At the Savoy Conference in 1661 one of the objections made to the Communion Service was that four of the Offertory sentences were "more proper to draw out the people's bounty to their ministers than their charity to the poor." [2] This shows that the offerings to ministers were at this time made separately from the offerings for the poor; and in fact we should have judged this to be the case from the Rubric, as the Churchwardens put "*the devotion of the people*" into "*the poor men's box*," whereas the people were to "*pay to the Curate*" their "*accustomed offerings.*" It may be that this objection points to some real abuse, but at any rate in the revision of 1662 a reform was made. In the revised Prayer Book, as we have it to-day, the Rubric after the Offertory agrees with the Scotch in substance, but a distinction is introduced with reference to the uses to which the Offertory is to be put. All mention is omitted of "the poor men's box," and of "offerings to the Curate," but in place of these two we have "*alms and other devotions of the people*," which are both to be received "*in a decent bason.*" This change was accompanied by two other alterations: firstly, for "alms" we have, in the Prayer for the Church Militant, "*alms and oblations;*" and secondly, the following

{Savoy Conference. Bounty to ministers, and charity to poor. Revised Prayer Book of Charles II. No mention of poor-box, or offerings to Curate; but "alms and other devotions" substituted.}

---

[1] "First Prayer Book of Edward VI." Parker and Co. See also Proctor, "History of Book of Common Prayer," p. 350. London, 1870.

[2] Proctor, "History of Book of Common Prayer," p. 120. London, 1870.

Rubric is added at the end of the whole service "as an explanation"
(so Dr. Cardwell says) "of the distinct purposes denoted by the two words 'alms and oblations.'"[1] Perhaps, as we shall show farther on, it would be more accurate to say, as an explanation of the way in which, under the new mode of collection, the proportion of alms was to be fixed, and in which such alms were to be distributed. This Rubric runs as follows: "*After the Divine Service ended the money given at the Offertory shall be disposed of to such pious and charitable uses as the Minister and Church-wardens shall think fit. Wherein if they disagree, it shall be disposed of as the Ordinary shall appoint.*"

<small>Two other changes: "alms and oblations" in Prayer for Church Militant: and a new Rubric.</small>

Dr. Cardwell's opinion is that both "alms" and "oblations" "refer to the offerings made in money." Mr. Proctor also writes: "The *other devotions of the people*, or *oblations* (. . .), as distinct from the *alms for the poor*, may be understood to refer to any gifts for pious purposes."[2] And he adds this valuable remark: "Whatever is included in the term (*i.e.*, oblations) has been received from the people in the bason, whether simply for the poor, or for the Minister, or for the service of the church, or for any charitable use. The elements for communion are not so gathered from the people. In the common case of a collection without communion, the words would be used in the prayer."[3] So, too, Mr. Purton defines alms and oblations as "The money offerings which have been collected during the reading of the sentences."[4] These opinions, it will be seen, are diametrically opposed to that propounded by Mr. Blunt. They all concur in regarding "oblations" as monetary offerings, nor is it easy to conceive how any one with the evidence before him could entertain any other opinion.

<small>Opinions of Dr. Cardwell and Mr. Proctor on "oblations."</small>

<small>Mr. Purton's opinion.</small>

<small>"Oblations" are certainly monetary offerings.</small>

To proceed now to the testimony of Durel's versions, we shall find that he also regards "oblations" as neither more nor less than

---

[1] Cardwell's "Conferences," p. 382.
[2] Proctor, "Common Prayer," p. 350, note 2. We consider this, however (see pp. 77, 79), rather too wide a description of the purposes to which the Offertory may be applied.
[3] Ibid. p. 351, note 3.
[4] "The Communicant," by W. O. Purton. Published by E. Stock, London.

monetary offerings. What he considered the terms of the Prayer for the Church Militant to mean is self-evident; and we must bear in mind that his interpretation was stamped with the authority of the King as Supreme Head of the Established Church, and moreover that the Latin Liturgy had been submitted to Dr. Sancroft's revision. This last point is very important, inasmuch as it was Archbishop Sancroft who, in 1661, made the fair copy of Bishop Cosin's corrections from his own book, now in the Cosin Library at Durham, and this copy was probably the one produced in Convocation in the November of that year. These corrections are made in a Prayer Book of 1634, imprinted at London by Robert Barker, King's Printer, and by the assigns of John Bill, which is now in the Bodleian Library, and which contains even minute instructions to the printer. We find at the commencement of this book a note in MS. saying, " This Book seems to have been corrected and prepared by a member of the committee appointed for the last Review," etc. "Several of the Corrections and Additions are taken into the Book as we have it now," etc. A letter dated Aug. 5, 1745, which is affixed, certifies to Dr. Sancroft's writing. It has now been ascertained that Dr. Sancroft made these MS. corrections from Bishop Cosin's copy;[1] and he made them when chaplain to him and prebendary of Durham together with Durel. Now it was in these MS. notes of Cosin and Sancroft that the words "and oblations" were first introduced into the Prayer for the Church Militant, and into the marginal note attached thereto. In the former we find (the words in italics in [ ] are, in the original, written over the line, with the mark of insertion after the word which they are to follow): "(to accept [*these*] our almes [*& oblations*] and)." And in the margin, "If there be no almes [*or oblations*] giuen to the poore, then shall the words (*of accepting our almes* [*& oblations*]) be left out vnsaid." The text thus altered shows clearly that

This shown by Durel's versions.

Importance of this evidence.

Cosin's corrections of Prayer Book in Sancroft's writing.

The insertion of " and oblations " is one of these corrections.

[1] Cardwell's "Conferences," pp. 390, 391. 3rd Ed. Clar. Press, 1849.

"oblations" were something of the nature of monetary offerings, though the words "giuen to the poor" were, in the final revision, omitted, because the "oblations" were given to the Minister. This fact gives great weight to Durel's version, as bearing upon this question; for Dr. Sancroft in his revision of the *Liturgia* would be likely to pay special attention to such parts as were renderings of or related to the suggestions of Bishop Cosin, which it had been his task to copy. It should also here be noted that it was Dr. Sancroft who was appointed by Convocation to superintend the progress of the English Prayer Book through the press.

Of the two Rubrics which are placed between the Offertory sentences and the Prayer for the Church Militant, the former reads thus in the English Prayer Book: "*Whilst these Sentences are in reading, the Deacons, Church-wardens, or other fit person appointed for that purpose, shall receive the Alms for the Poor, and other devotions of the people, in a decent bason to be provided by the Parish for that purpose; and reverently bring it to the Priest, who shall humbly present and place it upon the holy Table.*" Durel's Latin translation of this is as follows:—

Durel's Latin Version.

"*Dum ista recitantur, Diaconi, Ædituj,*[1] *aliive ad hoc idonei, quibus illud muneris demandatum est, Eleemosynam* "*Eleemosynam* ... *ut & alias populi oblationes.*" *erogatam*[2] *colligent, ut & alias populi oblationes in pios*[3] *usus, in Amula*[4] *seu lance idonea à Parochianis in hunc usum comparata, eamque ad Presbyterum reverenter afferent,*[5] *ab illo autem, gestu modesto ac humili super sacra Mensa collocabitur.*"

While those (things) are being rehearsed, (the) Deacons, Churchwardens, or other (persons) suitable for this, to whom that (portion) of service has been intrusted, shall gather (the) Alms appropriated unto (the) uses of (the) poor men, as also (the) other oblations of the people unto devout uses, in a Tankard or suitable dish provided by (the) Parishioners unto this use, and shall bring it reverently to (the) Presbyter, but by him, with a modest and lowly carriage it shall be arranged upon the holy Table.

[1] See p. 78 on "Œconomis."   [2] Or "asked for."
[3] Translated "devout" on the analogy of "pii Religionis" in the Dedication.
[4] "*Amula*" is retained in Eds. 1685, 1687, 1696, 1703; and in Parsell 1713 and 1716. G. Bowyer's Eds. 1733 and 1744 have simply "in lance idonea." Perhaps "*Amula*" was a misprint for "*Arcula*," diminutive of "Arca," a common word for "money-box." 'Amula' is translated "a Holy-water-tankard" in "A Dictionary English-Latin and Latin-English," by Elisha Coles, late of Magd. Coll., Oxon. Sixth Edition, Lond., 1708; and such a vessel may have been used for collecting, in those churches which possessed one. Baxter (1821) has "patellâ."
[5] Some Eds. have a misprint, "afferat."

Durel then translates "*Alms . . . and other devotions of the people*," by "*Eleemosynam . . . ut & alias populi oblationes in pios usus;*" he here brings out the full sense of the English "present and place," the latter being expressed by "collocabitur," the former by "oblationes in pios usus," an oblation of course implying a presentation.

<small>"Oblationes" are "devotions of the people."</small>

The next time this word "oblationes" occurs in Durel's Latin version is at the commencement of the Prayer for the Church Militant, where we find "eleemosynas atque oblationes" as his rendering of "alms and oblations." As only one short Rubric intervenes between that containing the words "Eleemosynam . . . ut & alias populi oblationes," and the prayer in which we have "eleemosynas atque oblationes," there can be no doubt that Durel used the term "oblationes" in the same sense in both passages; that is to say, it is evident that he understood the term "oblations," suggested by his patron Cosin and copied by his friend Sancroft, to refer to the "other devotions of the people," and in no way to an offering of bread and wine by the Priest.

<small>"Eleemosynas atque oblationes."</small>

Again, in Durel's French translation, the accuracy of which was, as we have shown, attested in due form by the Bishop of London's chaplain, and which became thereupon, in accordance with the king's ordinance, the only authorized French version, we find the following remarkable fact. In our English Prayer Book, it will be remembered, the passage in the Prayer for the Church Militant referred to above reads thus :—

<small>Durel's French version.</small>

"We humbly beseech thee most mercifully [*to accept our alms and oblations, and*] to receive these our prayers, which we offer unto thy Divine Majesty." Durel's version is this :—

<small>*If there be no alms or oblations, then shall the words* (of accepting our alms and oblations) *be left out unsaid.*</small>

"Nous te supplions bien-humblement qu'il te plaise [*accepter nos aumosnes & nos oblations &] recevoir nos Prieres que nous presentons à ta Divine Majesté." Here we see that Durel included under the "aumosne" or "alms" of the marginal note both the "aumosnes" and the "oblations" of the text of the prayer. His translation of the "*alms for the poor and other devotions of the people*" in the Rubric is "les aumosnes pour les povres & les autres charitez du peuple." We see from his retention of the two terms here that he did not consider "alms" and "devotions" or "oblations" as precisely the same, but it is also perfectly clear that he considered "oblations" to be nothing so generically distinct from "alms" as to be incapable of being included under the wide term "aumosne." In other words he here, as in the Latin "Liturgia," regards "oblations" as an offering of money.

* Ceci sera omis lors qu'il n'y aura point d'aumosne.

In Prayer for Church Militant, "aumosnes" & "oblations" included in marginal note in "aumosne."

"Oblations" therefore a monetary offering.

Nor did Durel act blindly in thus stamping the term "oblations" with the meaning of an offering of money and not of the elements. For we find that the Rubric "*And when there is a Communion*," etc., came in substance from the Rubric in the Scotch Liturgy of 1637: there, however, we have "*shall then offer up, and place*" with regard to the Elements; and we find from Sancroft's MS. notes that there was some proposition for retaining the words "*offer up;*" "but the words 'offer up' were not adopted," writes Dr. Cardwell;¹ and so we are met by the singular and significant circumstance that the term "oblations" with regard to money was inserted by the very persons who cut out the expression "offer up" with regard to the elements. This of itself is good evidence that the Revisers never conceived their word "oblations" to imply an offering of bread and wine.

A suggestion for introduction of "Oblation of Elements" rejected by Revisers.

So their term "oblations" must have a different meaning.

These statements derive further support from the fact that in none

---

¹ Cardwell's "Conferences," p. 382. Third Ed.

of Durel's works in defence of Church institutions and doctrines does he vindicate an Oblation of the Elements. We have his sermon, "The Liturgy of the Church of England asserted" (1662), where he defends the newly-revised Liturgy against the attacks of the Nonconformists; and again, his "View of the Government and Public Worship of God in the Reformed Churches beyond the Seas" (1662); and his subsequent work, published the year before his Latin Prayer Book, "Sanctæ Ecclesiæ Anglicanæ Vindiciæ," where, in chap. xxi., he treats expressly of "those things which the Presbyterians censure in the Administration of the Sacraments according to the Rite of the English Church." But in none of these does he defend an oblation of bread and wine, as he certainly would have done had the Nonconformists censured such an oblation; and the only possible reason why they did not censure it is that it was a thing unrecognized by the Church at the period of Revision. Durel's opponents, who asserted that "The Tables were turned into altars," would have been the first to censure an "offering" on those "altars;" but the only grounds of their complaint are the position of the Table, and the reverent replacing of the remainder of the elements after all had communicated. Moreover, we do not find a single reference to an oblation of the elements in the Nonconformist writers of that period. The "Patronus Bonae Fidei" and "Bonasus Vapulans" written in reply to Durel (1672), the "History of Conformity, or a proof of the mischief of Impositions" (1681), the "Plea for the Nonconformists" (1684), and other works attacking the rites and doctrines of the Church, contain no mention whatever of an Oblation of the Elements. Nor does Neal make any allusion to it in his "History of the Puritans," where he enumerates many of the alterations and additions made at the last Revision of the Prayer Book by Convocation.

Durel nowhere vindicates "Oblation of Elements."

The doctrine was not then recognized.

No reference to it in Nonconformist writers of the period.

The contemporaneous versions in Welsh and in Greek tend to support Durel in making the "oblations" an offering of money. In

the Welsh Prayer Book of 1664,[1] for "shall receive the alms," etc. in
the Rubric, we find "a dderbyniant yr Elusenau i'r tho-
dion, a defosionau eraill y Bobl mewn cawg gweddus."
Then in the Prayer for the Church Militant we have,
"gymmeryd ein eluseseni ["eluseni" in Ed. 1677] a'n
hoffrynımau," and in the marginal note "Oni bydd dim
eluseni nac offrymau, yna gadawer y geiriau hyn (gymmeryd ein eluseni ac offrymau) heb ddywedyd;" *i.e.*, "to
accept our alms and offerings," and "If there be no
alms or offerings, then shall the words (of accepting our
alms and offerings)," etc. Now the word used for
"offerings" or "oblations," is "hoffrymmau," or "offrymmau" (for the "h" is mutative), which is nothing but the plural
of "offrwm," the word in common use for the "offertory."

The view of "oblations" as "monetary offering" supported by Welsh version.

"offrymmau," or "oblations," is plural of "offrwm," or "offertory."

There is a somewhat singular custom obtaining in many of the
older parishes of the Principality of Wales. At a funeral
the mourners and friends, frequently comprising a
great proportion of the parishioners, walk in procession
past the minister, who, standing at the Communion rail, receives their
offerings. A Welsh clergyman informs us that in most cases the usual
sum to give is one penny, and little children, even those in arms, are
taught to give a halfpenny. These offerings are called by the very
same word, "offrymau," which is used here for "oblations;" so that
it is clear that the Welsh translators considered "oblations" to
refer to money given in the "offertory."

Welsh custom at funerals.

Turning now to the Greek version of Duport (1665), we find in
the Rubric τὰς τοῖς πένησι ἐσθείσας ἐλεημοσύνας, καὶ ἄλλα ἅτινα
οὖν τοῦ λαοῦ ἑκουσία λήψονται, κ.τ.λ.; "devotions" being here
"voluntary (gifts)." In the Prayer for the Church
Militant, Duport has [*τὰς ἐλεημοσύνας καὶ προσφορὰς ἡμῶν] καὶ
κ.τ.λ.; and in the margin * ἐὰν οὐδεμία ἐλεημοσύνη ποιηθῇ, χρὴ
παραλείπειν ταῦτα τὰ ῥήματα (τὰς ἐλεημοσύνας καὶ προσφορὰς ἡμῶν. So that

This view supported also by Duport's Greek version.

"Llyfr Gweddi Gyffredin," etc., MDCLXIV. See note on "qued nobis datur" in Catechism.

he includes both 'alms' and 'oblations' under ἐλεημοσύνη. This is more valuable than some portions of Duport's book, inasmuch as he does not here follow his predecessor Petley, who has ταύτην τὴν ὠροφο- ρίαν ἀναλαβεῖν, κ.τ.λ. As to the term προσφορὰς, then, which Duport uses for "oblations," we can find no instance of its use in anything like a sacrificial sense; the verb from which it comes, προσφέρω, is used principally in the sense of (1) "*to bring to*," and (2) "*to contribute, to bring in, to yield;*" τὰ προσφέροντα, being "*sources of income*" (Liddell and Scott). This probably covers very nearly the meaning of "obla- tions," as those "offerings" which formed one of the Curate's "sources of income."

Lastly, the view of "oblations" as a monetary offering is supported by a note made in MS. in an interleaved Prayer Book of 1663,[1] the year after the Revision; where after the word "oblations" in the Prayer for the Church Militant we find the mark of omission, and on the margin of the printed page "*omiss,*" which at the commencement of the book is said to mean that something is omitted; then, on the opposite page the words written in MS., as omitted after "oblations," are "*given to the poore.*" This shows that the annotator certainly regarded the "obla- tions" as an offering of money and not of the elements. *Also by annotated Prayer Book of 1663.*

We have now, we trust, shown conclusively, on the evidence of Durel's French and Latin versions, that the Revisers meant nothing but a monetary offering by their word "obla- tions;" and have supported this by grounds of literary propriety, by history, by cotemporaneous writings, by the Welsh and Greek versions, and by the opinions of high modern authorities. We may proceed, therefore, to try *More exact determination of the species of monetary offering denoted by "oblations."*
and determine still more accurately the meaning of the word; to trace the uses to which these "oblations" were to be put; and to see what species of monetary offering was designated by that term.

---

[1] The imprint of this book, which we have inspected in the Bodleian Library, is, "LONDON, Printed by *John Bill* and *Christopher Barker*, Printers to the Kings most Excellent Majesty. MDCLXIII. Cum privilegio."

Mr. Purton writes: "The money thus collected, to whatever pious use it may afterwards be applied, is regarded in the light of *alms* when viewed in respect of those who contribute it, and in the light of *oblations* when considered in reference to him to whom it is offered."[1] Mr. Proctor has a similar statement.[2]

View of Mr. Purton and Mr. Proctor.

We are unable to acquiesce in this interpretation of the word "oblations." In the first place, this explanation affords no sufficient reason for the insertion of the term "oblations" one hundred and ten years after the introduction of the mention of "alms" into the Prayer for the Church Militant. True it is that, as one of the sentences, taken from Prov. xix., has it, "He that hath pity upon the poor lendeth unto the Lord;" but this fact is sufficiently recognized in the Offertory sentences without the necessity for its insertion in the Prayer for the Church Militant by the introduction of the word "oblations."

(1) This explanation affords no reason for introduction of term "oblations."

Secondly, we conceive that the Offertory, Offering, or Oblation is made during the reading of the sentences, and not in the Prayer for the Church Militant. This is clear from the Rubrics; in the first Prayer Book of Edward VI. we have, "*whiles the Clerks do sing the Offertory*" ["Tempore quo canitur offertorium." Aless, 1551], and in our own Prayer Book, "*Then shall the Priest return to the Lord's Table and begin the Offertory, saying one or more of these Sentences,*" etc. ("*et offertorium incipiet,*" etc., Durel's "Liturgia.") So in the Prayer itself God is asked to "accept" (accipias) our alms and oblations, or devotions, as already given, whereas with regard to our prayers the words are added, "which we offer" ("quæ divinæ majestati tuæ offerimus, exaudias "). Thirdly, the term "alms," on the explanation of "oblations" given by Mr. Purton, is alone left to cover all the offerings made in the Offertory. As, however, offerings to the Curate were made at this portion of the service, the term "alms" appears inadequate. Gifts to the minister in charge would not carry with them the conno-

(2) The offertory, or oblation, takes place during the sentences.

(3) There are some offerings which are not "alms."

---

[1] "The Communicant." By W. O. Purton. Published by E. Stock, London.
[2] "Common Prayer."

tation attaching to the word "alms." If we consider "almoner," "almshouses," and the like, we shall see that "alms" could in no way include such "duties" as are referred to in the Offertory sentences taken from 1 Cor. ix. 7; 1 Cor. ix. 11; 1 Cor. ix. 13, 14; Gal. vi. 6, 7. Archbishop Secker brings out this distinction very clearly; contributions for the maintenance of ministers should be regarded "not as an Alms given to an Inferior, but as a Tribute of Duty paid to a Superior." And fourthly, such expressions as, "Die autem oblationum quilibet persoluet Pastori debitam pensionem" (Aless, 1551); "oblationes & decimas" (Q. Eliz.), etc., point historically to "oblationes" as the correct term for offerings to ministers. *Archbishop Secker's distinction.* *(4) Historic testimony.*

At first sight, we admit, Durel's French version seems to sanction the idea that "alms" included all the gifts made at the offertory. But his French Prayer Book differed from the English Book in the purpose for which it was intended. In England there was the parochial system, and the duties payable to the curates in charge; this system would not obtain in the same way where Durel's French Prayer Book was in use; for instance, the King provided, as we know, one minister (Durel himself) for the Savoy Chapel. *Durel's French version.*

The only purposes for which it is known that money might be collected at the Offertory are such as were prescribed by the Act of 1531 (*i.e.*, alms), by the Rubric which allows Briefs to be read, and by the sentences in the Offertory referring to provision for ministers. We trust we shall be able to show upon historical grounds that the "other devotions of the people," or "oblations," refer, partly perhaps to money raised on Briefs,[1] but chiefly to gifts made to ministers, and certainly in no way to offerings for Church expenses or the like. *The purposes for which money might be collected. (1) 22 Hen. viii. c. 12. (2) Briefs. (3) Offerings to Curate. "Oblations" chiefly the latter.*

In the Prayer Book of 1549 we have in the Rubric offerings to the poor-box, and to the Curate; the latter were to be made, says Aless, "Die oblationum;" we have the same two kinds of offerings in the Rubric in the Prayer Book of *History of change in Rubric.*

---

[1] See Appendix C for an example of a Brief.

1552; this is the same again in Queen Elizabeth's English Prayer Book, and in her Latin Prayer Book of 1560 we have still, in the Rubrics, of 1559, "oblatam a populo eleemosynam," alms offered by the people for the poor, and "oblationes & decimas," oblations or offerings to the Curate and tithes payable to him. We now come to the Prayer Book of Charles II. Here we find the Rubric omits "due and accustomed offerings" "to the Curate," or "oblationes & decimas," and inserts, "and other devotions of the people," or "et alias populi oblationes in pios usus," and also inserts "oblations," or "oblationes," in the Prayer for the Church Militant. The reason for this latter insertion was that up to this time gifts to the Curate were paid to him, and were not, as now, collected in the basin together with the alms. It seems evident from this that the "other devotions of the people," *i.e.*, the "oblationes" of Durel, are the "due and accustomed offerings," or "oblationes & decimas" of Queen Elizabeth's Prayer Books; that is to say, that both "other devotions of the people" and "oblations" refer principally, if not solely, to the offerings to the Curate in charge.

In 1662 "offerings" to Curate omitted, and "other devotions of the people" inserted.

Reason for insertion of "oblations."

"Oblations" were offerings to Curate in charge.

To complete our subject we must revert for a moment to the new Rubric of the Prayer Book of Charles II., which we have quoted before. It occurs at the end of the Communion Service: "*After the Divine Service ended, the money given at the Offertory shall be disposed of to such pious and charitable uses, as the Minister and Church-wardens shall think fit. Wherein if they disagree, it shall be disposed of as the Ordinary shall appoint.*" This is in Durel's version as follows :—

The new Rubric.

Durel's Latin version.	
"*Sacris peractis pecunia, in offertorio erogata collocabitur in pios usus, à Ministro et Œconomis*[1] *prout ipsis visum fuerit.*"	Service being ended (the) money, appropriated in (the) offertory shall be arranged unto devout uses, by (the) Minister and Churchwardens according as it shall have seemed good to themselves.

[1] "Œconomis" is here used for Churchwardens, whereas in the Rubric before the Offertory we have "Ædituii": it is perhaps worthy of remark that in *Janua Linguarum*, 1647, Ædituus is "sexton" or "clark." Justinian (Instit. I. tit. xiii.) says, "ædituii dicuntur, qui ædes tuentur."

Dr. Cardwell's opinion is that this Rubric was inserted "as an explanation of the distinct purposes denoted by the two words 'alms and oblations.'" Perhaps it would be more precise to say that its insertion was due to the same cause as was the change of "due and accustomed offerings" to the Curate into "other devotions of the people," and the introduction of the word "oblations." This cause was a laudable desire to render more exact the description, and the rules for the distribution, of the moneys collected. This new Rubric probably refers only to the proportion of the Offertory to be applied to charitable uses (alms) or pious uses (oblations), and to the distribution of the former. It in no way refers to gifts for Church expenses or non-parochial purposes. For Church expenses were provided for by Church rates; these existed in England by Common Law right; nothing is known of their commencement or introduction. Something equivalent to them was payable, at all events, in the reign of Canute, for his 63rd law is "de fano reficiendo," in which it is said that all persons ought of right to contribute to the repair of Churches. *Dr. Cardwell's view.*

The Rubric probably refers only to alms.

Church expenses met by Church rates.

With such moneys the Curate would have nothing to do; but with regard to the application of collections made under Briefs and of alms for the poor a diversity of opinion might very possibly arise between the Curate and Churchwardens. It was the custom, as we have shown, up to the date of the Last Review for the "alms" to be collected, and then put "into the poor men's box."[1] Now these poor men's boxes (several of which we have seen) had customarily three locks and three keys, so that they could only be opened by the joint consent of the Curate and of the *Possible diversity of opinion about alms.*

Before last Review alms put in trebly-locked box.

---

[1] An interesting account of the consecration of a church at Fulmer, in Buckinghamshire, is contained in "Howe's Continuation of 'Stowe's Annals' unto the ende of this present yeere, 1614." Lond., fol. 1615, p. 908. We are tempted to give an extract to illustrate these collections for the poor, and also to show how monetary offerings were regarded as "sacrifices." "This church thus fully finished and adorned, was consecrated the first day of November, this yeare 1610, by the right reverend father in God, Doctor Barlow, then L Bishop of Lincolne; . . . and in place of the collect was sayd this prayer. We beseech thee, . . . vouchsafe to receive the sacrifices of thy servants, whether of almes, or prayers, or thanksgiving, which shall be offred herein, . . . Then

two Churchwardens.[1] At the Last Revision, however, the Rubric orders that the money shall be brought to the Priest and be presented and placed upon the table. Whether this change was caused by representations made at the Savoy Conference, or was simply the embodiment of a custom which had begun already to obtain, we have not been able to discover. But this Rubric, which required the moneys collected to be brought to the Priest, instead of being placed in the trebly-locked poor men's box, necessitated the introduction of another Rubric to give the Churchwardens their due voice in the matter of distribution.

After last Review alms taken to Priest.

The examples we have now given will be sufficient for our purpose in showing the value of Durel's translations of the Prayer Book. All criticisms, explanations, or translations which are not contemporary with the original text are liable to a class of errors which every commentator has to dread. The most honest mind must approach with views more or less preconceived the text of writers of a previous age, and the almost inevitable result is that modern ideas are unconsciously sought, and are often conceived to have been found, in the original words of the text. This is no less the case in profane than in religious writings. Any student of Greek Philosophy will admit how often thoughts, of which Plato and Aristotle had probably no conception, are confidently pointed out in their works. The value of historical testimony is incalculable; its value is enhanced when the evidence is contemporaneous. On all points of dispute with regard to the English Prayer Book we would once more earnestly commend the inquirer to the contemporary testimony of Dean Durel.[2]

Value of contemporary evidence.

the bishop celebrated the communion, where the founder, by the byshop's direction, kneeled by himselfe in the middle of the quyer, right before the altar, and being a collection for the poore, he offered a piece of gōlde," etc.

[1] See Canon 84 (1603), where such a box is ordered.

[2] A few words may be added upon the *Credence Table*. With regard to the Western Church the earliest instance of the term "Credentia" in any ritual book is in the Pontifical of Leo X. The "Credence" was not fully established till the Bull of Clement VIII., A.D. 1604. In respect of the Eastern Church, it appears that it was not customary to use a "Credence Table" (said to be derived from "credenza," to "prove" or "taste" food to prevent poisoning), but to have a "prothesis" in a side chapel where the people used to make their offerings. As regards the Reformed Church of England, there can be no need or use of a Credence Table, if, as we have shown, there is no Oblation of the Elements.

APPENDIX C.

COPY OF A BRIEF.

"After our harty Commendations, &c.

"The Queens Majesty of her great Clemency and Goodness, hath granted unto one *Richard Kirford* of *Chard* Letters patents under her Highness great Seal, for the gathering of the charitable Devotion of well disposed persons, toward the relieving of the said poor Man, being undone, together with his Wife and Children, by means of sudden Mischance of Fire I am therefore, both in Consideration of my duty towards her Majesty, pitifully respecting the miserable Estate of the poor Man, as also for very Conscience sake and Christian Charity, very vehemently moved and enforced to seek some way that may help and succour his great Extremity and Need; which cannot be well done without your Assistance and Aid. Wherefore seeing the said *Richard* by reason of his Gout is not able to Travel personaily about his Business, I earnestly desire you, that you will take order with the Ministers and Church-Wardens of every parish within the Dioces of *Bath* and *Wells*, with as convenient speed as you may, that they will gather the Devotions of every the said Parish, and write upon the Back-side of the Copy of her Majesty's said patents the Summ of Money which shall be contributed: And that they will send or bring their Collections with the said Copies of the said patents, and deliver the same before *Whitsuntide* next to your Register; and he to keep the same until the said *Richard Kirford*, or his Deputy or Assign, shall receive the same Money so gathered and received at his Hands. The Copies of her Majesty's Patents are sent unto you by this bringer; so many as shall serve your Archdeaconries. I pray you be careful that this may be done speedily and effectually. And in so doing you shall give the poor Man, his Wife and Children, a good Cause to pray for you. And thus I bid you heartily fare-well. From *London* the 24th. of Febr. 1581.

"Your loving friend,
"WILL. AUBREY." [1]

ADDENDA.

I. ON THE USE OF PRESBYTER.

Letter of Alexander Nowell (Dean of St. Paul's, 1585): "I have thought good herein to enclose certain Words contained in Her Majesty's Foundation of Her Highness's Church at *Westminster;*" "*Eandem Ecclesiam Collegiatam, de uno Decano Presbytero, & duodecim Praebendariis Presbyteris, tenore praesentium,*

---

[1] "The History of the Life and Acts of the Most Reverend Father in God Edmund Grindal, etc., Archbishop of York and Canterbury," etc., pp. 267, 268. London, 1710.

re aliter & ad plenum, pro Nobis, haeredibus & Successoribus nostris, creamus, erigimus, fundamus, ordinamus, facimus, constituimus & stabilimus, perpetuis futuris temporibus duraturum, &c."

"That all the New Cathedral Churches, founded by Her Majesty's Father of most famous Memory ; and the Church of *Westminster*, founded by Her Gracious Majesty ; were (as they verily thought) according to these old Statutes by their Foundation, *De uno Decano Presbytero, & Praebendariis Presbyteris*." (Strype's "Life of Archbishop Whitgift," pp. 234, 235.)

II. On the Misuse of Priest.

"And lastly, that as for the Name of *Priest*, as they took it, [*i e.* as Sacrificers] he did likewise condemn in our Ministers, neither did they ascribe it to themselves. And that therefore the Libeller in these Points writ like himself." (The Archbishop's own Vindication.—Strype's "Life of Archbishop Whitgift," p. 305. London. MDCCXVIII.).

III. On Placing the Elements.

"For three centuries past the Church of England has eschewed the Romish Credence. Why now seek to overthrow the precedent of *three hundred years !*"

"But the rubric seems, they say, to require that the elements should be put on the Lord's Table just prior to celebrating the Supper. The precedent of 300 years surely is enough to settle this." ("Credence or Tasting Tables," pp. 19, 20. By the Rev. Mourant Brock, M.A. London : Seeley & Co. 1881.)

PART III.
THE CATECHISM.

THE CATECHISM.

"Cæteram quippe turbam non intelligendi vivacitas, sed credendi simplicitas tutissimam facit."—*Aug. C. Ep. Fund.* c. 4.

CATECHISMUS,	A CATECHISM,
Hoc est, *Institutio quam unusquisque addiscere tenetur, priusquam adducatur ad Episcopum ut ab illo Confirmetur.*	This is, *an Instruction which each one is bound further to learn, before that he be brought to a Bishop to be Confirmed by him.*
Quæstio.	*Question.*
QUOD est tibi nomen?	WHAT name have you?

CATECHISMUS. The Greek ἠχέω (cf. our "echo," which is the substantive form) means "to sound;" κατηχέω, "to resound," and so "*to sound* a thing *in one's ears, impress it* upon one *by word of mouth*" (Liddell and Scott).

In the New Testament, forms of the Greek verb are translated by means of the words "taught" (Gal. vi. 6), "teacheth" (ditto), "instructed" (Luke i. 4, and Acts xviii. 25).

Durel uses the masculine form "Catechismus." Queen Eliz. (1560, for the copies quoted see Part II. chap. i.) has the Catechism placed in the Confirmation Service, as in the First and Second Prayer Books of Edward VI. and in Elizabeth's English Prayer Book of 1559: "Confirmatio Puerorum, *cui insertus est Catechismus*," is the general heading; at the beginning of the Catechism itself we have "Catechesis, qua puer instituitur priusquam ad Confirmationem producitur." These headings are verbatim the same as those in Aless (see Part II. chap. i.). At the end of his larger Catechism (Parker Society's Edition, 1853) Nowell says, "*Catechismus*, vel potius Catechesis, Graec. Latine, prima institutio." The title of this Catechism is "CATECHISMVS, siue prima Institutio," etc., and the date, M.D.LXX. Norton's Translation is entitled, "A CATECHISME, or first Instruction," etc. Nowell's Middle Catechism is called, "Chris-

* * * * * * * * *

tianae Pietatis prima institutio," etc. His small Catechism is entitled "CATECHISMVS PARVVS," etc. In the Latin and Greek Prayer Book prepared by his nephew William Whitaker, who afterwards made the Greek version for Nowell's Small Catechism, the Catechism does not form a part of the Confirmation Service, but is separate: it is called "Catechesis," or Κατήχησις. The date of this book is M.D.LXIX. Petley (1638) uses the feminine form in his Greek version, as does also Duport (1665), who has ΚΑΤΗΧΗΣΙΣ as the heading of the Catechism. The feminine, in fact, appears to be the only correct form in Greek, though at the end of the Baptismal Service, and in the Rubric at the end of the Catechism, Duport employs the masculine form.

The Latin version printed by Vautrollier (1574) has "Confirmatio, in qua Catechismus ad Pueros instituendos continetur," with the subordinate heading "Catechismus memoriter à pueris ediscendus antequam ad confirmationem adducantur." The readings of this Prayer Book are given throughout the notes, it being here quoted as the representative of the three Prayer Books bearing the printers' names of Wolf, Vautrollier, and Jackson, the first of which Mr. Clay regards as "the earliest version into Latin of the whole Prayer Book." The authorized version of Queen Elizabeth is also quoted throughout, and the principal points are noted wherein Aless, the predecessor of Haddon, who was reputed the preparer of Queen Elizabeth's Latin Prayer Book, and Haddon's successor, Whitaker, differ from his translation. Nowell's Catechisms will be quoted on points of special interest, especially his Small Catechism (see Part II. chap. i.); as will also the private versions of Petley, and of his follower Duport, of Harwood, and of Messrs. Bright and Medd.

Hoc est. So Eds. 1685, 1687: Eds. 1696, 1703 have capitals.

Institutio: elementary instruction. "Puerilis institutio" (Cicero, de Or. 2. 1). Cf. the "Institutiones" or "Institutes" of Justinian, Cranmer's "Institution of a Christian man," Calvin's "Institutions," the "Institutiones Universales," by Philippus Mocenicus (1586), etc. So Archbishop Secker: "And not only in this Respect, but every other, is our Lord's Prayer an admirable *Institution* and Direction for praying aright" ("Lect. on Catech.," vol. ii. p. 147. London, 1769). Cf. Bishop Patrick's "Aqua Genitalis" (1658), p. 520: "The slackness of many Parents would

* * * * * * *

---

be much quickened who pass over the institution (or instruction) of their Children," etc. Συμβίβασις, " teaching," " instruction " (Petley and Duport).

The verb "instituere" occurs later on in Durel's Catechism in the sense (1) " to appoint," (2) "to begin."

Archbishop Secker's description of the Catechism is " that very good, though still improveable, Form of sound words, which we now use" ("Lectures on Catechism," vol. i. pp. 50, 51. London, 1769). In the same place he writes, " If Baptism had been administered to Children, without anything said to express its Meaning, it would have had too much the Appearance of an insignificant Ceremony, or a superstitious Charm. And if only the Privileges to which it intitled, had been rehearsed; they might seem annexed to it absolutely, without any conditions to be observed on the Children's Part." This is a most excellent reason for a Catechism : it should so explain ceremonies that they may be neither slighted on the one hand, nor superstitiously regarded on the other. To effect this golden mean of due observance, a Catechism must be simple and tempered to youthful understanding. Nor can it be said that our Catechism leaves this condition unfulfilled. It is nothing if not simple ; in it there is no Priest, no Confession, no Absolution, no Consecration ; but Repentance, Faith, and Forgiveness of Sins, without reference to a Sacerdotal Mediator, and the Baptism of Water and Receiving of Bread and Wine which the Lord commanded.

addiscere, "to learn in addition." English Version has simply, "to be learned." This is one place out of many which shows that this Latin version is not intended to be a slavish translation of the original, but to be explanatory of its meaning. Cf. notes on "salutis viam," "Spiritum Sanctum Deum," etc, etc. The preposition in "addiscere" refers to the end of " Public Baptism of Infants," " so soon as *he* can say the Creed, etc., and be further instructed in the Church-Catechism set forth for that purpose ; " in Durel's version, " & in Catechismo in eum finem edito, plenius instituatur " (where we observe that Durel has no word for " Church "). Duport there reads ἔτι δὲ καὶ πόρρω παιδευθῇ κ.τ.λ., but here in the Catechism he has simply " to learn," μανθάνειν. Whitaker has "*qua* puer instituitur," and ἣν ἕως τὸν παῖδα μανθάνειν, κ.τ.λ. Cf. " addidicerint " and " addiscere " in the second Rubric after the Catechism in Durel.

* * * * * * * *

---

tenetur. Cf. further on " te teneri ea credere," etc, and " quod promissum tenentur ipsi praestare." This usage is not classical ; but we may compare "quod quis spondet, etc., praestare tenetur," "What any one undertaketh as surety for another, etc., he is bound to perform ; " this passage is in a book to which we shall make frequent reference ; it is called "JANUA LINGUARUM RESERATA, etc., *authore Cl. Viro* J. A. COMENIO," revised by G. P., and published London, 1647 ; it is therefore almost contemporary with this Latin Catechism, and, being drawn up in parallel columns of English and Latin, often shows the relation of English and Latin terms at that date. The style of both books is very similar ; *e.g.,* we have in both " Imo," not " Immo," the unusual form of " Sabbatum " for " Sabbata," "gnavus " or "gnaviter," not "navus," etc. It is interesting to observe that the original edition of this book gained for Comenius such celebrity that he was invited to England, whence, however, he had to retire on the breaking out of the civil war.

ad Episcopum: perhaps "to the Bishop," *i.e.,* his own bishop.

Petley has εἰς τὸν Ἐπίσκοπον πρὸς τὸ Ἐπικυροῦσθαι. Duport has no words for " to the Bishop," but continues εἰς τὸ βεβαιωθῆναι ὑπὸ τοῦ Ἐπισκόπου, in place of " ut ab illo," etc. : as E.V., " BEFORE HE BE BROUGHT TO BE CONFIRMED BY THE BISHOP." Whitaker has no mention of the Bishop in either place.

Confirmetur. So Eds. 1685, 1687, 1696, 1703. Bagster (1866) has a comma after "Institutio" and after " Episcopum." The F. V. in Ed. 1578 had, " be confirmed, or admitted to receave the Holy Communion " (First Prayer Book of Edward VI. Parker and Co.).

Quæstio. Q. Eliz. has " Quaestio " and " Responsio," or shortened forms of these. Vautr. " Quæstio " and " Responsum." Whitaker, " Quæstio " and " Responsio." Nowell's Small Catechism is headed " *Voti Sponsio in Baptismo:*" then he has " Magister," and " *Auditor.*"

QUOD—nomen. "QUod" in Eds. 1685, 1687, 1696, 1703. "QVOD est tibi nomen ?" (Q. Eliz.). " QVod tibi nomen est ?" (Vautr.) " *QVo nomine appellaris?*" (Nowell's Small Catechism). " Nomen " is subject : cf. " nomen Mercurii est mihi " (Plautus Am. prol. 19) : " cui saltationi Titus

* * * * * * * * *

---

nomen est" (Cic. Brut.). Whitaker, Petley, and Duport have τί ἐστί σοι τὸ ὄνομα; which agrees with the Latin, except that τί is here "quid," not "quod." Harwood (1785) has "Qui vocare?"

It is to be remarked that the large capitals in Durel show the commencement of different divisions. "Q̲uod" begins the Introduction, "C̲redo," the portion on Belief; "E̲a," that on the Law; "P̲ater," that on Prayer; and "Q̲uot," that on the Sacraments. These correspond to the divisions of Nowell's Large Catechism: the prefatory part; "Secunda pars de Evangelio et Fide;" "Prima pars, de Lege et Obedientia;" "Tertia pars de Oratione, et Gratiarum Actione;" and "Quarta pars, de Sacramentis."

So Duport has capitals at Τί, Πιστεύω, Ἀς, Πάτερ, Πόσα. These correspond precisely to Eds. 1685, 1687, 1696, and 1703, which have "Q̲uod," "C̲redo," "E̲a," "P̲ater," and "Q̲uot." Petley has Τί, Ἀ, Πάτερ, Πόσα, thus making no separate division for the Creed.

Cf. Bishop Beveridge, in "The Church Catechism Explained," etc., London, 1705; he makes five divisions, as does Durel:—1. Our *Baptismal Vow;* 2. *The Apostles' Creed;* 3. *The Ten Commandments;* 4. *Our Lord's Prayer;* 5. *The Doctrine of the Sacraments.*

Bagster has "Quod," "Credo," etc., in Ed. 1821. Upon the divisions in Ed. 1834 the Rev. Sydney Thelwall, B.A., writes to us: "The principle of printing appears to be to mark certain leading divisions in the Catechism by certain differences in the position of these words (*Quæstio* and *Responsio*). At the outset we have *Quæstio* in a line by itself; but not *Responsio*. In the three cases of rehearsal, first of the Creed, next of the Decalogue, and thirdly of the Prayer, *Responsio* (but not *Quæstio*) has a line all to itself. Finally, to mark the Sacramental portion (a later addition) of the Catechism off from the rest, we have again a line allotted, not to *Responsio*, but, as at the beginning, to *Quæstio*, by itself. This arrangement has a certain degree of method, at all events, to recommend it; and such divisions, which strike the eye, have some distinct advantages."

Responsio.	*Answer.*
N. aut M.	N. or M.
Quæstio.	*Question.*
Quis tibi hoc nomen imposuit?	Who has placed this name upon you?
Responsio.	*Answer.*
Susceptores mei & Susceptrices in	My Godfathers & Godmothers

N. aut M. "N. vel N.," Queen Eliz. and Vautrollier. "N. aut M.," Nowell's Small Catechism.

"N. aut M." is probably for "N. aut NN." (Nomen aut Nomina), NN. being contracted into M, as CIↃ is also supposed to have been (though perhaps M. is for Mille); and as HS is for IIS or LLS. Queen Eliz. and Vautrollier have "N" both here and in the Marriage Service. In the latter place our present Prayer Book has "M" for the man, and "N" for the woman. Queen Elizabeth's English book has "N" for both.

In Aless we have in the Communion Service, "Epistola Sancti Pauli Apostoli, scripta ad N.N. cap. N.N.," and below, "Sanctum Euangelium, scriptum ab N.N. uel N. in N. & N. capite."

Whitaker, Nowell, Petley, and Duport have ὁ δεῖνα, ἢ ὁ δεῖνα.

Aut. This is more correct than "vel." "Aut" (alterum) should always be kept distinct from "vel" (velle), the latter implying that the alternative is still dependent on the will. Many other instances of the precision of Durel's style (cf. the Ciceronian "hoc est" above for "id est") will be remarked in reading the Catechism.

Quis—imposuit? "Quis indidit tibi hoc nomen?" (Queen Eliz.). "Quis tibi hoc nomen tribuit?" (Vautrollier). "*Quis hoc tibi nomen imposuit?*" (Nowell's Small Catechism). τίς σοι ἔθετο τὸ ὄνομα τοῦτο; (Duport). Whitaker and Petley have ἐπέθετο. Harwood has, "Quis istud nomen tibi indidit?"

Susceptores, etc. "Patrini, in Baptismo, quo factus sum membrum Christi, filius Dei, & haeres vitae aeternae" (Queen Eliz.). Whitaker, who usually closely adheres to Queen Elizabeth's version, here has "in quo." Vautrollier has "Susceptores mei in Baptismo, in quo membrum Christi, filius Dei, & haeres regni coelorum effectus sum."

Nowell, in his Small Catechism, has "Qui voti se sponsione Deo pro me obligarunt in Baptismo meo: In quo Christi membrum, filius Dei, & regni coelestis haeres sum institutus." In the Greek for "sum institutus" Nowell has ἀπεδείχθην, *i.e.*, "was shown, pointed out."

| Baptismo, in quo factus sum membrum Christi, filius Dei, & haeres regni coelorum. | in Baptism, in which I have been made a member of Christ, a son of God, & an inheritor of (the) kingdom of (the) heavens. |

"Susceptores" is literally "undertakers," or "contractors:" cf. the single occurrence of the verb "undertake" in our Bible, Isa. xxxviii. 14, "Undertake for me," where the Vulg. has "Responde pro me;" and compare the Hebrew word in Gen. xliii. 9, xliv. 32, Psa. cxix. 122, etc. "Susceptores" appears a late word; it is translated "godfathers" on the authority of *Janua Linguarum*. Duport has σύμπατρις (sic) καὶ συμμητρίς [συμμητόρις (sic) in Ed. 1818]: Whitaker and Petley had the same words. Nowell has οἱ ἐγγυηταὶ τῷ Θεῷ καταστήσαντες ἑαυτοὺς ὑπὲρ ἡμῶν, and below, οἱ ἐγγυηταί.

in Baptismo: "in" not "at" Baptism; "at Baptism" would have tied the change to a particular time and place; "in" leaves it an open question whether true Baptism, with the inward part, "Mori peccato," etc., has ever taken place. Nor is it "by" Baptism. Cf. *Paraphrasis cum Annotatis ad Difficiliora loca Catechismi Anglicani*, 1674: "*wherein* [not whereby, but by vertue of the Institution, and Word and God's promise in the New Covenant, as mighty as God Himself]."

factus sum. Probably a true perfect tense; the inward part of Baptism, "Mori peccato, et denuo nasci justitiae," by which "facti sumus Filii Dei," being *assumed* to have taken place by this time (postquam adoleverimus); but such assumption is hypothetical; "factus sum ... filius Dei" must refer to the same thing as "facti sumus Filii Dei." See note on "hâc ratione."

Petley and Duport have ἐγενήθην, the same *tense* as Nowell, but a verb of very different meaning from that of his ἀπεδείχθην.

membrum, or "part." Cf. the simile of the vine and branches, etc., in the New Testament. The word has no relation to the modern meaning of "member" of a sect. Duport (following Whitaker, Nowell, and Petley) has μέλος rightly.

haeres: "inheritor," not "heir:" a testator can appoint "haeredem," but not an "heir." κληρονόμος, Whitaker, Nowell, Petley, and Duport. Cf. *Paraphrasis cum Annotatis ad Difficiliora loca Catechismi Anglicani*, 1674: "*and an Inheritour of the Kingdome of Heaven* [not Absolutely and Irrespectively, but only upon condition of doing my endeavour to perform, keep, observe, and do my Baptismal vow, which follows presently after]."

coelorum: singular in Duport. Harwood has "coelestis." Queen

Quæstio.	*Question.*
Quid Susceptores tui & Susceptrices tum tuo nomine praestiterunt?	What have your Godfathers & Godmothers then performed on your account?
Responsio.	*Answer.*
Tria meo nomine promiserunt ac	Three things on my account they

Eliz., as we have seen, has "of eternal life" for "of the kingdom of the heavens:" "regni coelorum" (Vautrollier). Whitaker follows Queen Eliz. in the Latin, and in the Greek has ζωῆς αἰωνίου. Nowell and Petley have the adj. οὐρανίου.

Quid—praestiterunt? "Quid promiserunt pro te Compatres, & Commatres?" (Queen Eliz.).

"Quid tuo nomine tum susceptores fecerunt?" (Vautrollier).

"*Quid tunc pro te consponsores illi susceperunt?*" and τί τότε ἀνεδέξαντό σε ποιήσειν ἐκεῖνοι οἱ ἐγγυηταί. (sic) (Nowell's Small Catechism.)

tum. Mr. J. G. Fitch, M.A., Assistant Commissioner to the late Endowed Schools' Commission, and one of Her Majesty's Inspectors of Schools, said, in his Lectures on Teaching, delivered in the University of Cambridge, Lent Term, 1880, that he had recited this question many hundred times, all the while believing "then" was a verb meaning "pledge:" an excellent illustration of the way in which children are too often allowed to learn the words of the Catechism.

tuo nomine: "in your name," here equivalent to "on your account." Cf. "tuo nomine" (Cic. Phil. i. 12); "alio nomine" (Cic. Rosc. Com. 14); "suo nomine" (Cæsar B. G. i. 18); "meo nomine" (Tac. H. i. 29), etc.

So Queen Eliz. has "pro te." Whitaker, Petley, and Duport have ὑπὲρ σου, "on your behalf," whereas in the answer they have "in my name." Nowell's Small Catechism has "pro te" in the Latin; for the Greek see above on "Quid—praestiterunt?" Harwood, too, has here "tuâ vice," and in the answer "meo nomine."

praestiterunt, or "become surety for," "warrant," "undertake." Both this and the preceding question show that the child is responsible for fulfilling its part when it is grown up. This is also clearly shown by Nowell's Small Catechism: Τί τότε ἀνεδέξαντό σε ποιήσειν, "What did ... undertake that you would do," etc.

Tria—meae. "Tria meo nomine polliciti sunt."

"Primum, quod renunciarem Diabolo, mundo, & carnalibus concupiscentijs."

"Deinde, ut crederem omnes Articulos fidei Christianae."

voverunt; *Primùm, me abrenuncia-* | have promised and have vowed; *First,*
turum Satanae & omnibus operibus | that I would renounce Satan & all
ejus, pompis & vanitatibus hujus | his works, (the) shows & emptinesses

---

"Tertio, quod vellem obsequi praeceptis Dei, & ei seruire in sanctitate & iustitia, omnibus diebus vitae meae" (Queen Eliz.).

"Tria promiserunt, primùm, renuntiaturum me Diabolo & omnibus operibus eius, pompis & voluptatibus huius seculi & pravis concupiscentijs carnis. Secundùm, crediturum me omnibus fidei articulis. Tertiùm, sanctam Dei voluntatem, & omnia eius praecepta obseruaturum, in eisq'; per omnem vitam, perambulaturum" (Vautrollier).

"Tria DEO spoponderunt voveruntque meo nomine; Primum, quod Diabolum, cunctaque ejus opera, inanem pompam atque vanitatem impij mundi, & vitiosos omnes carnis appetitus funditùs repudiarem. Secundùm, quòd Christianae fidei Articulos universos crederem. Tertium, quod sanctissimae Dei voluntati obtemperarem, atque praeceptis ejus parere (*sic*, and in 1584), & ad illorum rationem totius vitae formam dirigerem" (Nowell's Small Catechism).

p r o m i s e r u n t refers to the Church; "voverunt," to God.

a b r e n u n c i a t u r u m : "adeò ut nec eas sequuturus sis nec iis te duci permissurus" (Baptismal Service in Durel).

The English Version of Edward and Elizabeth had "forsake," not "renounce." It is somewhat curious that the compilers of the Catechism have left this first promise and vow unexplained, except in so far as the explanations of the other parts throw light upon it. This, perhaps, partly accounts for the general ignorance on this subject.

S a t a n a e : "Diabolo," Queen Eliz., Vautrollier, Nowell, and Harwood. τῷ Διαβόλῳ, Whitaker, Nowell, Petley and Duport: the last three with small initial.

o p e r i b u s e j u s. So Norton, Petley, and Duport have αὐτοῦ, and Harwood, "illius."

In Eds. 1685, 1687, 1696, 1703 of Durel, "ejus" is omitted.

p o m p i s : "shows" in *Janua Linguarum*, where also "vanitas" is "lightnesse," and "nequam" "naught" or "vile." Cf. "The water is naught" (2 Kings ii. 19), and "the midst of a naughty world" in the present form of Ordinal. In the Baptismal Service Durel has "inani pompae et gloriae hujus saeculi, omnibus ejusdem cupiditatibus."

In Petley and Duport the words for both pomps and vanities are singular, and are under the vinculum of a common article. So Nowell's Small Catechism, τῇ κενῇ πομπῇ καὶ ματαιότητι. Petley and Duport have the same substantives.

mundi nequam; & omnibus pravis concupiscentiis carnis. *Secundùm*, me omnes fidei Christianae articulos crediturum. *Tertiùm*, me sanctam Dei voluntatem & illius mandata servaturum, & in iis ambulaturum omnibus diebus vitae meae.

of this naughty world; & all crooked longings of flesh. *Secondly*, that I would believe all points of Christian faith. *Thirdly*, that I would observe God's holy will & his commands, & walk in them on all days of my life.

The First Prayer Book of Edward VI. had "the devil and all his works and pomps," etc. (Parker and Co.).

For "vanitatibus" Harwood has "nugis."

Bagster has "scelerati hujus mundi," and a comma for the semicolon.

pravis. So in Tert. adv. Marc. iv. 36. cir. fin. "fidei . . . pravae," "a perverse faith," *i.e.*, directed to a wrong object.

concupiscentiis. Aless has after "concupiscentijs" "pugnantibus cum lege Dei," which Queen Eliz. did not retain. Nowell's definition of the word is "rerum malarum appetitus, vel appetitio" (Large Catechism).

articulos. Not the Articles of the Church, of course, but the "joints," clauses, sentences, or points of the Creed: in the Creed hereafter given each "articulus" is commenced by a capital letter. ἄρθρα, "joints" (Petley). κεφάλαια, "heads" (Whitaker, Nowell, and Duport).

crediturum. Note this verb with the acc. simply, as in the next question, and cf. with last clause of the Creed. Aless here has "quod crederem," not as Queen Eliz., "ut crederem."

mandata. Called in the Communion Service "Decalogum:" the word "mandates" might be kept. Cf. Maunday Thursday, the most reasonable explanation of which is perhaps that it is a corruption of Mandate, or Maudate Thursday, as being the day on which was given the New Commandment.

Whitaker has ἐντολαῖς, and so has Nowell's Small Catechism. Petley and Duport have ἐντάλμασι, a word which is only used in the New Testament of the commandments of *men*.

in iis ambulaturum: "iis" probably only refers to "mandata," but it might also refer to "voluntas."

Harwood, "ad illorum normam me totam vitam meam directurum."

An non—promiserunt? Bagster's Ed., "Nonne putas," etc. "Nonne putas te esse astrictum vt credas atque facias illa, quae ipsi tuo nomine promiserunt?" (Queen Eliz.). Aless had a different version: "Scis ne etiam quae debes credere, & facere?"

"Putásne te coram Deo deuinctum esse & obstrictum, vt ea omnia credas & facias quae tuo nomine illi susceperunt?" (Vautrollier).

Quæstio.	*Question.*
An non putas te teneri ea credere, & facere quae tuo nomine promiserunt?	Do you not think then that you are bound to believe those (things), and to do (those things) which they have promised on your account?

"*Tenerine te putas, ea credere & praestare, quae illi pro te receperunt?*" Nowell's Small Catechism, where the Greek is, Οὐκοῦν νομίζεις τὸ σὸν παντελῶς ἔργον εἶναι, κ.τ.λ.

In "An non," etc., there is an ellipsis of a prior question, such as, "Is that all?" "Are they alone bound?" The sense of "An" is represented by Arnold ("Lat. Prose Comp.," Part I. p. 36) by the insertion of "then."

οὔκουν νομίζεις ὑπόχρεως ὤν, καὶ ὅτι ὀφείλεις κ.τ.λ. (Duport). This is good as laying stress on the personal responsibility of the child baptized, and on the binding character of the ceremony.

Harwood has "An non."

e a   c r e d e r e. Probably the "ea" is intended to refer both to "credere" and "facere," but there should have been no comma after "credere," or else one also after "facere;" as in English Version "to believe, and to do, as," etc. Eds. 1685, 1687, 1696, and 1703, however, agree with this of 1670.

Bagster's Ed. has a comma after "facere."

Petley's pointing is like Durel's, πιστεύειν τε, καὶ ἐργάζεσθαι. So is Duport's πιστεύειν τε, καὶ πράττειν. Whitaker has no comma before the καί, nor has Nowell's Small Catechism. The latter has πράττειν, the former ἐργάζεσθαι. Harwood, "ad ea credendum et praestandum quae," etc.

t u o   n o m i n e. Here Messrs. Bright and Medd have "tuo nomine," but in the previous answer "in meo nomine."

I m ò — m e a e. "Ita certè: atq; id Dei auxilio sum facturus, & gratiam ago ex animo coelesti Patri, qui me ad hāc gratiam per Dominum nostrum Iesum Christum uocauit, eumq; toto pectore precor, ut porro largiatur mihi gratiam, ut in ea perseverem usq; ad finem uitae" (Queen Eliz.). Aless's version commenced differently: "Scio, & Dei auxilio uolo, & gratiam ago," etc., the rest being followed by Queen Eliz. Whitaker also differs here: "Ita certè: atque id Dei gratia facturus sum," etc.

"Equidem puto, Deóq; adiuuante ita faciam. Patri item coelesti gratias ago immortales, quòd me dignatus sit per Dominum Iesum Christum ad hanc salutis viam vocare, ipsumq; vehementer oro, vt me ita sua gratia confirmet, in eadem vt permaneam ad finem vsque vitae meae" (Vautr.).

THE CATECHISM.

Responsio.

Imò sanè, Deóque adjuvante faciam. Et ex animo Patri nostro cœlesti gratias ago quod me ad hanc salutis viam vocaverit, per Jesum

Answer.

Yea surely, and God helping (me) I will do. And from (my) heart I give thanks to our heavenly Father that he has called me unto this way

---

"Maximè profecto. Et Deo opem mihi atque auxilium ferente, enitar quantum quidem facere potuero. Coelesti vero patri maximas ex animo gratias ago habeóque, quòd me per Iesum Christum Servatorem in hunc salutis statum deduxerit. Simúlque Deum precor ut divina me virtute sua imbuat, quò eundem usque ad extremum spiritum, & ultimum vitae finem, perpetuò retineam" (Nowell's Small Catechism).

Bagster has "Immo sane;" and a comma after "adjuvante." Also commas after "ago," "Christum," and "rogo."

ex animo: heartily. Whitaker, Petley, and Duport, ἐκ καρδίας.

gratias ago: I give, render, return, or *express* my thanks. "Habere gratiam" is to *feel* grateful; "referre gratiam," to *requite* a favour.

Nowell has "ago habeóque." Duport has εὐχαριστῶ, Whitaker and Petley having the participle.

hanc salutis viam. So Eds. 1680, 1685, 1687, 1696, 1703: so, too, Vautrollier (see above), and J. W. Parker's Prayer Book, and Bagster. Not "state of salvation," as our English Version, but "*way*," or "*path*." There is no assertion here of complete salvation in this life, but the contrary is directly implied in the words "ut in ea," etc., "that I may continue in that (way) right on up to my life's end." Aless, Queen Eliz., and Whitaker have "ad hanc gratiam," "unto this grace," which agrees with the sense given by Vautrollier and Durel. In the Greek, Whitaker has, in his own Prayer Book, εἰς ταύτην ἐμὲ τὴν χάριν. Petley, too, has εἰς ταύτην ἐμὲ τὴν τῆς σωτηρίας χάριν, "unto this grace of salvation." Duport, however, who usually follows him closely, has εἰς ταύτην τῆς σωτηρίας κατάστασιν, which is at least not good Greek. Nowell's Small Catechism has also εἰς ταύτην τῆς σωτηρίας (*sic*, but σωτηρίας in 1584) κατάστασιν, & "in hunc salutis statum" in the Latin; and this latter Parsell, 1713 and 1716, G. Bowyer, 1733 and 1744, and Harwood also have; so, too, have Messrs. Bright and Medd.

Compare for Durel's version Acts xvi. 17. "Isti homines serui dei excelsi sunt qui annuntiant vobis viam salutis," Vulgate (Ed. MDLXXIII. in the Bodleian); English Version, "These men are the servants of the most high God, which show unto us the way of salvation."

For "salutis," translated "safety" in theological writings, see Nowell,

Christum Servatorem nostrum. Deum | of safety, through Jesus Christ our

"quae enim nobis spes esset reliqua salutis per illum, qui seipsum non servarit?" "for what hope of safety should we have had left by him that had not saved himself?" Norton's translation (1570).

In *The Catechism Set forth in the Book of Common-Prayer, Briefly explained*, etc. (Tho. Marschall, D.D., Rector of Lincoln College), "Printed at the THEATER in OXFORD. *Anno Dom.* 1679," we find upon "state of salvation :"—"Common Calling is that whereby a nation, city or family are called to the knowledge of the meanes of salvation. Special, or effectual Calling, is that whereby God calleth his elect, out of their natural state of sin, unto holyness and salvation, through Christ Jesus; and that ordinarily by meanes of the Gospel preached." The Imprimatur of Joan. Nicholas Vic-Can. Oxon. is dated March 20th, 1678.

Again, in "A Comment on the Book of Common-Prayer," W. Nicholls, D.D., 1710, there is a note as follows : " Called me to this state of Salvation.] *By calling us to a state of Salvation is meant*, God's admitting us at our Baptism into that Holy Religion which we profess, and by which we enjoy all the necessary means of Salvation." Again, Bishop Beveridge, in " The Church Catechism explained," 1705, writes : " *into this state of Salvation*, that is, into such a state and condition of life wherein he may be saved, and shall certainly be so, if he doth but perform what he promised, when he was by Baptism admitted or brought into it, and what he hath now promised again. . . . But though he be now in a state of Salvation unless he continue in it he cannot be saved."

v o c a v e r i t. Eds. 1685 and 1687 have no comma, but Eds. 1696 and 1703 have.

S e r v a t o r e m. Better Latin than " Salvator," which Cicero thought did not express the Greek σωτήρ. Nowell says, " neque enim aliud Hebraeis est JESUS, quam Σωτὴρ Graecis, Latinis SERVATOR." Messrs. Bright and Medd have " Salvator."

u t — c o n f i r m e t. So, too, Vautrollier (see above). Remark the difference from the English Version, "to give me his grace :" here it is said, we may note, to be the office of God (not of the Bishop) to " confirm " or " strengthen."

Whitaker has χαρίζισθαι μοι. Petley has χαρίζισθαί μοι ; Duport, again differing from him, has ζοῦναί μοι τὴν χάριν αὐτοῦ. Harwood, " ut mihi suam gratiam impertiat."

Nowell's Small Catechism has " ut divina me virtute sua imbuat," and in the Greek τὴν θεϊκὴν αὐτοῦ ζύναμιν ἐμοί ἐμποιεῖν.

g r a t i â. Never translated " grace," but " favour " in *Janua*. So Arch-

etiam rogo ut me ita suâ gratiâ con- | Saviour. I also ask God so to
firmet ut in ea permaneam usque ad | strengthen me by his favour that I
finem vitae meae. | may continue in that (way) right on
| up to my life's end.

---

bishop Secker defines the inward part of a sacrament as "some favour freely bestowed on us from Heaven:" again, "a Sacrament expresses ... some Grace or Favour towards us:" once more, "a sacrament is a Sign or Representation of some heavenly Favour" ("Lecture on Catechism," vol. ii. p. 209). Norton, also, occasionally translates "gratia" by "favour."

confirmet. Eds. 1685, 1687 have comma; Eds. 1696, 1703 have no stop.

ad finem: "ad extremum spiritum meum," Harwood; which appears to be taken from Nowell's Small Catechism, "ad extremum spiritum, & ultimum vitae finem."

Catechistes. The more correct Greek word is Κατηχητής, which, however, appears not to have been Latinized. Hieronymus uses "Catechista." Queen Elizabeth has "Question" in English Version, and "Quaestio" in Latin: Vautrollier and Whitaker have "Quaestio." Cf. note on "CATECHISMUS" above. The reason why we have "Catechist," and not "Question," in our present Prayer Book of 1662, in this passage and where the child is requested to say the Lord's Prayer, is that these sentences are hortatory or imperative, and not interrogative.

Petley of course has Ἐρώτησις, which Duport alters in accordance with the revision of 1662, and he has Κατηχιστής.

Recita—articulos: "Recita articulos Fidei." (Queen Eliz.) "Recita fidei articulos" (Vautrollier). "*Recita mihi articulos fidei Christianae*" (Nowell's Small Catechism). "Recitare" is used for "rehearse" in *Janua Linguarum,* and it is rendered by "rehearse" in Norton's translation of Nowell's Large Catechism. "Recita—memoriter" (Harwood).

fidei. See next note. "When we beleeve another's report, that is beleefe [faith]," Lat. Fides: *Janua Linguarum.* This is a kind of faith; Christian faith differs, being a special gift of God, and the fruit of His Spirit.

tuae. In Eds. 1685, 1687, 1696, 1703, for "tuae" we find "tui," the genitive of the pronoun: in the next question we have, however, "tuae" the pronominal adjective. These editions also have "Fidei" and "Articulos."

Bagster's Edition has "tui." Harwood has "tuae."

THE CATECHISM.

Catechistes.
Recita fidei tuae articulos.

Responsio.
CREDO in Deum Patrem omnipotentem, creatorem coeli & terrae: Et in Jesum Christum Filium ejus unicum Dominum nostrum, Qui conceptus est de Spiritu sancto, Natus

Instructor.
Rehearse (the) points of your faith.

Answer.
I BELIEVE on God (the) Father almighty, creator of heaven & earth : And on Jesus Christ his only Son our Lord, Who was conceived from the holy Ghost, Was born of

CREDO—*Amen.* The Eds. 1685, 1687, 1696, 1703 have "CRedo."
"Credo in Deum Patrem Omnipotentem," etc., Queen Eliz. The Creed in the Morning Service there, is the same as Durel's, with some differences in pointing and capitals, *e.g.*, "natus," "crucifixus," and two divergencies, "ad inferna" and "Et vitam." Aless had given the Creed in full in the Catechism: he has "ad inferos," and "Et in Spiritum sanctum, sanctam Ecclesiam Catholicam," etc. The Creed in Vautrollier, which is given in full in the Catechism, and not the first words only, as in Queen Eliz., is the same as that in the Morning Service of Queen Eliz., but again with differences of pointing.

The Creed given in Nowell's Large Catechism agrees in the main with Queen Eliz., but with five divergencies, mentioned below. These same divergencies occur in his Small Catechism, with one other notable point (see note on "Sanctam Ecclesiam Catholicam").

P a t r e m. Nowell's Greek (Small Catechism) is here pointed Θεὸν, πατέρα παντοκράτορα, κ.τ.λ.

o m n i p o t e n t e m. Ed. 1696 has no stop here. Eds. 1685, 1687, and 1703 have a semicolon.

u n i c u m. Eds. 1685, 1687, 1696, 1703 have a comma here.

d e. Nowell also has "DE" in both Large and Small Catechisms, but in his explanation in the former he has "e."

Whitaker, Nowell, Petley, and Duport have ἐκ. For "de," cf. "Deum de Deo," in Nicene Creed.

s a n c t o. So Eds. 1696, 1703; but Eds. 1685, 1687 have "Sancto."

N a t u s : "natus," Queen Eliz.; it being part of the same "articulus" as "conceptus."

V i r g i n e. Whitaker, Nowell, Petley, and Duport have "the (τῆς) Virgin," rightly. Cf. the Greek of Matthew i. 23 with the Hebrew and Greek of Isaiah vii. 14.

Harwood has "de" here.

8

ex Maria Virgine, Passus sub Pontio Pilato, Crucifixus, mortuus & sepultus, Descendit ad inferos; Tertia die Resurrexit à mortuis, Ascendit ad coelos, Sedet ad dexteram Dei Patris omnipotentis: Indè venturus est judicare vivos & mortuos.

Credo in Spiritum Sanctum, Sanctam Ecclesiam Catholicam, Sanctorum Communionem, Remissionem peccatorum, Carnis resurrectionem, ac Vitam aeternam. *Amen.*

Mary (the) Virgin, Suffered under Pontius Pilate, Was crucified, died & was buried, Went down unto those below; On (the) third day Rose again from (the) dead, Went up to (the) heavens, Is sitting at (the) right hand of God (the) Father almighty: Thence is to come to judge living & dead.

I believe on (the) Holy Ghost, (The) Holy Catholic Church, (The) Fellowship of (the) Holy, (The) Remitting of sins, (The) rising again of Flesh, and (the) Life everlasting. *Amen.*

---

sub Pontio Pilato. Whitaker, Nowell, Petley, and Duport have ἐπὶ Ποντίου Πιλάτου, "in the time of," etc. The First Prayer Book of Edward VI. has "Ponce Pilate."

Crucifixus: "crucifixus," Queen Eliz.; so making it part of the same "articulus" as "Passus."

mortuus (*sc. est*): "died," not "was . . . dead," as English Version.

sepultus: Nowell "SEPULTUS EST," in both Large and Small Catechisms. In the latter, however, the Creed is in small type.

ad inferos: or, "unto the other world," as *Janua* translates "inferos:" a good rendering, as implying in no way the place of torment, which all such expressions as "the world below" or "beneath," "the lower," or "nether world," etc., more or less do imply. The "inferi" are simply the dead, as opposed to those who are "super terram" (see Commandment V.). For the place of torment *Janua* uses "Orcus," "Erebus," "Avernus," and "Gehenna." Nowell has the same as Durel, and Norton translates "inferos" by "hell;" but in his explanation Nowell (Large Catechism) shows he meant simply that place where both "the souls of the unbelieving" and "the dead, which, while they lived, believed in Christ," were to be found. Tho. Marschall, D.D., in "The Catechism, etc., Briefly explained," 1679, says on the word "hell," "after Christ was dead and buried, his Soul and Body continued for a time in a separate condition under the dominion of death: which condition is sometimes signified by the Grave or Hell."

Queen Eliz. and Whitaker have "ad inferna" (sc. loca), "unto the

* * * * * * * * *

---

places below." Whitaker, Nowell, Petley, and Duport have εἰς ᾅδου, "unto (the abode) of Hades," which is as indefinite as "ad inferos."

à mortuiis. "a" is "from," not "out of," Cic. Caec. 30. Nowell also has "a," but Whitaker, Nowell, Petley, and Duport ἐκ.

"mortuiis" may be a misprint, but more probably is like "hijs" for "his," and such forms, which occur in abundance in Queen Eliz., etc. Eds. 1685, 1687, 1696, 1703 have "mortuis."

The definite article is only inserted before "dead" because the English idiom unfortunately demands it: "dead ones" would perhaps be better, but harsh. Whitaker, Nowell, Petley, and Duport rightly omit the article both here and below in "to judge," etc., where the English also allows the omission.

coelos. So Whitaker, Nowell, Petley, & Duport have οὐρανούς. Nowell has "COELUM."

Sedet: "is sitting," present. The king "sitteth (sedet) the Queen standing by," *Janua*. Nowell (Large Catechism, Norton's translation) says, "Kings use to set them on their right hands to whom they vouchsafe to do highest honour, and make lieutenants of their dominion."

ad dexteram Dei. Whitaker and Nowell (Small Catechism) have simply ἐκ δεξιῶν τοῦ πατρός, κ.τ.λ. Duport and Petley have Θεοῦ Πατρὸς.

Indè: "UNDE," Nowell.

venturus est: the subject is "Qui," which is the subject also of all the verbs from "conceptus." Duport, after using participles for the other verbs, has here ὅθεν μέλλει κ.τ.λ.

judicare: "AD JUDICANDUM," Nowell.

in Spiritum Sanctum: called "holy," says Nowell, "Not only for his own holiness, which yet is the highest holiness, but also for that by him the elect of God and the members of Christ are made holy. For which cause the holy scriptures have called him 'the Spirit of Sanctification'" (Large Catechism).

Sanctam Ecclesiam Catholicam. It is worthy of close attention that, in the Greek, Whitaker, Nowell, Petley, and also Duport have

* * * * * * * * *

———

πιστεύω τήν (not εἰς τήν) ἁγίαν ἐκκλησίαν καθολικήν, repeating πιστεύω, but without the εἰς; thus making all the subsequent nouns dependent upon this verb, and at the same time, by the omission of the εἰς, drawing an emphatic distinction between our belief *in* the Father, *in* the Son, and *in* the Holy Ghost, and our belief *that there is* a Holy Catholic Church, etc. We cannot without idolatry believe *on* any person or thing except God. So Nowell in his explanation writes, "Now remaineth the fourth part, of the *Holy Catholic Church*," etc.; clearly dividing the latter part of the Creed from the three former divisions on the Trinity; and further on he writes, "credere [not 'in'] Sanctam Catholicam Romanam Ecclesiam." So in his Vocabulary at the end of his Catechism, Nowell writes, "*Credo*, cum accusativo, et praepositione; nostrum; ut credere in Deum, i.e., Deum vere agnoscere, illi fidem habere, illi confidere, spem et fiduciam omnem in illo collocare; nam haec omnia simul complectitur. Credo item, cum solo accusativo, ut Credo resurrectionem mortuorum, et vitam aeternam, id est, certo expecto, vel spero; nostra sunt." He therefore drew a sharp distinction between "Credo in," which is used of the Deity, and means to acknowledge, have faith in, trust, and place hope and confidence in him, and "Credo" with the accusative, meaning to expect or hope for. He evidently regards, then, the last two clauses of the "fourth part" of the Creed as dependent on "Credo," and not "in," and therefore presumably the other three clauses of that part are also dependent upon "Credo" simply.

There are reasons for thinking that Durel also intended "Sanctam Ecclesiam," etc., to depend directly on "Credo," in the same way that in the Creed in the Communion Service he puts " in " before each person of the Trinity, but not before the Catholick and Apostolick Church; just as Petley and Duport there also make the Church, etc., to be governed simply by πιστεύω. Durel there has "Et unam sanctam, Catholicam, & Apostolicam Ecclesiam." So here Durel probably meant "Ecclesiam" to be governed directly by "Credo." Otherwise he would have repeated the preposition, as Classical usage requires and as he does elsewhere: cf. "de terra Ægypti, de domo servitutis;" and again, "ex toto corde, ex tota mente, ex tota anima, & ex totis viribus;" and "ab omni peccato, ac malitiâ, ab hoste animorum & ab aeterna morte."

* * * * * * * * *

It may be added that in Queen Elizabeth's Latin Prayer Book, in that printed by Vautrollier, and also in the English Book of Queen Eliz., there is a full stop after the clause of belief on the Spirit. "I believe in the Holy Ghost. The holy Catholic Church. The," etc., Queen Eliz. English Version. In the Latin versions at all events it is improbable that the preposition "in" was intended to govern any words after a full stop; whereas "Credo" might well be understood as in the second part of the Creed : " Et (*sc.* Credo) in Iesum Christum," etc.

That this construction, "Credo Sanctam Ecclesiam Catholicam," is intended in the Latin versions, also appears from the following facts. Firstly, in Whitaker's Greek and Latin Prayer Book (parallel columns) we find in the Latin "Credo in Spiritum Sanctum. Sanctam ecclesiam Catholicam. Sanctorum," etc.; and in the Greek column, Πιστεύω εἰς πνεῦμα ἅγιων, πιστεύω τὴν ἁγίαν ἐκκλησίαν κ.τ.λ.

Again, in Nowell's Small Catechism, we have the Greek and Latin in parallel columns. In the former we find πιστεύω εἰς πνεῦμα ἅγιον πιστεύω τὴν αγίαν (sic) ἐκκλησίαν καθυλικήν, κ.τ.λ. In the Latin we have "Credo in Spiritum sanctum : sanctam Ecclesiam catholicam, sanctorum communionem," etc.; *i.e.*, a colon dividing the first clause from the rest, which are only divided from one another by commas. This is the same in both Ed. 1584 and 1633.

So, too, in "Catecheticae Versiones Variae," etc., "The common Catechisme in foure Languages," London, 1638, we find in the English column, "I beleeve in the holy Ghost : the holy Catholique Church :" etc.; and in the Latin, "Credo in Spiritum Sanctum : credo sanctam Ecclesiam catholicam," etc.; showing that, even where a colon divided the clauses in the English, "in" was not supposed to govern "Church," but "Church" was thought to be governed directly by "believe."

Again, in "A Comment on the Book of Common-Prayer," etc., by William Nicholls, D.D., London, MDCCX, we find as follows : "XV. *By believing in the Holy Ghost*, we profess him to be very God," etc. "XVI. *From the Article of the Catholick Church we believe*, That there is a number of Men," etc. "XVII. *By the Article of the Communion of Saints we believe*, That there is a Communion," etc. : this clearly shows

4. * * * * * * * * *

---

that Nicholls did not think the Creed expressed "belief *in*," but simply belief of the *existence* of a Church.

Before leaving the subject we may compare "Peres the Ploughmans Crede" (circa 1394), "CREDO. LEUE thou on oure Louerd God ... And on gentyl Jesu Crist ... And in the heighe holly gost holly y beleue, And generall holy Chirche also hold this in thy mynde," etc.

Sanctorum Communionem. Nowell in his explanation gives this clause of the Creed in the form " CREDERE SANCTORUM COMMUNIO-NEM" (Large Catechism), showing that he did not consider "Communionem" at all events to be governed by "in :" "we believe 'the communion of saints'" (Norton's translation). It follows the previous clause " Sanctam Ecclesiam Catholicam", "Because these two belong all to one thing" (ditto).

This clause was explained at the attempted Revision of 1689 as the "fellowship of all true Christians in faith, hope, and charity."

As the words "Sanctum" and "Sanctam" are used immediately before or " Holy," it seems better to retain the word " Holy " here. " Saints " in the modern sense is " coelitibus " in *Janua;* where also " communionem " is " fellowship." Cf. note on " sanctificavit" in the next answer, and in the Fourth Commandment. "Sanctificare" is to make holy, or hallow, and "Sancti" are the hallowed. Cf. "All Hallows," *i.e.*, "Omnium Sanctorum."

In the additional notes in Nicholl's Commentary on the Prayer Book, we find "Sancti (h. e. fideles."

Remissionem peccatorum. The Rev. E. Daniel writes ("The Prayer Book," etc., London, p. 368) : "At first sight the connection between this article and the Holy Ghost may not strike the reader. It is this. The Church is the instrument which God has appointed to convey to man the forgiveness of sins and it is to the Holy Spirit the Church owes its existence and its powers. It is the regeneration effected by the Holy Spirit in Baptism which secures the remission of sins ; it is by the gift of the Holy Ghost that the ministers of the Church are empowered to authoritatively declare to those who are truly penitent and believe his holy gospel the forgiveness of sins which they commit day by day." With this we cannot agree. The very fact that such connection might "not

*　　*　　*　　*　　*　　*　　　　*

---

strike the reader" is an argument against the implication of any such connection in a Creed quoted in a Catechism or simple form of Instruction for the young and unlearned.

The keys, which are given unto the Church, says Nowell (Large Catechism, Norton's translation) are "that power of binding and loosing, of reserving and forgiving sins, which standeth in the ministry of the word of God" (quae in verbi Divini ministerio sita est). Again, "*M.* What meanest thou by this word 'forgiveness'? *S.* That the faithful do obtain at God's hand (a Deo impetrare) discharge of their fault and pardon of their offence: for God, for Christ's sake, freely forgiveth them their sins," etc.

Dr. Harrison writes to us: "Our Nicene Creed is quite wrong on the doctrine of Baptism. Cyril, Bishop of Jerusalem, recites an article from an earlier form of it as follows: 'I believe *in* one Baptism of Repentance for the remission of sins.' This is the obsolete Baptism of John, and not Christian Baptism. Cyril, accordingly, in his exposition of this article, distinctly maintains that John's Baptism conveyed the remission of sins. Now John's Baptism was for, or in order to, repentance or conversion; and repentance was for, or in order to, remission. The error, when discovered, was only partially corrected by leaving out the words 'of repentance.' By this omission the Creed ceased to teach John's Baptism, but it was made to teach Christian Baptism as being for, or in order to, the remission of sins, which I am sure is neither the phraseology nor the doctrine of Scripture."

Carnis: the same word used to translate "flesh" in "lusts of the flesh" in the third answer; for the latter, cf. the use of "pulpa" in Persius Sat. ii. l. 63, with the attribute "scelerata," "this sinful pampered flesh of ours" (Conington). Nowell (Vocab. to Large Catechism) gives two senses of "Caro": (1) "pro genere humano," (2) "pro vitiosa et corrupta natura."

resurrectionem: "rising again." So Wiclif, "again—rising." Here, again, Nowell's Large Catechism has "CREDO RESURRECTIONEM CARNIS, ET VITAM AETERNAM" in his explanation: this also shows that these two clauses are governed by "Credo," not "in." "I believe the resurrection of the flesh," etc. (Norton).

Quæstio.	*Question.*
Quid potissimùm doceris in his fidei tuae articulis?	What are you especially taught in these points of your faith?
Responsio.	*Answer.*
Primò, doceor credere in Deum Patrem, qui me & mundum universum condidit.	Firstly, I am taught to believe on God (the) Father, who has made me & (the) whole world.

ac Vitam: the last "articulus" begins at "Vitam." Queen Eliz. has "et vitam," making "Carnis—aeternam" one clause. Nowell, Petley and Duport omit καὶ, but Whitaker has it.

aeternam: or "eternal."

Before leaving the Creed we must note the differences, though slight, in the Latin version given in Bagster's Polyglot Prayer Book (Ed. 1866), which in the main follows Durel verbatim.

In his first edition (1821), the edition "first published by *W. Bowyer* in 1720" is said to be followed (see Part II. chap. i.), but in the edition of 1866 no acknowledgment of the authorship is made. Singularly enough there is no copy of Ed. 1821 in the Bodleian.

His text in the main follows Durel verbatim, but there are considerable divergencies of pointing, capitals, etc., and some few very important differences in the language itself. For the latter, at all events, there is no warrant in any edition of Durel published during his lifetime or for the remainder of that century. We shall endeavour to note most, if not all, the divergencies throughout the Catechism, except such as "et" for "&" and the changes in accentuation.

In the Creed we find commas after "Deum," "Christum," "mortuus," "Dei," and "venturus est;" a semicolon for a comma after "nostrum;" a colon for a semicolon after "inferos;" a colon for a comma after "mortuis" and "coelos;" a full stop for a comma after "sepultus;" and lastly, small letters instead of capitals in "Et," "Qui," "Natus," "Passus," "Crucifixus," "Tertia," "Resurrexit," "Ascendit," "Sedet," "Indè," and "Sanctam."

Owing to the want of inflections in our language, stops are of the utmost importance. It is only in the precision of legal language that we can dismiss them. In ordinary sentences the insertion or omission of even a comma may completely alter the doctrine they teach; a notable instance of this we shall have occasion hereafter to remark (see note on "quod nobis datur"). Nor are capitals unimportant: there is, for example, a great difference between "Verbum" and "verbum;" the latter, "the word" of God; the former, His "Word."

Secundò, in Deum Filium, qui me & totum genus humanum redemit.	Secondly, on God (the) Son, who has ransomed me & (the) whole human race.
Tertiò, in Spiritum sanctum Deum, qui me & omnes electos Dei sanctificavit.	Thirdly, on (the) Holy Ghost (as) God, who has hallowed me & all God's elect ones.

Quid potissimùm. "Quid praecipue didicisti ex his articulis fidei?" Queen Eliz. Aless had no "fidei." Whitaker has "discis." "In illis fidei articulis quid praecipuè discendum arbitraris?" (Vautrollier). "*Quid ex hijs fidei articulis potissimùm discis?*" (Nowell's Small Catechism). In connection with the note above on "Sanctam Ecclesiam Catholicam," it is interesting to note that no mention is made of the Catholic Church, etc., in this summary.

Primò, doceor, etc. "Primùm, didici credere in Deum Patrem, qui creauit coelum & terram.

"Deinde in Deum Filium, qui me redemit, & totum genus humanum.

"Tertiò, in Spiritum sanctum, qui me sanctificat, & uniuersum electum populum Dei" (Queen Eliz.). Whitaker has "disco," not "didici."

"Primùm, disco credendum mihi esse in Deum Patrem, qui & me & vniuersum hunc mundum condidit. Secundò in Deum filium, qui & me & totum genus humanum redemit. Tertiò, in Spiritum sanctum Deum, qui me & omnes Dei electos sanctificat" (Vautrollier).

"Primò in Deum Patrem credere, qui me, & mundum universum fabricatus est. Secundò, in Deum Filium, qui me, & universum genus humanum redemit. Tertiò, in Deum Spiritum sanctum, qui me, & omnes à Deo electos sanctificat" (Nowell's Small Catechism).

mundum: this word, and also "universus," "condere," and "redimere" occur in *Janua* translated as here. Whitaker's, Petley's, and Duport's word for "qui condidit" is $\delta\eta\mu\iota\text{ουργήσαντα}$.

redemit: or, "redeemed."

Spiritum sanctum Deum. "Deum," being placed after "Spiritum sanctum" is emphatic. This clause in the Creed was originally introduced on account of doubts of the Deity of the Holy Ghost. Duport has $\Theta\epsilon\grave{o}\nu\ \tau\grave{o}\ \Pi\nu\epsilon\tilde{\upsilon}\mu\alpha\ \tau\grave{o}\ \text{"}\Alpha\gamma\iota o\nu$, but it is to be remarked that, whereas he uses the definite article here and in $\Theta\epsilon\grave{o}\nu\ \tau\grave{o}\nu\ \text{'}\Upsilon\iota\grave{o}\nu$, he omits it before "Father," saying simply $\Theta\epsilon\grave{o}\nu\ \Pi\alpha\tau\acute{\epsilon}\rho\alpha$: and strictly in the case of the Son and of the Holy Ghost $\Theta\epsilon\grave{o}\nu$ is used predicatively. The versions of Vautrollier and Harwood agree with Durel's. Queen Eliz., as we have seen, has not "Deum" at all; nor has Whitaker, who has only $\epsilon\grave{i}\varsigma\ \pi\nu\epsilon\tilde{\upsilon}\mu\alpha\ \tau\grave{o}\ \ddot{\alpha}\gamma\iota o\nu$ in the Greek. Nowell's Small Catechism has $\Theta\epsilon\grave{o}\nu$ and the article with all three.

Quæstio. Dicebas Susceptores tuos & Susceptrices tuo nomine promisisse, te mandata Dei Servaturum. Dic mihi quot sunt illa?	*Question.* You were saying that your Godfathers & Godmothers had promised on your account, that you would Observe (the) commands of God. Tell me how many are those?
Responsio. Decem.	*Answer.* Ten.
Quæstio. Quae sunt illa?	*Question.* What are those?
Responsio. EA ipsa quae Deus tradidit capite	*Answer.* THOSE very ones which God has

sanctum. So Ed. 1696; Eds. 1685, 1687, 1703 have "Sanctum."

omnes electos. The word "omnes" (not "cunctos") carries the idea of individuality. Here again the Latin somewhat differs from the English Version, which has, "all the elect people of God;" to this Petley's and Duport's Greek adheres: πάντα τὸν (Duport; Petley, συνόλον and no article) τοῦ Θεοῦ ἐκλεκτὸν λαόν: and Whitaker's also, who, however, has ὅλον for πάντα. So, too, "universum electum populum Dei" (Queen Eliz.). But similar to Durel's are the versions of Nowell, "omnes à Deo electos," and συμπάντας ἔτι τοῦ Θεοῦ ἐκλεκτοὺς (Small Catechism), of Vautrollier, "omnes Dei electos," and of Harwood, "cum omnibus Dei electis." "*Electi Dei,*" Nowell says (Large Catechism), is "pro electi a Deo."

sanctificavit. So Eds. 1685, 1687, 1696, 1703. Perfect, not as English Version, present tense; another mark of independence of this Latin version. The perfect assumes that the "denuo nasci justitiae" has by this time taken place. "The common Catechisme in foure Languages," 1638, has, "who hath sanctified" in the English.

The other versions collated (Queen Eliz., Nowell, Vautrollier, Petley, etc.) have the present, adhering to the English Version. So Duport, too, has ἁγιάζον. For "sanctificavit" see note on "**Sanctorum Communionem.**"

Dicebas. Bagster has "Dixisti," followed by a comma. "Cùm responderis, Patrinos nomine tuo promisisse te seruaturum esse praecepta Dei, dic quot sunt?" (Queen Eliz.). "Dixeras susceptores tuo nomine promisisse, te mandata Dei obseruaturum, dic igitur quot sunt illa?"

vigesimo Exodi, dicens, Ego sum Dominus Deus tuus, qui eduxi te de terra Ægypti, de domo seruitutis.	delivered in (the) twentieth chapter of Exodus, saying, I am thy Lord God, who have brought thee out from (the) land of Egypt, from a house of thraldom.

(Vautrollier). "*Dicebas sponsores illos tuos tuo nomine in se recepisse praecepta te divina esse observaturum. Dic mihi quot ea sunt.*" (sic in 1584 also.) (Nowell's Small Catechism.) In the Greek he has Εἶπις ἄνω for "Dicebas."

S u s c e p t o r e s.   Petley and Duport, Σύμπατρας (sic). Nowell's Small Catechism has οἱ κατασπάντες ὑπὲρ σου ἐγγυηταί.

S e r v a t u r u m : small "s" in Eds. 1685, 1687, 1696, 1703.

s u n t : not "sint," but the mood shows there should be a comma after "Dic mihi," "quot" etc. being a direct question. But the pointing is the same in Eds. 1685, 1687, 1696, 1703. Bagster inserts a comma after "mihi." Queen Eliz. has the same mistake in pointing, and Nowell and Vautrollier also. So has Whitaker, λέγε πόσα ἐστι ; so has Duport, λέγε μοι πόσαι εἰσί ; Petley is right here, λέγε ἄρα, πόσα ἐστί ; Nowell's Small Catechism has, in the Greek, λέγε δή, πόσα ἐστὶν αὐτά.

D e c e m.   "Decem," Queen Eliz., Vautrollier, and Nowell's Small Catechism.

Q u a e s u n t i l l a ?   "Quae sunt?" (Queen Eliz.). "Dic quae sunt?" (Whitaker). "Quae sunt illa?" (Vautrollier). "*Quae ?*" (Nowell's Small Catechism).

E A   i p s a   e t c.   So Eds. 1685, 1687, 1696, 1703. "Ea quae Dominus recensuit Exodi vicesimo, dicens : Ego sum Dominus Deus uester, qui eduxi te de terra Ægypti, ex domo seruitutis, &c. vt supra, ante Communionem" (Queen Eliz.). Note "uester—te." In the Communion Service we have "Deus tuus." Aless had no preface, but began at once with the Commandments. Whitaker retains "vester."

"DEUS AD HUNC MODUM EFFATUS EST. AUDI ISRAEL ; EGO SUM DOMINUS DEUS TUUS, QUI TE EDUXI EX DOMICILIO SERVITUTIS ÆGYPTIAE" (Nowell's Large Catechism). In his Small Catechism he commences, "Eadem, quae in vigesimo capite Exodi extant : quae Deus ipse ad hunc modum effatus est. Ego sum," etc., as in the Large Catechism ; but in Ed. 1584 he has "ΛEgiptiae."

Bagster's Edition inserts a comma after "ipsa," and "in" before "capite," and has a colon instead of comma after "dicens."

t r a d i d i t : "spake," English Version. "recensuit," Queen Eliz. "pro-

I. NON habebis Deos alienos | I. THOU shalt not have another's

---

didit," Vautrollier. ἰλάληοιν, the LXX., Whitaker, Petley, and Duport; the latter continues ἐν τῷ (τῇ in Ed. 1818) εἰκοστῷ Κιφαλαίῳ, κ.τ.λ. Harwood has " quae Deus, ut in capite vigesimo Exodi habetur, effatus est ad hunc modum."

E g o s u m : the version of the Commandments given by Durel is the ordinary Vulgate version, with some differences in pointing and capitals, and three small divergencies which are noted below. (The edition of the Vulgate which we have consulted is 1573. See note on PATER noster.) Messrs. Bright and Medd, in these three passages, have the same divergencies as Durel. It is somewhat remarkable that in Vautrollier we find two versions of the Commandments. The one in the Communion Service is substantially the same as that in Queen Eliz., with divergencies which we shall note. That in the Catechism, on the other hand, is in parts the same as Nowell's.

"Quae Deus ipse prodidit capite vigesimo Exodi, dicens: Ego sum Deus tuus, qui te eduxi ex Ægypto ex domo seruitutis" (Vautrollier in Catechism).

de terra, etc. Here again Nowell, Petley, and Duport have ἐκ where Durel has "de." So, too, ἐξ οἴκου, LXX., Nowell, and Duport, and ἐκ ἑώμου, Petley.

Queen Eliz. has " de terra" and " ex domo."

Harwood, following Nowell, has " ex domicilio servitutis Ægyptiae."

servitutis : "thraldome" in *Janua* ; "thraldom" or "bondage" in Norton's translation of Nowell's Large Catechism.

I. N O N. Eds. 1685, 1687, 1696, 1703 have "Non" throughout; Bagster also has "Non."

"Deos nullos alios habebis praeter me," Queen Eliz. (Communion Service); whereas Aless had "Nullum praeter me Deum habebis."

"NON HABEBIS DEOS ALIENOS CORAM ME," Nowell's Large Catechism, and also in the small one. We shall note the differences between them in words, but not those in pointing, etc. After each Commandment is given the response, " Miserere nostri," etc.

Vautrollier in Catechism has the same as Nowell; in Communion Service, the same as Queen Eliz.

habebis : the future used for a gentle and courteous imperative ; for the usage compare Cicero In Cat. I. *sub fine*, where he employs the future in an appeal to Jupiter Stator. This explanation is supported by "Memento" of the fourth, and "Honora" of the fifth Command-

coram me.	Gods in my presence.
II. NON facies tibi sculptile, neque	II. THOU shalt not make for thyself

ments. It is, however, equally probable that these are simple (not hortative) futures throughout the Commandments: "Thou wilt," not "thou shalt have," etc. One of the chief grounds that tend to this conclusion is the form of the negative particle in the Hebrew. By way of illustration it may be observed that a very dignified and authoritative style of injunction among ourselves is similarly expressed, *e.g.*, in the Queen's speeches to Parliament. And in the Commandments we must remember that we have "the King of kings" and "Lord of lords," from whom comes all that is essentially noble and gentle, in style as in everything else; and that he is addressing those whom he is pleased to choose for "a kingdom of priests, and an holy nation."

Queen Eliz., Nowell, and Vautrollier have "habebis." Harwood has "habeto," "facito," etc. οὐκ ἔσονταί σοι, κ.τ.λ., LXX., Nowell, Petley, and Duport, who, however, have the imperatives Μνήσθητι and Τίμα in the affirmative commands.

alienos: or "alien." "Deos alienos habere" is Nowell's synonym for "Idololatria." The Rev. E. Daniel explains "other gods" by such as the Gentile nations had. But if, as he says, the Ten Commandments are binding on Christians now, "other gods" must be such as should be had by any at any time anywhere, including the paste idol of the Romish Church.

coram me: coram is "in his presence," as in *Janua*. So Nowell and "The common Catechisme in foure Languages," 1638. Petley, too, and Nowell's Small Catechism, and "The common Catechisme," etc., have ἐνώπιόν μου; and our English Bible has "before me." Queen Eliz., however, has "praeter me." So has Harwood; and the LXX. and Duport have πλὴν ἐμοῦ. The English Version is "none other God but me." Vautrollier, we have seen, has both "praeter" and "coram." Nowell explains "CORAM ME" as follows: the words mean, he says, "That we cannot once so much as tend to revolting from God, but that God is witness of it; for there is nothing so close nor so secret that it can be hid from him. Moreover, he thereby declareth that he requireth not only the honour of open confession, but also inward and sincere godliness of heart, for that he is the understander and judge of secret thoughts" (Norton's Translation).

II. NON facies. "Non facias tibi sculptile, neque similitudinem alicuius rei in coelo superne, uel in terra inferne, neque in aquis subtus terram, non procides ante haec, nec coles illa" (Aless).

omnem similitudinem quae est in coelo | a carved (thing), nor any likeness

"Non facies tibi scuIptile, neque ullam similitudinem ullius rei quae est supra in caelo (*sic*), aut infra in terra, aut in aquis sub terra: non adorabis ea nec coles. Ego enim Deus tuus fortis, zelotes sum, uisitans iniquitates patrum in filios, in tertiam & quartam generationem eorum qui oderunt me, & faciens misericordiam in milia, hijs qui diligunt & custodiunt praecepta mea" (Queen Eliz.: Communion Service).

"SIMULACHRUM ULLIUS REI, QUAE AUT SUPRA IN COELO, AUT INFRA IN TERRA, AUT IN AQUIS INFRA TERRAM SIT, NON EFFINGES; EA NON VENERABERIS NEQUE COLES. NAM EGO SUM DOMINUS DEUS TUUS, ZELOTYPUS, QUI PARENTUM INIQUITATEM ETIAM IN LIBERIS VINDICO, AD TERTIAM USQUE QUARTAMQUE PROGENIEM OSORUM MEI; CLEMENTIAQUE UTOR AD MILLESIMAM USQUE PROGENIEM, ERGA MEI AMANTES, MEAQUE PRAECEPTA CONSERVANTES" (Nowell).

Vautrollier in the Catechism has, "Non facies tibi simulachrum ... coelo sit, aut ... terram. Non veneraberis ea neque ... tuus zelotypus, ... mei, clementiáq; ... progeniem erga ... praecepta obseruantes." The portions omitted here are verbatim the same as Nowell's. In the Communion Service his version is the same as Queen Eliz., except that for "caelo" he has "coelo," and for "Deus tuus fortis, zelotes" he reads "Dominus Deus tuus, Deus zelotes;" he also has "millia," and inserts "me" after "diligunt."

This longer form of the Commandments was introduced into the Catechism in the Second Prayer Book of Edward VI., 1552. His First Prayer Book of 1549 has the short form, as has Aless in his version. The longer form of our English books is that which is given in Cranmer's Bible (1540).

f a c i e s. The Rev. E. Daniel says, "It was not the making of images that was forbidden, but the bowing down to them and worshipping them." The Latin, however, is plain and peremptory: "NON facies."

s c u l p t i l e, "carved:" similitudo, "likenesse:" colo, "reverence:" in *Janua*. εἴδωλον, LXX., Nowell, Petley, and Duport.

n e q u e o m n e m : "neque ullam" or "neque quamquam" would have been better Latin; but cf. Cicero "sine omni sapientia" (de Or. 2. 1), etc. The same form of expression is used again in the fourth and tenth Commandments.

Probably such phrases in passages like the present are directly to be traced to the Hebrew. The *rationale* of these Hebrew forms is very clearly given in Lee's Hebrew Grammar. He points out that to the Orientals generally (who perhaps derive their habits of thinking and expressing themselves from Hebrew sources), such phrases as "thou

desuper, & quae in terra deorsum, nec eorum quae sunt in aquis sub terra. Non adorabis ea neque coles; Ego enim sum Dominus Deus tuus fortis, Zelotes, visitans iniquitatem patrum in filios in tertiam & quartam generationem eorum qui oderunt me, & faciens misericordiam in millia his qui

which is in heaven above, & which is on earth below, nor of those (things) which are in waters under earth. Thou shalt not adore them nor reverence (them); for I am thy Lord God strong, Jealous, visiting unfairness of fathers on sons till (the) third & fourth generation of those who hate

---

shalt *have none*" would be unnatural, as it would seem to imply the possibility of *having* what does not *exist*. And hence he contends that their phrases "thou shalt not have any" and the like are the more strictly logical ones.

similitudinem quae est. So the Vulgate. Aless has "similitudinem alicuius rei." "ullius rei, quæ est" (Queen Eliz.). "ULLIUS REI, QUAE ... SIT" (Nowell and, in small type, Vautrollier). English Version, "the likeness of any thing that is," etc. So, too, Nowell, Petley, and Duport have οὐδὲ παντὸς ὁμοίωμα, following the LXX. Harwood has "ullius rei, quae extet."

There are, however, no words in the Hebrew for "of any thing."

desuper, deorsum: or, "from above," "from beneath."

Non adorabis. "*M*. What manner of worshipping is that which is here condemned? *S*. When we, intending to pray, do turn ourselves to portraitures or images; when we do fall down and kneel before them with uncovering our heads, or with other signs shewing any honour unto them, as if God were represented unto us by them;" etc. (Nowell, Norton's Translation).

adorabis ea neque coles. Here there is rightly no comma after "adorabis ea." Cf. note on "ea credere, & facere."

enim. This word is not in the Vulgate in this passage.

sum Dominus: not "sum—fortis," for then "sum" would also go with "visitans," which would not be good Latin.

fortis. There is no equivalent for this word in the English Version of the Prayer Book; "for I the Lord thy God am a jealous God." There should be a comma before "fortis." The divergence from the English Version is here probably due to following the Vulgate.

Nowell, Petley, and Duport also have Θεὸς ἰσχυρός. The LXX. version has not ἰσχυρός.

Zelotes: "zelotes," Eds. 1685, 1687, 1696, 1703. Nowell gives "Socii impatiens" as an equivalent, in Vocabulary to Large Catechism.

| diligunt me & custodiunt praecepta mea. | me, & showing mercy till thousands to these who love me & guard my commandments. |

---

in filios. Eds. 1685, 1687, 1696, 1703 have a comma here.

in tertiam. This "in" is not like "in filios," which corresponds to "his," but like "in millia," to which it is parallel.

misericordiam: or "tenderheartedness."

in millia: *i.e.*, of generations. Queen Eliz. agrees with Durel. "CLEMENTIAQUE UTOR, AD MILLESIMAM USQUE PROGENIEM, ERGA MEI AMANTES," etc., Nowell. Harwood has "ad millesimam usque stirpem erga mei amantes."

LXX., Nowell, Petley, and Duport have εἰς χιλιάδας.

"*M.* Where afore we speak of revenging, he nameth but three or four generations at the most; why doth he here, in speaking of mercy, contain a thousand? *S.* To shew that he is much more inclined to mercifulness and to liberality, than he is to severity; like as also in another place he professeth that he is very slow to wrath, and most ready to forgive" (Nowell, Norton's Translation of Large Catechism).

his: "these," not "those" as English Version. The Vulgate, however, has "iis."

praecepta: "decem praecepta," "the Ten Commandments," *Janua.* So, in the Rubric before the Commandments in Communion Service, Queen Eliz. has "Decem praecepta," and further on, "post singula mandata."

III. NON assumes. "Non assumes nomen Domini Dei tui in uanum: non enim habebit insontem Dominus eum, qui assumpserit nomen Domini Dei sui frustra." Queen Eliz. (Communion Service). Aless had simply "Non accipies nomen Dei tui uane."

"NOMEN DOMINI DEI TUI INANITER NON USURPABIS; NEQUE ENIM SINET IMPUNITUM JEHOVA, QUI EJUS NOMEN INANITER ADHIBUERIT" (Nowell).

Vautrollier, in Catechism, has the same as Nowell, but a comma after "usurpabis," and "Deus impunitum" for "impunitum Jehova." In the Communion Service he has the same as Queen Eliz., except that for "Domini Dei sui" he has simply "eius."

in vanum. Vanitas, "emptiness;" vanus, "a liar," *Janua.* So "in vanum" perhaps "unto a lie." Cf. "ex vano," Livy 33, 31. frustra, "to no purpose," *Janua.*

Nowell gives "inaniter" both here and for the "frustra" at the end. Why the Vulgate, which Durel here follows, should have "in vanum" in

III. NON assumes nomen Domini Dei tui in vanum, nec enim habebit	III. THOU shalt not take (the) name of thy Lord God in vain, for

the first place and "frustra" in the second we cannot tell, unless to show that they are equipollent. A comparison of passages in which the Hebrew word occurs (mostly in Jeremiah) seems to show that it was an adverbial form, and that "inaniter" is hardly so good an equivalent as "frustra" or "in vanum."

LXX., Nowell, Petley, and Duport have ἐπὶ ματαίῳ in both places. Harwood, "inaniter ne adhibeto."

n e c e n i m : the Vulgate has "non enim."

n o m e n : Rev. E. Daniel includes under this Commandment everything God has set His name upon, including His Sacraments and Ministers. This, however, contradicts the teaching of the Church, inasmuch as the Church places duty to Ministers in the Second Table, and not in the First: "Ministers" coming under "patrem" in the fifth Commandment.

IV. M E M E N T O.—"Memento," Eds. 1685, 1687, 1696, 1703. Bagster also has "Memento." He also has commas after "operaberis," "tu," "filius tuus," "servus tuus," "coelum," "mare," and "Sabbati": putting also a full stop for a comma after "sanctifices" and "est," with the accompanying change of "sex" to "Sex," and "non" to "Non:" he also reads "septimo. Idcirco" for "septimo; idcirco."

Aless has "Memento ut diem Sabbati sanctifices." See note on "II. NON facies," sub fine.

"Memento ut diem Sabbati sanctifices. Sex diebus operaberis, & facies omnia opera tua, septimo autem die Sabbatum Dñi Dei tui est. nullum in eo facies opus, tu & filius tuus & filia tua, seruus tuus & ancilla tua, iumentum tuum, & aduena qui est intra portas tuas. Sex enim diebus fecit Dominus coelum & terram & mare, & omnia quae in eis sunt, & requievit die septimo. Idcirco benedixit Dominus diei Sabbati, & sanctificauit eum" (Queen Eliz., Communion Service).

"DIEM SABBATI SANCTE AGERE MEMENTO. SEX DIEBUS OPERABERIS, ET FACIES OMNIA OPERA TUA; SEPTIMO VERO DIE, QUOD EST DOMINI DEI TUI SABBATUM, NULLUM OPUS FACIES; NEC TU, NEC FILIUS TUUS, NEC FILIA TUA, NEC SERVUS TUUS, NEC ANCILLA TUA, NEQUE JUMENTUM TUUM, NEQUE APUD TE DEGENS PEREGRINUS. NAM SEX DIEBUS PERFECIT DEUS COELUM ET TERRAM, ET MARE, ET QUICQUID IN ILLIS CONTINETUR. SEPTIMO QUIEVIT. ITAQUE DIEM SABBATI SACRUM, SIBIQUE DICATUM ESSE VOLUIT." Nowell's Large Catechism; in the small one, "sibique dicatum esse voluit" (Ed. 1633), but in Ed. 1584, "dicatum." So in Middle Catechism, "dicatum."

In the Catechism, Vautrollier agrees with Nowell in the main: the

insontem Dominus eum qui assump- | (the) Lord wi l not hold guiltless him
serit nomen Domini Dei sui frustrá. | that shall have taken (the) name of
| his Lord God to no purpose.

IV. MEMENTO ut diem Sabbati | IV. REMEMBER to hallow (the)

---

portions denoted by the dots are the same in both, Vautrollier, however, having "th" for "t" in "Sabbati" and "Sabbatum:" "Diem . . . transigere memento, sex . . . tua. Septimo . . . facies, nec . . . nec iumentum . . . continetur, septimo . . . sacrum sibíq; . . . voluit."

In the Communion Service, Vautrollier agrees with Queen Eliz.

Sabbati: it should be "Sabbatorum," but in *Janua* we have "Sabbatho," and Queen Eliz., Nowell, and Vautrollier all have the singular. LXX., Nowell (Greek of Small Catechism), Petley, and Duport have the plural τὴν ἡμέραν τῶν σαββάτων.

omne: see note on "neque omnem." Nowell and Duport have πᾶν, following the LXX.

servus: one of the reasons which Nowell gives for this Law is "to, provide for the state of servants, that it be made tolerable."

ancilla: "dairy-maid" (*Janua*).

jumentum: "labouring beasts or working cattell" (*Janua*): "a beast of burthen," Dr. Smith's Latin Dictionary, where it is added that it is "not an ox, to which it is freq. opp." The derivation is probably from jungo (jugumentum): it has, however, been suggested that jumentum is related to "juvo" (help) in the same way that momentum (movimentum) is to "moveo." This may be hinted at in *Janua*, "Jumenta sunt animalia, . . . nos juvantia."

Petley and Duport have a singular version here: ὁ βοῦς καὶ τὸ ὑποζύγιόν σου, καὶ πᾶν κτῆνος. In this they follow the LXX. version, which, however, has σου after βοῦς and κτῆνος, as also has Nowell.

advena: or, "immigrant." προσήλυτος, Duport, as also Nowell and Petley.

sunt: here Eds. 1685, 1687, 1696, 1703 have a semicolon.

requievit, etc. "Requievit die septimo eumque benedixit" (Lactantius). "Benedicere" with the acc. is "to hallow," with the dative, as here, "to bless:" and this is better Latin.

Upon this rest of God, Nowell remarks, "Why hath God set herein before us an example of himself for us to follow?" "Because notable and noble examples do more thoroughly stir up and sharpen men's minds," etc. (Norton's Translation, Large Catechism).

"seriatus est die septimo: Quâ de causâ diem septimum faustum sacrumque fecit" (Harwood).

sanctifices, sex diebus operaberis & facies omnia opera tua: septimo autem die Sabbatum Domini Dei tui est, non facies omne opus in eo, tu & filius tuus & filia tua, servus tuus & ancilla tua, jumentum tuum, & advena qui est intra portas tuas. Sex enim diebus fecit Dominus coelum & terram, & mare & omnia quae in eis sunt : & requievit die septimo; idcirco benedixit Dominus diei Sabbati & sanctificavit eum.

day of (the) Sabbath, on six days thou shalt work & do all thy works : but on the seventh day is thy Lord God's Sabbath, thou shalt not do any work on it, thou & thy son & thy daughter, thy servant & thy handmaid, thy beast of burden, & (the) stranger who is within thy gates. For on six days (the) Lord hath made heaven & earth, & sea & all (things) which are in them : & rested on (the) seventh day ; therefore (the) Lord hath blessed (the) day of (the) Sabbath & hath hallowed it.

---

septimo: Eds. 1685, 1687, 1696, 1703 have a comma here.

sanctificavit: see note on "Sanctorum Communionem." Nowell gives two uses of "Sanctificare :" (1) "*Sanctificare*, et glorificare ad Deum relata," etc. (2) "*Sanctificare*, et justificare, ad homines relata," etc. We find a similar use to the first in the Lord's Prayer, and to the second in the answer after the Creed. But neither is precisely the sense here.

V. HONORA, etc. "Honora," Eds. 1685, 1687, 1696, 1703. So Bagster "Honora patrem tuum & matrem tuam, ut sis longaevus super terram, quam Dñs deus tuus dabit tibi" (Queen Eliz.). Aless had simply "Honora patrem, & matrem."

"HONORA PATREM ET MATREM ; UT SIS LONGAEVUS SUPER TERRAM, QUAM DATURUS EST TIBI DOMINUS DEUS TUUS" (Nowell).

Vautrollier, as usual, agrees with Nowell in the Catechism, and with Queen Eliz. in the Communion Service, only he has "Deus" for "deus," and "ut prolongentur dies tui" for "ut sis longaevus," and "dat" for "dabit."

patrem: "we must understand all those to whom any authority is given, as magistrates, ministers of the church, schoolmasters ; finally, all they that have any ornament, either of reverent age, or of wit, wisdom, or learning, worship or wealthy estate, or otherwise be our superiors, are contained under the name of fathers ;" etc. (Nowell, Norton's Translation).

tuam. Eds. 1685, 1687 have no comma after "tuam ;" but Eds. 1696, 1703 have.

longaevus: μακροχρόνιος (LXX., Nowell, Petley, and Duport).

V. HONORA patrem tuum & matrem tuam, ut sis longaevus super terram, quam Dominus Deus tuus dabit tibi.

VI. NON occides.

VII. NON moechaberis.

V. HONOUR thy father & thy mother, that thou be long-lived above (the) earth, which thy Lord God will give thee.

VI. THOU shalt not kill.

VII. THOU shalt not commit adultery.

---

s u p e r : or, "upon," but not the same as "in terra." Harwood has "in terrâ, quam tibi Dominus Deus tuus donat."

ἐπὶ τῆς γῆς [ἐπὶ τῆς γῆς τῆς ἀγαθῆς, LXX.], Nowell, Petley, and Duport, which is the expression used in Ephes. vi. 3, "and thou mayest live long on the earth."

d a b i t : "donat," Harwood following Parsell.

VI. N O N o c c i d e s. "Non occides" (Queen Eliz.). So, too, Nowell, and also Vautrollier.

o c c i d e s : "murther" (*Janua*). Harwood has "Ne hominem occidito."

VII. NON m o e c h a b e r i s. "Non committes adulterium" (Queen Eliz.), whereas Aless had "Non moechaberis."

"NON ADULTERABERIS" (Nowell). Vautrollier, as usual, agrees with Queen Eliz. in the Communion Service, and with Nowell in the Catechism.

VIII. N O N f u r t u m : "Non furtum facies" (Queen Eliz.). Aless, however, had "Non fureris."

"NON FURABERIS" (Nowell).

Vautrollier follows Queen Eliz. in Communion Service, and Nowell in Catechism.

"Ne furator" (Harwood).

f u r t u m . See note on "furto" below.

IX. N O N l o q u ê r i s. "Non loquêris," etc. as Durel, Queen Eliz.; whereas Aless had "Non dices falsum testimonium."

"NON ERIS ADVERSUS PROXIMUM TUUM TESTIS MENDAX" (Nowell).

In the Communion Service, Vautrollier follows Queen Eliz.; in the Catechism he has "Non dices falsum testimonium contra proximum tuum."

l o q u ê r i s. Eds. 1685, 1687, loqueris. Eds. 1696, 1703 have the accent.

p r o x i m u m : neighbour, but not quite like "vicinum" ("nigh-dweller," *Janua*). The term embraces, says Nowell, "eos etiam, qui nobis sunt incogniti, adeoque inimicos etiam nostros."

VIII. NON furtum facies.	VIII. THOU shalt not commit theft.
IX. NON loquêris contra proximum tuum falsum testimonium.	IX. THOU shalt not speak against thy neighbour false witness.
X. NON concupisces domum proximi tui, nec desiderabis uxorem ejus, non servum, non ancillam, non bovem, non asinum, nec omnia quae illius sunt.	X. THOU shalt not long for thy neighbour's house, nor shalt thou yearn for his wife, not servant, not maidservant, not ox, not ass, nor all (things) which are his.

X. NON concupisces: "Non concupisces domum proximi tui, nec desiderabis vxorem eius, non seruum, non ancillam, non bouem, non asinum, nihil deniq'; quod sit alterius" (Queen Eliz.).

This is the same as Durel's with the exception of the last clause. Aless's version was considerably different: " Non concupisces uxorem proximi tui, non seruum, neque ancillam, neque bouem, neque asinum, neque quicquam quod est ipsius."

"NON CONCUPISCES CUJUSQUAM DOMUM, NON UXOREM, NON SERVUM, NON ANCILLAM, NON BOVEM, NON ASINUM, NEC QUICQUAM OMNINO ALIUD, QUOD ALTERIUS SIT" (Nowell).

In the Communion Service, Vautrollier agrees with Queen Eliz., except that "concupisces" is repeated in place of "desiderabis," and he has "nec quicquam eorum quae illius sunt." In the Catechism he has "Non concupisces domum proximi tui, non vxorem, non seruum, non ancillam, non bouem, non asinum, nec quicquam omninò aliud quod alterius sit." This partly follows Queen Eliz., partly Nowell.

Nowell's Greek (Small Catechism) is here noteworthy: Οὐκ ἐπιθυμήσεις τὴν οἰκίαν τοῦ πλησίον σου, οὐκ ἐπιθυμήσεις τὴν γυναῖκα τοῦ πλησίον σου. οὐδὲ τὸν παῖδα αὐτοῦ, οὐδὲ τὴν παιδίσκην αὐτοῦ, οὔτε τοῦ βοὸς αὐτοῦ, οὔτε τοῦ ὑποζυγίου αὐτοῦ, οὔτε παντὸς κτήνους αὐτοῦ, οὔτε κ.τ.λ.

Petley and Duport omit the first clause, and after the second have, οὐδὲ τὸν ἀγρὸν αὐτοῦ. Duport also has οὐδὲ for οὔτε throughout.

The LXX., from which these are taken, has Οὐκ ἐπιθυμήσεις τὴν γυναῖκα τοῦ πλησίον σου. Οὐκ ἐπιθυμήσεις τὴν οἰκίαν τοῦ πλησίον σου, οὔτε τὸν ἀγρὸν αὐτοῦ, οὔτε τὸν παῖδα αὐτοῦ, οὔτε κ.τ.λ.

tui. Bagster has semicolons after "tui" and "ejus."

desiderabis. It is difficult to see why the Vulgate has "concupisces" in one place, and "desiderabis" in another. It is neither sanctioned by the Hebrew nor by the Septuagint.

"desiderare," in *Janua*, is "to miss and desire" "has miss, finds lack."

Quæstio.	*Question.*
Quid potissimùm ex his mandatis discis?	What do you especially learn out of these commands?

non servum: not "nec," the verb (probably " concupisces ") being understood. So Eds. 1685, 1687, 1696, 1703.

non bovem, non asinum. Here, again, Nowell has οὔτε τοῦ βοὸς αὐτοῦ, οὔτε τοῦ ὑποζυγίου αὐτοῦ, οὔτε παντὸς κτήνους αὐτοῦ, κ.τ.λ. See notes on "jumentum" and "X. Non," etc., above.

nec omnia, etc. See note on "neque omnem," in Commandment II. There is considerable divergency in the readings of this clause. Durel (Eds. 1670, 1685, 1687, 1696, 1703) and the Vulgate have "nec omnia quae illius sunt." Aless has "neque quicquam quod est ipsius." Queen Eliz. has "nihil deniq'; quod sit alterius." Nowell has "nec quicquam omnino aliud, quod alterius sit," and he is followed by Vautrollier. Harwood follows Queen Eliz., as also did Parsell (1713, 1716) and G. Bowyer (1733, 1744).

Nowell's Small Catechism has the longer form of Response after this Tenth Commandment.

οὔτε ὅσα τοῦ πλησίον σου ἐστί (Nowell, Petley); and with υἱέι, Duport. The LXX. version has τῷ, not τοῦ, otherwise it is the same.

Quid potissimùm. "Quid potissimum ex his praeceptis discis?' (Queen Eliz.)

"Quid ex istis mandatis tibi praecipuè discendum arbitraris?" (Vautrollier.)

"*Quid ex istis mandatis praecipue discis?*" (Nowell's Small Catechism.)

Duo; etc. "Duo: Primum, quid Deo: Alterum quid proximo debeam" (Queen Eliz.).

"Equidem duo ex illis disco. Officium scilicet, primum in Deum, deinde etiam & in proximum" (Vautrollier).

"Duo: Pietatem primum erga Deum, deinde meum erga homines officium addisco" (Nowell's Small Catechism). In Ed. 1584 "*Duo? Pietatem,*" etc.

Duport, Δύω μανθάνω· κ.τ.λ.

nempe: "to wit" (*Janua*).

& meum etiam officium. Bagster has "simulque officium meum." Harwood has "erga alterum" for Durel's "erga proximum."

Quodnam: "Quid Deo debes?" (Queen Eliz.). "Quod est in deum officium tuum?" (Vautrollier.) "*Pietas adversus Deum quae est?*" (Nowell's Small Catechism.) Τί σοι ἔιον ἐστι πρὸς κ.τ.λ. (Duport); but in the answer, Ἐμὸν ἔργον ἐστί κ.τ.λ.

Responsio.	*Answer.*
Duo ; nempe officium meum erga Deum, & meum etiam officium erga proximum.	Two (things) ; to wit, my duty towards God, & my duty also towards a neighbour.
Quæstio.	*Question.*
Quodnam est officium tuum erga Deum?	What duty pray is yours towards God?

"Quodnam" is from "quinam," not "quisnam," and so goes with "officium ;" not "what is?" etc. Cf. QUOD in the first question.

O f f i c i u m , e t c.   "Fidem, timorem, amorem ex toto corde, tota mente, anima, & omnibus uiribus : cultum, gratiarum actionem, ut omnem fiduciam meam in eum collocem, eum inuocem, glorificem, nomen & uerbnm (*sic*) suum sanctum honore afficiam, ac seruiam ei omnibus diebus uitae meae" (Queen Eliz.).

"Vt in illum credam, illum timeam, diligam ex toto corde, ex tota mente, ex totis viribus, vt illum colam, illi gratias agam, in illum solum fiduciam collocem, illum inuocem, illius nomen & sacrosanctum verbum adorem, illi'que semper seruiam omnibus diebus vitae meae" (Vautrollier).

"Pietas erga Deum est, in eum credere, eum timere, eum toto pectore, mente tota, tota anima, viribus totis amare : illum venerari : illi omnia accepta referre : in illo fiduciam omnem collocare : ipsius implorare opem : ipsius sanctissimo nomini, et verbo summam venerationem praestare : & illi per omnem vitam studiosè fideliterque inseruire" (Nowell's Small Catechism).

i p s u m : probably emphatic ; not as "eum," or "illum :" though in the Vulgate, at all events, there is a great laxity in the use of pronouns.

t i m e a m & d i l i g a m : "timeam, ipsumque diligam" (Bagster).

c o r d e , e t c.   Durel here has "cor," "mens," "anima," and "vires," corresponding to the English Version, heart, mind, soul, and strength. Durel's list is the same as that of Queen Eliz. ; but Vautrollier omits "anima." Nowell, referring to Mark xii. 30, has "ex toto corde tuo, ex tota anima tua, ex tota mente tua, et ex totis viribis tuis," the English Bible having in that passage, heart, soul, mind, and strength. This agrees with Queen Eliz. and Durel. In continuing the subject, however, Nowell asks, "Totum cor, anima tota, totaeque vires quid significant?" (Large Catechism). Here, then, he omits "mens," as Vautrollier after him omits "anima." It is possible that they considered the two words synonymous, and it is interesting to remark that in the original passage, Deut. vi. 5, we have only heart, soul, and might : "ex toto corde tuo, & ex tota anima tua, & ex tota fortitudine tua" (Vulgate).

Responsio.

Officium meum erga Deum est, ut in ipsum credam, ipsum timeam & diligam ex toto corde, ex tota mente, ex tota anima, & ex totis viribus; ut ipsum colam, ipsi gratias agam, in ipso solo confidam; ipsum invocem; ipsius sanctum nomen ejusque verbum honorem; & ipsi verè serviam omnibus diebus vitae meae.

Quæstio.

Quodnam est officium tuum erga proximum?

Answer.

My duty towards God is, that I believe on himself, fear & love himself out of a whole heart, out of a whole mind, out of a whole spirit, & out of whole strength; that I reverence himself, give thanks to himself, trust in himself alone; invoke himself; honour his own holy name and his word; & truly serve himself on all days of my life.

Question.

What duty pray is yours towards a neighbour?

There is, however, a real difference in all the terms. "Cor" is the heart, as the seat of passions or affections. "Mens" is the pure intellect, the wholly intellectual part of the soul: it is connected with "memini," and is literally the faculty of memory, recollection, or association of ideas. "Anima" is literally "air" (cf. Greek, ἄνεμος, "wind"); so it is the breath of life: see Gen. ii. 7, where it is said God "breathed into his nostrils the breath of life; and man became a living soul"; "inspiravit in faciem eius spiraculum vitae, & factus est homo in animam viventem" (Vulgate). It should be carefully distinguished from "mens," and also from the masculine form "animus:" "anima" is the principle of animal life, "animus," the principle of spiritual life, the rational spirit; "animus" is also often used as almost equivalent to "cor," and so we find it in the fourth answer of Durel's Catechism, "ex animo" corresponding to the ἐκ καρδίας of Whitaker, Petley, and Duport, and "heartily" in the English Version. In the explanation of the Lord's Prayer, Durel has "ab hoste animorum" in the first edition; the later editions however, have "animarum."

The Greek Testament (Mark xii. 30) has ἐξ ὅλης τῆς καρδίας σου, καὶ ἐξ ὅλης τῆς ψυχῆς σου, καὶ ἐξ ὅλης τῆς διανοίας σου, καὶ ἐξ ὅλης τῆς ἰσχύος σου.

Petley and Duport have the words καρδία, διάνοια, ψυχή, and ἰσχύς, which correspond closely to Durel's "cor," "mens," "anima," and "vires." Nowell and Whitaker have the same words, but in a different order, ψυχή coming second, and διάνοια third, as in the Greek Testament.

Harwood has "toto corde, totâ mente, toto animo, summâque ope."

confidam. Eds. 1685, 1687, 1696, 1703 have a comma after this word.

Responsio.	Answer.
Officium meum erga proximum est, ut eum diligam sicut meipsum, & id omnibus hominibus faciam, quod ab iis vellem mihi fieri. Et ut Patrem meum & Matrem meam diligam & honorem, iisque succurram. Ut regem honorem, ipsique atque iis omnibus qui sub ipso aliquâ pollent	My duty towards a neighbour is, that I love him just as myself, & do that for all men, which I would wish to be done by them for me. And that I love & honour my Father & my Mother, and help them. That I honour the king, and submit to himself and all those who have power

invocem. "*The Preacher out of the pulpit calleth upon* [invocat] *the holy Ghost : he expoundeth the originall text of the Bible,*" etc. (*Janua*).

nomen ejusque verbum. So Eds. 1685, 1687, 1696, 1703. Bagster has commas after "nomen" and "verbum." He retains the small initials.

It is of some importance here whether "nomen" and "verbum" should have small or capital initials. Aless, Queen Eliz., Whitaker, Vautrollier, Nowell, and Durel all have a small initial. Duport has Ὄνομα and λόγον, but his predecessors, Whitaker, Nowell, and Petley, have small initials in their Greek versions. Messrs. Bright and Medé, however, have "Nomen et Verbum."

omnibus diebus. The Puritans complained in 1661 that there was no reference made in this answer to the Fourth Commandment. This the bishops denied, saying that the last words of the answer "do orderly relate to the last commandment of the first table, which is the fourth."

Quœstio, a misprint for *Quæstio*. Eds. 1685, 1687, 1696, 1703 have "*Quaestio.*"

Quodnam, etc. "Quid uero debes proximo?" (Queen Eliz.) "Quod tuum est in proximum officium?" (Vautrollier.) "*Quod est tuum erga proximum officium?*" (Nowell's Small Catechism.)

Officium meum, etc. "Vt amem eum perinde ac me ipsum : & ut faciam omnibus hominibus, prout uelim mihi fieri ab illis : ut honore afficiam Patrem & Matrem, eis succurram & subueniam, ut obediam Regi & ipsius Ministris, ut me subiiciam meo Magistratui, Doctoribus, Pastori spirituali, & Magistro, vt me modestè geram, & reuerenter erga maiores & meliores, ut nullum laedam uerbo aut facto, vt sim fidelis & iustus in omnibus negotijs, ut nulli inuideam, nullum odiam, ut manus contineam à furto, linguam à maledicentia & obtrectatione, ut me ipsum castum & sobrium seruem. Ne concupiscam aliorum bona, sed discam meo labore mihi uictum parare, & ut Deo obediam in quacunque uocatione, ad quam me dignabitur uocare" (Queen Eliz.).

authoritate obsequar; omnibus meis superioribus, Doctoribus spiritualibus, Pastoribus ac praeceptoribus meipsum subjiciam; submissè ac reverenter me	with some authority under himself; put myself under all my betters, spiritual Teachers, Shepherds and masters; bear myself humbly and

"Vt illum aequè atque meipsum diligam : ita me erga alios geram, quemadmodum & illos erga me se gerere cupio. Parentes amore, veneratione, & subsidio complectar. Regalem maiestatem eiúsque ministros honore & obedientia prosequar : erga omnes gubernatores, institutores, pastores spirituales, & magistros morigerum me & obedientem praebeam. Submissè me & reuerenter geram erga maiores. Neminem verbo aut facto laedam. In omnibus me iustum, fidelem & integrum ostendam. Odium intus in animo occultum non foueam. Manus à furto, linguam à mendacio, calumnia & obtrectatione contineam. Corpore me temperantem, sobrium, castum praebeam. Aliena denique vt bona non concupiscam, sed proprio labore & industria studeam ad victum necessaria comparare, ei'que vitae rationi satisfacere, ad quam me Diuina prouidentia vocarit " (Vautrollier).

"Illum eadem, qua meipsum, benevolentia & charitate complecti. Omnibus hominibus facere, quod mihi ab illis fieri velim. Parentes charos, & in honore habere, eos fovere, & tueri : principi & magistratibus honorem tribuere & illorum me imperio & potestati subjicere : authoritate praeditis omnibus, doctoribus, Ecclesiae ministris, & praeceptoribus dicto audientem esse : superiores omnes observare & revereri. Neminem dicto factóve laedere, veritatem retinere, servare aequitatem in rebus omnibus : mentem ab omni malitia odióque vacuam atq'; integram servare : manus a fraude, furto, latrocinijs : linguam ab omni maledicentia, mendatio, & ab infamia cuiquam inferenda abstinere. Corpus temperatè sobriè, & castè habere : aliena non concupiscere, neque appetere. Res ad vivendum necessarias justè mihi, & cum fide acquirere : & in eo vitae statu, in quo me Deus collocabit, officium non deserere " (Nowell's Small Catechism).

Nowell then gives an expansion (*fusiùs paulo dicere*) of the duties towards one's neighbour, under these heads : the duty of subjects to prince, of children to parents, of spiritual children to spiritual parents or pastors, of servants, of parents to children, of masters and heads of houses, of husbands to wives, and of wives.

meipsum. Bagster here has a colon in place of Durel's comma. He also has a colon for Durel's full stop after "fieri," "succurram," "antecellunt," "lædam," "foveam," "calumnia," & "custodiam :" semicolon for comma after "honorem" and "aveam :" colon for semicolon after "subjiciam :" and a comma is inserted after "ipsique," "auctoritate," and "praeceptoribus."

geram erga omnes qui re ullâ me antecellunt. Neminem verbo factóve laedam. Fidelem ac justum me in omnibus praestem : neque maliciam neque odium in animo meo foveam. Manus meas à furto & latrocinio cohibeam ; & linguam à maledicentia,

reverently towards all who in any thing surpass me. That I hurt no one by word or deed. That I show myself faithful and just in all (things): nor cherish badness nor hatred in my heart. That I keep in my hands from theft & open robbery; & (my)

Patrem. Bagster has small initials in "Patrem," "Matrem," "Doctoribus," and "Pastoribus."

regem. "Regi," in Queen Eliz., should of course be "Reginae." Mr. Clay ("Lit. Serv. Queen Eliz.," Parker Society) regards this as an error of Haddon, who "ought to have substituted '*Reginae*' for Aless's '*Regi;*'" but Queen Eliz. English Prayer Books of 1559 have "King." This shows a want of care in the preparation of both the Latin and English Prayer Books of Queen Eliz. Whitaker has "Reginae," and Vautrollier "Regalem maiestatem," which Harwood follows.

iis omnibus qui, etc. τοῖς αὐτοῦ διακόνοις (Petley). πᾶσι τοῖς ὑπ' αὐτοῦ ἐν ἐξουσίᾳ τεταγμένοις (Duport). "et quibus officium suum delegavit" (Harwood). Whitaker's is the same as Petley's, but αὐτῆς. Nowell, τοῖς ἄρχουσι. Before 1662 the English Version was simply "and his ministers."

aliquâ : almost "special," or "specific;" "aliquis" is more definite than "quispiam," less definite than "quidam" (See Dr. Donaldson, Introd. to Longer Ex. in Lat. Prose, p. xxiv.).

authoritate. Bagster, "auctoritate."

obsequar : or, "be loyal to." *Janua*, "be ruled by." Durel here differs from the English Version, "To honour and obey the King, and all that are put in authority under him;" where "honour and obey" are both enjoined with reference to the King's officers: as the wide term "all that are put," etc., includes the lowest officials, Durel's expression may be thought to be the more correct, as enjoining obedience only, and not honour, to be shown to subordinate officials.

Queen Eliz. has simply "ut obediam Regi & ipsius Ministris," so far agreeing with Durel. Nowell has only "honour" for both ("honorem tribuere" and τιμὴν ἀποδοῦναι). Vautrollier has "Regalem maiestatem ciúsque ministros honore & obedientia prosequar." Harwood, "Regiam Majestatem, et quibus," etc., "honore et obedientiâ prosequar." The Greek versions of Petley and Duport also enjoin both honour and obedience with regard to subordinate officers.

superioribus : "superioribus obediens" is obeying one's "betters"

mendacio, ac calumnia. Ut corpus meum temperanter, sobrie, atque castè custodiam. Bona aliena neque concupiscam neque aveam, sed discam artem ad vitam sustentandam idoneam, & in ea gnaviter laborem. Et meo officio fungar in eo vitae statu, ad quem Deo visum fuerit me vocare.

tongue from ill-speaking, lying, and slander. That I keep my body temperately, soberly, and chastely. That I neither long for nor crave for another's goods, but learn a craft fit to maintain life, & therein labour actively. And that I discharge my duty in that estate of life, to which it shall have seemed good to God to call me.

(*Janua*). "meo Magistratui" is the equivalent in Queen Eliz. Whitaker, who has "Magistratui" in the Latin, has τῷ ἐμοῦ ἄρχοντι in the Greek.

spiritualibus: "spirituales cantelenas," "spirituall songs" (*Janua*). Aless has not "spirituali," as Queen Eliz. has.

Pastoribus. In the "Forma & Modus Faciendi," &c., in Durel's Prayer Book we have "Pastor" for the English Version "Shepherd." Pastoribus is "*Shepheards*" only, in *Janua;* praeceptoribus, "*masters*." Bishop Stillingfleet (1664) writes: "'occidere' is not 'pascere' in any sense; 'Lanii id est, non Pastoris,' that's the Butcher's not the Shepheard's part." Duport, ποιμίσι, and ἐισπόταις. Whitaker and Petley have the singular. So have Aless and Queen Eliz. Nowell (Small Catechism) has "Ecclesiae ministris," and τοῖς διακόνοις τῆς ἐκκλησίας.

reverenter: "*Be . . . submissively obedient to thy betters, reverencing them awfully* (reverenter cole);" "*Rise up to thy elders, put off thy hat, make a leg* (flecte genu)," *Janua*.

The Rev. E. Daniel says that "lowly" relates to the estimate we set upon ourselves; but in Durel's version at all events ("submissè ac reverenter me geram") "submissè" seems to refer to the way in which we regard the claims of our superiors.

ullà: "quapiam" (Bagster).

antecellunt. So translated in *Janua*. So also are "laedam" and "foveam."

maliciam. Eds. 1685, 1687, 1696, 1703, "malitiam."

"malitia" is properly "badness;" here it probably is equivalent to "spite." Cf. *Janua*: "calumniatores maligni [malitiosi]," "*spitefull slanderers* (false accusers)." Nowell (Vocab. to Large Catechism) says, "*Malitia,* κακία, quam vitiositatem Cicero mavult appellare, quam

Catechistes.	Instructor.
Mi puer, scias hoc, te ex te-ipso ista praestare non posse, neque in Dei mandatis ambulare & ipsi servire absque gratia illius speciali, quam	My child, know this, that you of yourself are not able to perform those (things), nor to walk in God's commands & serve himself without his

Malitiam. Malitiam enim certi cujusquam vitii, vitiositatem omnium nomen esse."

Bagster has "malevolentiam."

Harwood's version here is remarkable, "nemini in animo meo male velim."

furto: "privie theft," or "filching" (*Janua*).

latrocinio: "open robbery," *Janua*: where also "cohibere" is "keep in." For Durel's "latrocinio" Bagster has "compilatione." Nowell (Small Catechism) has "a fraude, furto, latrocinijs," and φρινακισμοῦ, καὶ κλοπῆς, καὶ λῃστείας. Queen Eliz. has simply "manus ... à furto," and Vautrollier, "manus à furto," taking no account of the distinction in the English Version, "picking and stealing." Messrs. Bright and Medd also have simply "manus a furto." Shakespeare, who often drew from the Bible, seems to have drawn from the Catechism here in his words, put in the mouth of Hamlet, "By these pickers and stealers."

maledicentia. "*Maledicere*" is "execrari, devovere, diris devovere, diras obnuntiare" in Nowell (Large Catechism). The Rev. E. Daniel makes "evil-speaking" a generic term including lying and slandering, but Durel's words do not admit of this.

discam. Note the difference from the English Version, "to learn and labour truly to get my own living." Bagster has "discam et enitar mea ipsius opera vitam sustentare." "discam meo labore mihi uictum parare" (Queen Eliz.). "sed proprio labore & industria studeam ad victum necessaria comparare" (Vautrollier). μαθεῖν ἐκ τοῦ ἰδίου πόνου τὰ ἐπιτήδεια προσπορίζειν (Petley). So Whitaker, but μανθάνειν. μανθάνειν καὶ ἐργάζεσθαι ἐπὶ τῷ ἀδόλως τὸν βίον πορίζεσθαι (Duport). "proprio labore studeam victum exercere" (Harwood).

artem: "nam artem aliquam nemo non factitat," "artem" being "trade, craft or profession" (*Janua*). "Sustentare" is to "maintain" in ditto.

gnaviter: not "naviter;" so, too, in *Janua*, "gnavus" for "navus."

Et meo. This is a separate sentence, and not dependent upon the preceding one. The construction in the English Version appears at first sight to be "to learn and labour ... to do my duty;" but Durel is probably right in conceiving "to do" as parallel to, and not dependent

omni tempore diligenter invocare discas oportet. Audiam itaque num orationem Dominicam possis recitare.

peculiar favour, which (favour) at all times you ought to learn to invoke carefully. Let me hear accordingly whether you can rehearse the Lord's prayer.

---

upon, "to learn and labour." This is supported by the fact that before 1604 the sentence ran, "But learn," etc.; at that date the word "to" was added, perhaps to show the parallelism with "to do." Queen Eliz., taking the same view as Durel, has not the infinitive, but "& ut Deo obediam in quacunque uocatione, ad quam me dignabitur uocare." Vautrollier takes the opposite view, and reads "ei'que vitae rationi satisfacere, ad quam me Diuina prouidentia vocarit." Harwood follows this verbatim with differences of spelling. In the Greek versions Whitaker has τὸ πείθεσθαι τῷ θεῷ, which is certainly a separate sentence: it is difficult to say whether the infinitive ποιεῖσθαι in Petley does or does not depend upon "to learn." Duport's πράττειν is also independent of μανθάνειν, as his subordinate verb is put in a prepositional phrase ἐπὶ τῷ ... πορίζεσθαι. Nowell (Small Catechism), in both Latin and Greek, has a colon dividing "to do," etc., from the former clause, thus showing that he, like Durel, Queen Eliz., Whitaker, and Duport, regarded it as independent. Messrs. Bright and Medd, however, take the opposite view, and have "meo officio fungi," etc., depending upon "discam et bona fide studeam."

Fungar: "perform," or "discharge:" and "status," "estate," or "state," *i.e.*, position, rank, in *Janua*.

Mi puer. So Eds. 1685, 1687, 1696. Ed. 1703 has the misprint "peur."

Bagster has a semicolon after "posse," and commas after "ambulare" and "servire."

"Cum scire debeas, te ista ex tuis uiribus, & sine speciali Dei gratia praestare non posse, ac propterea continuò orandum esse pro gratia, dic mihi bone puer, Orationem Dominicam" (Queen Eliz.).

"Hoc velim scias, optime fili, tuis te viribus ista praestare non posse, neque in Dei mandatis versari, & illi prout decet, seruire, nisi singulari eius gratia adiutum: quam etiam discere oportet te ardentissimis precibus semper ab illo contendere. Audiam igitur an memoriter teneas orationem Dominicam?" (Vautrollier.)

"*Iam verò mi fili, quum non sit situm in hominis cujusquam potestate, ut istis similibúsque Dei Praeceptis per se pareat, illíque ex sanctissimo legum suarum praescripto inserviat, nisi ipsi (sic, but in 1584 ipse) virtutem nobis divinitùs largiatur, quae noctes diésque assiduis est efflagitanda*

THE CATECHISM.

Responsio.	*Answer.*
PATER noster, qui es in coelis: Sanctificetur Nomen tuum. Ad-	OUR Father, who art in (the) heavens: Hallowed be thy

precibus, an precationem illam, quae dominica dicitur, teneas, intelligere, & eam à te proinde mihi recitari velim" (Nowell's Small Catechism).
For "*ipsi*" Nowell has in the Greek ἐκεῖνος (no accent).
 puer. In the First Prayer Book of Edward VI. the English Version is "My good son," etc.
 speciali: "speciale symptoma," "an accident properly befalling," *Janua*: so "peculiar." τῆς ἰδίας τοῦ Θεοῦ χάριτος, Whitaker and Petley. τῆς ἐξαιρέτου χάριτος τοῦ Θεοῦ, Duport.
Note that this special grace is to be obtained, not by confession to or absolution by a priest, but by the due use of the Lord's Prayer. "Our Father" is to be directly approached, without a sacerdotal mediator.
 diligenter: "ardentissimis precibus," Vautrollier. So too Duport, δι' ἐπιμελοῦς προσευχῆς. Petley and Whitaker have ἀδιαλείπτως. In the Latin, Nowell's Small Catechism has "*assiduis est efflagitanda precibus,*" and in the Greek, ἀδιαλείπτως δι' εὐχῶν, κ.τ.λ. The English Version is, "by diligent prayer."
 Audiam itaque: or, "And so I will hear." But the English Version, and Queen Eliz., "dic mihi," rather support the other rendering: so Whitaker, λέγε μοι. ἡδέως ἀκούσαιμι ἄν, Duport and Petley: ἀκοῦσαι βούλομαι, Nowell.
Bagster has "Fac ergo audiam," etc.
 num: perhaps implies a doubt whether the child can say the Lord's Prayer. Cf. the Greek of Nowell, Petley, and Duport.
 orationem Dominicam. So Queen Elizabeth and Vautrollier. "Dominicus Dies," "the Lord's day," *Janua:* "oratione," "prayer," ibid.
Εὐχὴν τὴν Κυριακήν, Duport. See Rev. i. 10, ἐν τῇ Κυριακῇ ἡμέρᾳ, contrasted with Acts ii. 20 [τὴν] ἡμέραν Κυρίου, and compared with 1 Cor. xi. 20, Κυριακὸν δεῖπνον.

PATER noster: In Eds. 1685, 1687, 1696 and 1703, we have considerable changes in pointing, etc. (See below.)
Eds. 1685, 1687, 1696, 1703 have "P<small>A</small>ter."
Bagster here simply gives "Pater noster, qui es in coelis, &c."
In the Vulgate we find two versions of the Lord's Prayer. "Pater noster qui es in coelis, sanctificetur nomen tuum. Adueniat regnum tuum. Fiat voluntas tua sicut in coelo & in terra. Panem nostrum supersubstantialem da nobis hodie. Et dimitte nobis debita nostra, sicut

veniat regnum tuum. Fiat voluntas tua, Sicut in cœlo & in terra. Panem nostrum quotidianum da nobis hodié. Et dimitte nobis debita nostra, Sicut	Name. Arrive may thy kingdom. Done be thy will, Like as in heaven also on earth. Our daily bread give us to-day. And dismiss for us our

& nos dimittimus debitoribus nostris. Et ne nos inducas in tentationem, sed libera nos à malo. Amen." (Ed. Paris, 1573.) This is in Matt. vi. The other version is in Luke xi. : "Pater, sanctificetur nomen tuum, adueniat regnum tuum, fiat voluntas tua, panem nostrum quotidianum da nobis hodie, & dimitte nobis peccata nostra, siquidem & nos dimittimus omni debenti nobis : & ne nos inducas in tentationem." (The Revised Version also concludes the Lord's Prayer at "temptation" in Luke xi. 4.)

The first of these is precisely the same as that of the Romish Missal, with differences of pointing, etc., and one remarkable divergence, "quotidianum" being read for the Vulgate's "supersubstantialem."

Aless gives the Lord's Prayer only as far as "nomen tuum." Queen Eliz. says simply, "Pater noster qui es in coelis. &c. ;" but in Morning Prayer her version is verbatim the same as that of the Missal, with differences of pointing, etc. So is that of Whitaker in Morning Prayer, of Vautrollier, and that of Durel.

Nowell's version (Large Catechism) is somewhat different. He has, "PATER NOSTER QUI ES IN CŒLIS, SANCTIFICETUR NOMEN TUUM. VENIAT REGNUM TUUM, FIAT VOLUNTAS TUA, SICUT IN CŒLO, SIC ETIAM IN TERRA. PANEM NOSTRUM QUOTIDIANUM DA NOBIS HODIE. ET REMITTE NOBIS DEBITA NOSTRA, SICUT ET NOS REMITTIMUS DEBITORIBUS NOSTRIS. ET NE NOS INDUCAS IN TENTATIONEM, SED LIBERA NOS A MALO. QUIA TUUM EST REGNUM, ET POTENTIA, ET GLORIA IN SECULA. AMEN."

His version in the Small Catechism is the same, but in small type.

Harwood gives a different version: "Pater noster, qui es in coelis, sanctè colatur nomen tuum. Veniat regnum tuum. Fiat voluntas tua, ut in coelo, sic et in terrâ. Victum nostrum alimentarium da nobis hodie : Et remitte nobis debita nostra, ut et nos remittimus debitoribus nostris : Neve nos in tentationem inducito, sed à malo tuere. *Amen.*" This is the version given by Parsell.

Whitaker, Nowell, Petley, and Duport give the text of Matt. vi. verbatim in the Lord's Prayer ; but Duport has not the doxology. Nor has Durel, nor the English Version ; and it is omitted also in Matt. vi. in the Revised New Testament.

PATER: Augustine says, "oratio fraterna est."

coelis : below we have "Sicut in coelo." This change from plural to

& nos dimittimus debitoribus nostris.	debts, Like as also we dismiss (debts)
Et ne nos inducas in tentationem : Sed	for our debtors. And do not lead us
libera nos à malo. *Amen.*	into trial: But free us from evil.
	Amen.

singular is in accordance with the New Testament (Matt. vi.), where we have ὁ ἐν τοῖς οὐρανοῖς, but ὡς ἐν οὐρανῷ.

Eds. 1685, 1687, 1696 have a comma, and 1703 a full stop here.

The Revised Version omits "our" and "which art in heaven" in Luke xi. 2.

Sanctificetur. Cf. the notes on "Sanctorum Communionem," on "sanctificavit" in the next answer after the Creed, and on "sanctificavit" in Commandment IV.

Eds. 1696, 1703 have a capital, 1685, 1687 a small "s" in this word.

Nomen. Eds. 1685, 1687, 1696, 1703 have "nomen."

Adveniat: Nowell, "VENIAT;" but afterwards he says, "Secundo loco petimus, ut ADVENIAT REGNUM DEI." Cf. our expression "the Second Advent."

Fiat. The Revised New Testament omits "Thy will—earth" in Luke xi. 2.

Sicut in coelo. Eds. 1685, 1687, 1696, 1703 have "sicut." There is much difference in pointing here. The Vulgate has no stop from "Fiat" to "terra." The Missal usually has a comma after "coelo ;" in a Salisbury book, however, which we have consulted ("Sacra Institutio Baptizandi," etc., MDCIIII.), there is no comma. Queen Eliz. has commas both before "sicut" and after "coelo." So has Nowell. Vautrollier has a comma after "coelo." Durel has a comma before "Sicut," but not after "coelo," in the Catechism, in Eds. 1670, 1696, and 1703 ; but in 1685 and 1687 a comma also after "coelo," and in its first occurrence in the book he has a comma after "coelo."

It has been suggested by Mr. Boys that ὡς—γῆς refer to all the first three clauses of the Lord's Prayer, and not merely to the third.

quotidianum: the most probable meaning of the Greek τὸν ἐπιούσιον, which only occurs in Matt. vi. 11 and Luke xi. 3. Philologically the word is probably connected with ἡ ἐπιοῦσα, the following day. The Vulgate here has "supersubstantialem" in Matt. vi., " quotidianum " in Luke xi.

"quotidianum," daily, in *Janua*. Harwood has "alimentarium."

hodié. This follows Matt vi. ; Luke has τὸ καθ' ἡμέραν, day by day.

dimitte: Nowell "remitte." "Dimittere" is only used of dismissing a congregation in *Janua*; but "debitorem dimittere" occurs in Ulpianus

Quæstio.	*Question.*
Quid petis à Deo in hac oratione?	What do you seek from God in this prayer?

the lawyer, and "tributa alieni dimittere," in Tacitus H. 3. 55. On the latter place Orelli notes upon "dimittere," "in perpetuum eos tributis liberabat edicto suo: *remittere* foret unam alteramve pensionem iis ita condonare, ut tamen tributarii manerent." So that "dimittere" is the higher word, as expressing a full and complete dismissal for ever.

debita. Revised Version has "debts" in Matt. vi., and "sins" in Luke xi. The Authorized Version has "trespasses" in the former. Cf. "sin is the transgression of the law" (1 John iii. 4), a word of similar derivation.

Sicut. Eds. 1685, 1687, 1696, 1703 have "sicut."

There should, perhaps, strictly be no "sic," as the Greek is simply ὡς. Nowell goes farther from the Greek by writing "sicut in coelo, sic" etc. Harwood has "ut in coelo, sic" etc.

The sense of the Greek is "like as," or rather, "as ;" not "just as ;" for we should evidently not pray to be forgiven only so far, and as much, as we forgive others.

dimittimus: this follows Luke, who has the present; Matthew, according to the best MSS., has the perfect tense; but the Rec. has the present. Revised Version has perfect.

inducas: subjunctive, not imperative. So the Greek μὴ εἰσενέγκῃς, which however the Revised New Testament translates "bring us not into," etc. Harwood also changes this to the imperative "inducito."

tentationem. After this word Eds. 1685, 1687 have a comma; 1696 and 1703 a full stop.

A good illustration of the use of "temptation" in English is in Fuller, "Church History" iv. i. 29: "Though may it (New Coll. Oxon) never have a temptation in that kinde (a siege) to trie the strength of the walls thereof."

"Tenta" is "try, assay," and "tentat caput," "makes the head ache," in *Janua*. "Tentare" is properly to handle (tenere) frequently, so to "test;" especially of feeling the pulse, "tentare venas" (Quint. 11. 3. 38, etc.); so "tentatio perseverantiae" "proof," or "test (Livy 4. 42);" exactly the Greek πειρασμός, and not like the English Version "temptation;" but the Greek is masculine, whereas "tentatio" is feminine, and expresses the process of "testing" or "trial." Nowell (Vocab. in Large Catechism) says, " *Tentatio*, pro sollicitatione ad vitia."

libera. The Greek is ῥῦσαι, middle voice. It may be remarked here

Responsio.	Answer.
Peto à Domino Deo meo, Patre nostro coelesti, omnis boni largitore,	I seek from my Lord God, our heavenly Father, the lavisher of every

how difficult it is to translate such a Scripture as the Lord's Prayer. In the Greek original we have ἁγιασθήτω, ἐλθέτω, and γενηθήτω, all aorists imperative, the first and last being first aor. pass., the intervening one, a second aor. act. or neuter. Then we have ὡς and ἄφες, two second aor. act. Then (μή) εἰσενέγκῃς (a negative with) a first aor. subj. act. Then again ῥῦσαι, a first aor. imper. middle. All these are rendered in the Latin by present imperatives; passive, neuter, and neuter passive in the case of the first three, and active in the case of the rest; excepting only εἰσενέγκῃς, which becomes a present subj. active.

à malo: may be either masculine or neuter, just like the Greek ἀπὸ τοῦ πονηροῦ. But it is more probably neuter. In this case it may be "evil" generally, and this use of the Greek adjective and article is too common to need illustration; one example may be given (Arist. N. Eth. ii. 6): τὸ γὰρ κακὸν τοῦ ἀπείρου, ὡς οἱ Πυθαγόρειοι εἴκαζον, τὸ δ᾽ ἀγαθὸν τοῦ πεπερασμένου; or on the other hand, "malum" and τὸ πονηρὸν might conceivably be "the evil," *i.e.*, "the evil of the day." Cf. "quotidianum," and in the last verse of this same chapter of Matthew, "Sufficient unto the day *is* the evil thereof." The view that the word is neuter, or at all events that it is so in the Catechism, is supported by the explanation of "à malo," which is "ab omni peccato, ac malitiâ, ab hoste animorum & ab aeterna morte:" and this view is also supported by Augustine, Ep. cxxx. c. 11. (21) vol. ii.: "Cum dicimus *libera nos a malo*, nos admonemus cogitare, nondum nos esse in eo bono, ubi nullum patiemur malum. Et hoc quidem ultimum quod in dominica oratione positum est, tam late patet, ut homo Christianus in qualibet tribulatione constitutus in hoc gemitus edat, in hoc lacrymas fundat, hinc exordiatur, in hoc immoretur, ad hoc terminet orationem."

The Revised Version of the New Testament has "the evil *one*," and "evil" in the margin; but with so many words available for "Devil" in Hellenistic Greek, it would be somewhat remarkable for τοῦ πονηροῦ to be employed in that sense. Had the word been in the nominative, ὁ πονηρὸς would have carried no ambiguity; but it is not customary in Greek to use an oblique case of an adjective or participle for the masculine, where it might be mistaken for the neuter. A full criticism of this question is beside our purpose, but we may quote the opinions of Canon Cook (editor of "The Speaker's Commentary"), that the neuter is here, upon critical and grammatical grounds alone, distinctly preferable to the

ut gratiam suam mihi, & omnibus largiatur, ut ipsum colamus, ipsi serviamus & obsequamur prout tenemur. Deum etiam oro ut nobis ea omnia impertiatur quae sunt menti & corpori good, that he may lavish upon me, and upon all his favour, that we may reverence himself, serve himself & submit (to him) in proportion as we are bound. I also pray God that he may

---

masculine; and of the Lord Bishop of Derry and Raphoe, who urges the preference for the Authorized Version on the higher grounds that the idea of a Christian closing the prayer of prayers by a request to be delivered from him, from whom both the individual and the whole Church *has been* delivered already, is against the analogy of the faith.

We may add that St. Paul appears to be alluding to the Lord's Prayer in 2 Tim. iv. 18 : Καὶ ῥύσιταί με ὁ Κύριος ἀπὸ παντὸς ἔργου πονηροῦ, καὶ σώσει εἰς τὴν βασιλείαν αὐτοῦ τὴν ἐπουράνιον· ᾧ ἡ δόξα εἰς τοὺς αἰῶνας τῶν αἰώνων. ἀμήν. If the first clause of this be parallel to and founded on καὶ ῥῦσαι ἡμᾶς ἀπὸ τοῦ πονηροῦ, it is a strong argument for "the evil," or "evil," and not "the evil one;" just as the concluding words seem to support the genuineness of the doxology, ὅτι σοῦ ἐστιν ἡ βασιλεία καὶ ἡ δύναμις καὶ ἡ δόξα εἰς τοὺς αἰῶνας· ἀμήν.

In the edition of 1818 Duport is made to omit τοῦ before πονηροῦ in the last clause. This however he does not do in his edition of 1665.

It is noteworthy that the Latin here keeps the exact order of the Greek, with the exception of "qui es" for ὁ, and "nos" before instead of after "inducas."

Quæstio. Eds. 1696, 1703 have "*Questio;*" Eds. 1685, 1687, "*Quæstio.*"

Quid petis: "Quid petis à Deo hac precatione?" (Queen Eliz.) Whitaker has "in hac precatione?"

"In hac oratione quid à Deo petis?" (Vautrollier.)

Quid à Deo in hac Precatione expetis?" (Nowell's Small Catechism.)

Peto: "Peto ut coelestis pater, dator omnis boni, det mihi & omnibus hominibus, ut eum colamus, ei seruiamus, & obediamus, ut donet nobis omnia quae necessaria sunt ad hanc uitam, remittat nobis peccata, ac ut defendat nos in omnibus periculis corporis & animae. Postremò, ut nos liberet ab omni peccato, ab insidijs Diaboli, & morte aeterna. Credo etiam Deum Patrem pro sua bonitate & misericordia hoc facturum, per Dominum nostrum Iesum Christum, ideóque dico Amen : id est, ita fiet." (Queen Eliz.)

"Equidem contendo à Domino Deo Patre coelesti, bonorum omnium largitore, ita me omnésque alios sua gratia velit augere & confirmare, vt illum colamus, illi seruiamus, & pro eo atque decet in omnibus obtem-

necessaria ; utque sit nobis propitius, & peccata nostra nobis dimittat; ut nos etiam versantes in quolibet periculo tam animae, quam corpori immi-

give us a part of all those (things) which are necessary to mind & body; and that he may be favourable to us, & dismiss for us our sins; that he

---

peremus : peto etiam, vt omnia nobis largiatur tum ad corporis incolumitatem, tum ad animae salutem necessaria, vt sua nos misericordia complectatur, nobisque nostra peccata condonet, dignetur nos ab omnibus periculis & animae & corporis tueri, ab omni'que peccati & sceleris contagione, ab hoste spirituali Satana, morte & damnatione aeterna liberare. Quae quidem omnia spero pro sua misericordia & benignitate faciet, per Dominum nostrum Iesum Christum. Ideóque in extrema clausula addo. Amen" (Vautrollier).

"Precor Dominum Deum meum, Patrem coelestem, bonorum omnium authorem, ut ego, & universi mecum mortales divino illius spiritu afflati, eum piè sanctóq; colamus & veneramur (*sic*, and in 1584 also) illi inserviamus : & ejus voluntati, ut par est, obediamus. Oróq; Deum, ut omnia in universum, vel quae ad usum vitae pertinent, nobis largiri velit ; ut supplicum misereri, & peccatis nostris ignoscere, pericula omnia tam ab animis quàm corporibus nostris depellere, à vitijs & flagitijs omnibus avocare, à Satanae vi atque impetu tueri, & ab interitu sempiterno conservare nos velit. Atque haec eum pro paterna sua clementia, atque bonitate, per Dominum nostrum Iesum Christum largiturum esse, spem bonam concipio : ideóq; Amen, id est, ita fiat, ad finem precationis adjungo " (Nowell's Small Catechism).

Bagster has no comma after "mihi," "animae," or "peccato;" but he has commas after "obsequamur," "oro," "impertiatur," "etiam," "imminente," "animarum," "ipsum," and "sua :" a semicolon for a colon after "dignetur," and three other divergences mentioned below.

omnis boni: "τῆς πάσης ἀγαθότητος," Duport. πάντων ἀγαθῶν, Whitaker, Nowell, and Petley.

largitore: "largior" is "to give bountifully" (largus), as it is rightly used in *Janua* with "non rogatus" and "ex munificentia." Nowell (Small Catechism) has αἰτίῳ ; Whitaker and Petley, χορηγὸν ; Duport, ἐστῆρα καὶ χορηγὸν.

gratiam—largiatur: "det mihi . . . , ut" etc. (Queen Eliz.) "ita me . . . sua gratia velit augere & confirmare, vt," etc. (Vautrollier). "ut ego, & universi mecum mortales divino illius spiritu afflati, eum," etc., Nowell, who in the Greek has, τὸ θεῖον αὐτοῦ πνεῦμα . . . ψαρίσασθαι (*sic* in 1584 also). Whitaker and Petley have χαρίζεσθαι. Duport, τὴν χάριν αὐτοῦ καταπέμψαι.

nente custodire ac tueri dignetur : & nos servare ab omni peccato, ac malitiâ, ab hoste animorum & ab aeterna morte. Et hoc confido ipsum pro clementia ac benignitate sua praestiturum, per Dominum nostrum Jesum Christum. Ideóque dico, *Amen.* Sic fiat.

may vouchsafe also to keep and defend us when we are in any danger hanging over as well soul as body : & to preserve us from every sin, and badness, from the enemy of spirits & from everlasting death. And this I am confident himself will perform according to his graciousness and goodness, through our Lord Jesus Christ. And therefore I say, *Amen.* So be it.

---

e t i a m . In Ed. 1687 there is a misprint, "etium," as also in 1685; this is corrected in Eds. 1696 & 1703.

i m p e r t i a t u r : "to give part" (*Janua*).

p r o p i t i u s : or "propitious." "Favouring their cause, wel-pleased, reconciled" (*Janua*). "dignetur" is "vouchsafe" in ditto.

d i m i t t a t . For "dimittat," and a semicolon, Bagster has "remittat," and a colon. Harwood has "remittat."

v e r s a n t e s : "versari" almost equals "esse :" in *Janua* used for "to converse with," in the old sense of "conversation."

i n q u o l i b e t p e r i c u l o : ἐν πᾶσι τῆς τε ψυχῆς καὶ τοῦ σώματος κινδύνοις, Duport, and so Whitaker, but with τοῦ τε σώματος καὶ τῆς ψυχῆς, and thus also Petley. Nowell (Small Catechism) has πάντων κινδύνων τάς τε ψυχὰς καὶ τὰ σώματα ἀπαλλάττειν.

i m m i n e n t e : "hanging over" (*Janua*).

a b o m n i : ἀπὸ πάσης (not τῆς πάσης) ἁμαρτίας, Duport ; so Whitaker, ἀπὸ πάσης ἡμᾶς ἀνομίας ; and Petley, ἀπὸ πάσης ἀνομίας. Nowell, however, has τῶν κακιῶν καὶ πλημμελημάτων ἁπάντων ἀπάγειν.

m a l i t i â : in the answer before the Lord's Prayer, we have "maliciam" in this first Ed. of 1670.

πονηρίας, Duport. Whitaker has no word for it. Petley, ἁμαρτίας. Nowell, πλημμελημάτων.

For "ac malitiâ" Bagster has "et nequitia."

a b h o s t e a n i m o r u m : in Eds. 1685, 1687, 1696, 1703, we have "animarum."

Bagster has "animarum." So has Harwood.

Duport has ἀπὸ τοῦ πνευματικοῦ ἐχθροῦ ἡμῶν. Whitaker has ἀπὸ τῶν Διαβόλου ἐνέδρων (insidijs Diaboli). ἀπὸ τῶν πνευματικοῦ τοῦ πολεμίου ἐνέδρων (Petley). τῆς τοῦ Σατανᾶ βίας καὶ ὁρμῆς (Nowell). Messrs. Bright and Medd have "ab inimico spirituali."

Quæstio.	*Question.*
QUOT Sacramenta instituit Christus in Ecclesia sua?	HOW many Sacraments hath Christ appointed in his Church?

For "ghostly" in English Version, used for "spiritual," here and above with "dangers," cf. Shakespeare, "Romeo and Juliet," "Hence will I to my ghostly father's call."

a e t e r n a : Duport, θανάτου αἰωνίου, without the articles. So Whitaker and Petley; Nowell too has ἐξ αἰωνίου ὀλέθρου.

c l e m e n t i a : "mildnesse" (*Janua*).

d i c o. Eds. 1685, 1687 have a full stop after "dico;" Eds. 1696 and 1703 a comma.

A m e n : "Amen" in *Janua* is translated "*Amen* [So be it]."

S i c f i a t. Aless has "ita fiet," and Queen Eliz. retains this: Whitaker, on the contrary, who usually adheres to the latter, has "ita fiat," and so too Harwood has "sic fiat," just as Durel.

Whitaker and Petley have οὕτω γενηθήτω.

οὕτω γένοιτο, Duport : the contrary of St. Paul's expression μὴ γένοιτο, which our English Bible translates "God forbid."

At this point we have reluctantly to part company with the versions of Queen Elizabeth's reign, except in so far as concerns the Catechisms of Nowell.

Q U O T : Quot in Eds. 1685, 1687, 1696, and 1703.

"*Quot in Ecclesia sua Sacramenta instituit Dominus?*" (Nowell's Small Catechism.) The quotations up to this point have been given from an edition of 1633 (see Part II. chap. i.), on account of some superiority in spelling, etc., the divergences from the earlier text being mentioned where they appeared sufficiently noteworthy. Throughout this part upon the Sacraments, however, it has been thought more advisable to give the text of 1584.

This portion of the Church Catechism was introduced in 1604. The authorship is ascribed to Bishop Overall (see App. E.). It is interesting to note throughout how the author copied the phraseology of Nowell's Small Catechism, and the very order of the questions.

S a c r a m e n t a : μυστήρια is Nowell's word in the Greek: also Petley's and Duport's, who, however, have a capital M.

For Augustine's view of the Sacraments, see App. F. And for an Analysis of the Sacraments as explained in the Catechism, see Appendix G.

"This is in general, an Account of a Sacrament This, it is true, is none of those Words that are made use of in Scripture, so that it has no determined Signification given to it in the Word of God ; yet it was very

Responsio.	*Answer.*
Duo tantùm, quae quidem in genere	Two only, to be indeed in general

---

early applied by *Pliny* to those Vows by which the Christians tied themselves to their Religion, taken from the Oaths by which the Soldiery among the *Romans*, were sworn to their Colours or Officers; and from that time this Term has been used in a Sense consecrated to the Federal Rites of Religion" ("An Exposition of the Thirty-nine Articles," etc., by Bishop Burnet, MDCXCIX, p. 269).

It is interesting to compare the ancient form of judicial proceeding called "actio Sacramenti." Mr. Sandars writes ("Instit. of Justinian," Introd. p. lx. Fifth Ed.) : "The most ancient and most important of the actions of law, the *actio sacramenti*, brings before us, in the most marked manner, the delight in appeals to the external senses, and the use of symbolical acts, sanctioned by long usage and expressive in themselves, which belongs to the early times of so many nations. It was originally the only form of action; and every species of right could be enforced by it."

"a Sacramento arcet," etc., "he driveth away the impenitent from the Sacrament ; he leaveth hypocrites to their own conscience" (*Janua*).

i n s t i t u i t : παρέδωκεν ὁ Κύριος τῇ ἐκκλησίᾳ αὐτοῦ (Nowell's Small Catechism).

Duport has διέταξε for Durel's "instituit ;" Petley has κατέστησε.

"instituit" however is a true perfect ; see note on "sint" below.

Rev. E. Daniel says, "the question is not How many Sacraments are there? but How many Sacraments hath *Christ ordained* in His Church?" But is it not the same thing? Who else has power?

Duo tantùm. Nowell's Small Catechism has simply, *Duo : Baptismum.* (sic, but a comma in 1633) *& Coenam Domini.* Δύο : (sic in both editions) τὸ βάπτισμα, καὶ τὸ Κυριακὸν (κυριακὸν, 1633) δεῖπνον. Duport has, Δύω μόνον, ὡς καθόλου πρὸς τὴν σωτηρίαν ἀναγκαῖα, Βάπτισμα δήπου, καὶ Δεῖπνον τὸ Κυριακόν. Petley before him had precisely the same, only Βαπτισμόν.

Harwood has the same as Durel, but "sunt," not "sint," and "ad salutem consequendam" comes after "quae quidem." This change occurs also in Parsell (1713).

tantùm : "onely," *Janua*. Rev. E. Daniel says, "the answer is not Two only, but 'Two only as generally necessary to salvation.'" This opens the door for the other Sacraments of Rome. But Durel's version gives the simple answer "Two only," and then adds, "to be indeed," etc., showing their use.

in genere: "De Ethicâ in genere."—"Of morall Philosophy [*ordering of manners*] in generall" (*Janua*). So too in the same book, "De

necessaria sint ad salutem consequendam, nempe Baptismum & Coenam Domini.	necessary to attaining safety, to wit Baptism & (the) Lord's Supper.

Mechanicis in genere."—"Of Handy-craft Trades in generall." So in Centini, "Disput. Scolast," Tom. Sec. MDCXXXIX., we have : "De Sacramentis in genere, & in Specie de Baptismo, Confirmatione, & Eucharistia."

This expression "in genere" is used in Eds. 1680, 1685, 1687, 1696, and 1703 of Durel. Also in Parsell, Eds. 1713, 1716, 1733, 1744.

Harwood also has "in genere" in this passage, and in fact the whole answer is practically the same as Durel's with the exception of "sunt" for "sint."

Bagster (1821) has the same as Durel.

Messrs. Bright and Medd have "Duo tantum velut ad salutem generaliter necessaria ; Baptismum, et Cœnam Dominicam."

Durel's version shows that "generally necessary" in the English Version means "necessary in general." It has of late been asserted that "generally" means "universally ;" but we shall support Durel's rendering "in genere," *i.e.*, "in general," by certain points which will, we trust, show that "generally" here was never conceived at the time of the Last Revision to have any other meaning than "on the whole," or "under ordinary circumstances," or the like. The controversy is of the highest importance, as may be seen from Dr. Harrison's letter given in App. I. We shall proceed to examine, first, the reasons why the term "generally" is used ; secondly, the view taken of the subject by writers of the period ; thirdly, the renderings of other contemporary versions ; and lastly, shall criticize the arguments of those who assert that "generally" means "universally," and endeavour to show that the sense of "in general," or "on the whole," is a common, perhaps the most common, meaning of the word in the seventeenth century.

Firstly, then, why was the word "generally" introduced? The Church of England interprets her own Liturgy : "Beloved, ye hear in this Gospel the express words of our Saviour Christ, that except a man be born of water and of the Spirit, he cannot enter into the kingdom of God. Whereby ye may perceive the great necessity of this Sacrament, where it may be had" (Publick Baptism of such as are of Riper Years). "Dilecti, auditis in hoc Evangelio, Christi Servatoris nostri expressa verba, quod nisi quis renatus fuerit aqua, & Spiritu, ingredi non potest in regnum coelorum ; ex quibus potestis intelligere quanta sit hujus Sacramenti necessitas, ubi copia illius conceditur" (Durel's version). The words "where it may be had," "ubi copia illius conceditur," express a *condition* which

* * * * * * * * *

renders the Sacraments *conditionally*—not absolutely—necessary, and, if *conditionally* necessary, then "*generally*," or "*in general*" necessary; and certainly not "*universally*" necessary. And this agrees with the passage which the Baptism Service proceeds to quote: "He that believeth and is baptized shall be saved; but he that believeth not shall be damned." St. Mark (chap. xvi. 16) does not add here, "and is not baptized," as Dean Alford points out: the Dean thereupon remarks, "our Lord does not set forth here the *absolute*, but only the *general* necessity of Baptism to salvation, as the Church of England also teaches. But that general necessity extends to all to whom Baptism is accessible;" etc. In this answer the Church of England is guarding against two errors of the Romish Church. First, the latter said there were *seven* Sacraments (Concil. Trid. Sess. 7. Can. 1); our Catechism says, "Two only." Secondly, the Romish Church says, "a Sacrament is a sensible thing which by the institution of God hath a power as well of causing as of signifying holiness and righteousness" (Catech. Rom. par. 2. cap. 1. n. 11); "the Sacraments contain the grace which they signify, and confer grace (ex opere operato) by the work itself upon such as do not put an obstruction" (Concil. Trid.); "For these sensible and natural things work by the almighty power of God in the sacraments what they could not do by their own power" (Catech. Rom.); now on this system of the Sacraments *causing, containing,* and *conferring* grace, the Sacraments were of course necessary, simply and absolutely; but the Church of England guards against this by saying that they are "generally necessary," thus *qualifying the necessity* to allow of such a condition as "where they may be had."

Secondly, let us look what was the opinion of cotemporary writers upon this subject. Bishop Stillingfleet writes in "A Rational Account of the Grounds of Protestant Religion," p. 561, London, 1665: "And what they say of (defect of) intention, is much more true of Baptism itself; for in case it (the omission of baptism) be not done out of contempt I say that summus Sacerdos supplebit (the High Priest will supply that defect): it is not the meer want of Baptism will damn the soul of the Infant, (as you suppose) when you make it so necessary, to use such shifts as you speak of, to save the soul of a dying Infant." The Bishop of London's

"Imprimatur," affixed to this book is dated 1664, two years after the Last Revision. So, too, before the Revision, a Divine writes in the year 1636, "Baptisme" is "Necessary in divers and sundry regards. As the lawfull use thereof is a note whereby the true Church of God is discerned and distinguished from the false Church. Not that the Church of God cannot be a true Church without this Sacrament. For it may want Baptisme for a time and yet remaine a true Church, as well as the Church of the Jewes in ancient times wanted circumcision for the space of fourty yeeres Josh. v. 6 and yet ceased not to be a true Church & loved of God": and then four reasons are appended why Baptism is not absolutely or simply, in other words universally, necessary. Again, in "Paraphrasis cum Annotatis ad Difficiliora loca Catechismi Anglicani," etc., A.D. 1674, we find "Two only, as generally necessary to salvation" explained as "those things, in the devout, frequent, and constant use whereof, the generality of men obtain Salvation, and no otherwise :" not "all men," but "the generality of men." Again, in "A Comment on the Book of Common-Prayer," etc., by William Nicholls, D.D., London, MDCCX., a copy of which is in the Bodleian, our passage is thus explained : "Generally necessary.] *By generally necessary we understand,* That (1) all Persons, of what Rank and Quality soever, are obliged to the Performance of them, unless they labour under an Incapacity, by reason of their Age or otherwise, or are hindered therefrom by an invincible Necessity." Again, in the "Supplement to the Commentary on the Book of Common Prayer," Wm. Nicholls, D.D., published MDCCXI. (a copy is in the Bodleian), are certain Puritan objections answered ; these answers are stated in this book to be by Tho. Hutton, and to have been "*Printed* Anno Dom. 1606.*"* Exception 13 is "*There are two* Sacraments as generally necessary to Salvation. *This word* generally, *importeth other and more Sacraments; in particular implying the Popish Sacraments, and so is contrary to the Fifteenth Article of Religion, which saith there are Two Sacraments only.*" Then follows the Answer : " It is to be understood *generally necessary to Salvation,* noting it to be every Man's Duty in submitting unto them ; because every one is either an Infant, or of more Years : And if both, both generally necessary for Salvation for both. Besides the Word *As*, is as a Partition Wall, betwixt the Sacraments and Generally, giving a Reason why two Sacraments are received, and no more. There are two Sacraments as *generally necessary* in a Signification taken at large, meaning no more but two, and these two not simply and absolutely necessary, as if a Christian were damned without them; but as Generally necessary, that is, when they may be had according to Christ's Institution."

Again, Archbishop Secker, who was born towards the close of the seventeenth century, writes in his " Lectures on the Catechism," vol. ii. p. 222 : " and even these two, our Church very charitably teaches us not to look upon as indispensably, but as *generally necessary*. Out of which general necessity, we are to except those particular cases, where believers in Christ, either have not the means of performing their duty in respect to the Sacraments, or are innocently ignorant of it, or even excusably mistaken about it." His cotemporary John Wesley says that Baptism " was intended to last as long as the church into which it is the appointed means of entering. In the *ordinary* way there is no other means of entering into the church or into heaven" (vol. xiii. p. 401); and again, " If outward baptism be generally, in an ordinary way necessary to salvation," etc. (p. 404). So, too, the Rev. James Stillingfleet, a descendant of Bishop Stillingfleet and the intimate friend of Joseph Milner, the Church historian, writes : *Q.* " Why do you term them generally necessary?" *A.* " Because Christ has appointed them to be observed by all who are not deprived of the opportunity of receiving them."

So that we see that from 1606, two years after the passage containing " generally necessary" was first introduced into the Catechism, through the period of the Last Revision, and through the next century, "generally necessary" was held to mean "necessary in general;" and moreover that this accorded with the views of Divines of the period who regarded the Sacraments as necessary, but not simply, absolutely, or universally so.

In the third place, we must examine contemporary versions. The Welsh Prayer Book of 1664 has " Dau yn unig megis yn gyffredinol anghenrhaid i Jechydwriaeth, sef, Bedydd, a Swpper, yr Arglwydd." It is not a little remarkable that the word used for " generally" is " gyffred-

* * * * * * * * *

---

inol," which is the adverbial form of "gyffredin," the adjective used for "Common" in the title of the Book of Common Prayer, "Llyfr Gweddi Gyffredin." So that the Welsh Prayer Book takes "generally" to mean "commonly," which is still the ordinary sense of "gyffredinol." A Welsh clergyman writes to us, "The explanation in one of the two Welsh Catechisms, or rather Commentaries on the Catechism, in use in our Sunday schools is '*generally*, not *indispensably* ;' in the other, 'necessary in every instance where they may be had.'"

Petley and Duport both have Δύω μόνον, ὡς καθόλου πρὸς τὴν σωτηρίαν ἀναγκαῖα, κ.τ.λ. This appears at first sight, perhaps, to support the view of those who hold that "generally" is equivalent to "universally :" such, however, is not actually the case.

Used as an adverb καθόλου means "*on the whole, in general.*" These are the only two senses of its adverbial use given by Liddell and Scott (fourth edition), who further tell us that it is "for καθ' ὅλου, as it is written in authors before Arist. (*e.g.* Philipp. ap. Dem. 251. 3)." The substantive phrase τὸ καθόλου is often translated "the universal" in Logical works, sometimes perhaps rightly, but more often inaccurately : it will be as well, therefore, to see what are Aristotle's definitions of καθόλου in its logical uses. First, with regard to terms, he says, λέγω δὲ καθόλου μὲν ὃ ἐπὶ πλειόνων πέφυκε κατηγορεῖσθαι, καθ' ἕκαστον δὲ ὃ μή, κ.τ.λ. (de Interp. c. 7, p. 17, a 38): "I mean by καθόλου what has been so constituted naturally that it can be predicated of a greater number ("de pluribus," Trendelenburg), and by singular that which has not." Secondly, with regard to propositions he writes, λέγω δὲ καθόλου μὲν τὸ παντὶ ἢ μηδενὶ ὑπάρχειν ἐν μέρει δὲ τὸ τινί, κ.τ.λ. (Anal. pr. I. 1. p. 24, a 16) ; this means that by καθόλου he denoted a general proposition (all A is B, or no A is B), as opposed to particular propositions. We must compare with this another passage (Top. I. 12, p. 105, a 13), where Aristotle is defining Induction as ἡ ἀπὸ τῶν καθ' ἕκαστον ἐπὶ τὰ καθόλου ἔφοδος : the illustration he gives here is as follows :—if the pilot who possesses knowledge is the best, and if the same is the case with the charioteer, then on the whole (καὶ ὅλως) he who has knowledge upon each subject is the best. These Inductions are arrived at, according to Aristotle, sometimes διὰ πάντων,

* * * * * * * * *

---

sometimes διὰ πλειόνων, or διὰ πολλῶν. We fear that the word "universal" is used more loosely by logicians than it is in ordinary language. There is a real and important distinction between "universal" and "general" propositions. That Mr. J. S. Mill clearly apprehended this distinction one passage will suffice to show: "It is of importance to remark, that when a sequence of phenomena is thus resolved into other laws, they are always laws more general than itself.... Not only are the laws of more immediate sequence into which the law of a remote sequence is resolved, laws of greater generality than that law is, but (as a consequence of, or rather as implied in their greater generality) they are more to be relied on; there are fewer chances of their being ultimately found not to be universally true" (Logic, Bk. III. ch. xii. § 4. Eighth edition). General propositions admit of degrees of truth; even "all men are mortal" is not a universal truth, if we look but at the case of Enoch: but a universal proposition, such as the Law of Universal Causation, enunciates a truth coextensive with human experience. Keeping this distinction in mind, τὰ καθόλου in Aristotle should be, at all events for the most part, translated by general, not universal, propositions. This logical and substantival use is, however, rather beside our subject: we will revert to the meaning of καθόλου, when employed as in the Catechism in an adverbial form. A few passages from the Ethics of Aristotle will suffice to show the sort of meaning which he attached to the word. καθόλου μὲν οὖν εἴρηται ὅτι ὡς δεῖ ὁμιλήσει, ἀναφέρων δὲ, κ.τ.λ. (Eth. iv. 6. 6): "We have said generally that (the good man) will associate with people as he ought, but we may add (δὲ) that," etc. (Sir A. Grant's transl. in note on passage). καθόλου μὲν τὸ ὀφείλημα ἀποδοτέον, ἐὰν δ᾽ ὑπερτείνῃ, κ.τ.λ. (Eth. ix. 2. 5): "as a general rule the debt should be repaid, but if the giving (to some one else) preponderates in moral glory, or in the urgency of the case (over repaying), one must incline to this" (Sir A. Grant's transl. in note). καθόλου μὲν γὰρ τῷ πυρέττοντι συμφέρει ἡσυχία καὶ ἀσιτία, τινὶ δ᾽ ἴσως οὔ (Eth. x. 9, 15): "As a general rule, a fever must be treated by repose and low diet, but still to this rule there may none the less be individual exceptions" (Williams' transl.). Cf. Eth. i. 11. 2, etc. All these passages show that καθόλου means "as a rule," or "on the whole,"

✻ ✻ ✻ ✻ ✻ ✻ ✻ ✻ ✻

---

with the full possibility of exceptions. So that the versions of Petley and Duport support Durel's rendering of "generally" by "in genere." Had they meant "universally," or "absolutely," there is no lack of such words in Greek; ἁπλῶς, τὸ ἅπαν, πανταχῇ, πανταχῶς, παντελῶς, πάντῃ, πάντως, and many others were ready to their hand.

Again, in a book published twenty-two years before the Last Review, "The common Catechisme in foure Languages," London, 1638, a copy of which is in the Bodleian, we find "Duo solum, ut summatim necessaria ad salutem," for the Latin version, and Δύω μόνον, ὡς ἐπὶ πολὺ, καὶ ἐξαιρίτως (sic) εἰς τὴν σωτηρίαν ἐπιτήδεια in the Greek. The meanings given for "summatim" in Smith's Dictionary are "*on the top or surface, slightly:*" and "*slightly, summarily, compendiously,*" etc.: probably here, however, it is the same as "ad summam," "*on the whole.*" The Greek is sufficiently plain: ἐπὶ πολὺ is "*mostly, usually*" (See Liddell and Scott), and the translator does not use the word ἀναγκαῖα, "necessary," at all, but ἐπιτήδεια, "serviceable," "convenient," "useful," to which, however, he adds the adverb ἐξαιρέτως (accented thus), "specially:" so that his Greek means "Two only, as usually and specially serviceable unto salvation." So this work, as well as the Welsh Prayer Book and the Greek versions of Petley and Duport, show that "generally" does not mean "universally."

Fourthly, we must now examine certain statements made upon this word "generally" in the Catechism. Mr. Blunt ("Annotated Book of Common Prayer") writes: "The use of the word 'generally' in the sense of 'universally,' may be illustrated by the two places in which it is to be found in the Holy Bible. The first is in 2 Sam. xvii. 11, 'Therefore I counsel that all Israel be *generally* gathered unto thee, from Dan even to Beersheba:' the expression in the Vulgate being 'universus Israel,' and the LXX. πᾶς Ἰσραήλ. The second is Jer. xlviii. 38: 'There shall be lamentation *generally* upon all the housetops of Moab;' where the Vulgate reads 'super *omnia tecta Moab*,' and the LXX. ἐπὶ πάντων τῶν δωμάτων Μωάβ." Now before proceeding we must just remark that the "universus" and "omnia" of the Vulgate, and the πᾶς and πάντων of the LXX., are parallel to the "all" of the English Version, so that the Vulgate

* * * * * * * * *

and LXX. versions of these passages only tend to the conclusion that the word "generally" in the English Version has no equivalent in the original. Indeed in Coverdale's Bible we find simply "that thou gather together all Israel" and "upon all the houses toppes," and the probability is that the translators of the Authorized Version of 1611 added the word "generally" to *qualify* "all," because all Israel would not be gathered, but only the males above the age of twenty years; and so too lamentation would hardly be made upon all the housetops of Moab without a single exception.

Mr. Blunt further says, "There are probably no instances to be found of any writer in the sixteenth or seventeenth centuries who used the word 'generally' otherwise than with the meaning 'universally;' and such is its meaning in this place." Mr. Blunt here laboured under a complete misapprehension. That "generally" was then used precisely in its present sense of "commonly," or "in general," and that too in this very passage, is sufficiently proved by the quotations given above from writers of the seventeenth century : *e.g.* Hutton (1606, two years after the introduction of this answer) writes on this very passage that the Sacraments are "not simply and absolutely necessary, as if a Christian were damned without them ; but as Generally necessary, that is, when they may be had according to Christ's Institution." For other instances of the use of "generally" and cognate words in their present sense, see Appendix H.

The Rev. E. Daniel, M.A., Principal of St. John's College, Battersea, in his work, "The Prayer Book ; its History, Language, and Contents," writes thus :—"'Generally' has now the force of *in most cases.* In Old English it is used in its literal sense of *universally.*" He then quotes the two passages (2 Sam. xvii. 11, we presume "xvi." is meant for xvii., and Jer. xlviii. 38) ; and he adds Esth. xv. 10, Apoc., "Thou shalt not die though our commandment be *general*," (where by the by the word in the LXX. is κοινὸν, "common"). He then quotes Art. XVII. : "We must receive God's promises in such wise as they are generally set forth" ("ut nobis in sacris literis generaliter propositae sunt") : but "generally set forth" is here opposed to "expressly declared" further on in the Article,

* * * * * * * * *

"generaliter propositae" to "diserte revelatam;" the distinction is between promises made generally, in general terms, and the Will of God expressly, specifically, and positively enjoined; if the promises are "*universally* set forth," what is the opposition to "*expressly* declared," which is said of God's will?

Mr. Daniel then quotes "'The *General* Confession,' *i.e.*, the Confession to be used by *all*. The '*General* Thanksgiving,' *i.e*, the Thanksgiving that may be used on *all* occasions, as distinguished from the Special Thanksgivings intended to be used on particular occasions." With regard to the second, Durel has "Gratiarum Actio Generalis" for the heading, and the parenthesis is "(erga eos maximè, qui jam laudes et gratiarum actiones suas, etc)": in the parenthesis the benefits are particularized, in the prayer itself, as in the heading, the benefits are generalized, commencing with the fact of creation, ending with the hope of glory, and sweeping through the space between; this is the meaning of "General Thanksgiving." With regard to the first, "The General Confession," it is so called because it is (to use Mr. Daniel's own words) "A confession of sins in general terms."

Mr. Daniel then quotes Mr. Blunt's opinion that writers of the sixteenth and seventeenth century only used "generally" in the sense of "universally:" an unfortunate statement which we have shown to be altogether without foundation. He also quotes John iii. 5 and John vi. 53 to prove the universal necessity of the Sacraments, but the former probably refers to Ezek. xxxvi. 25-27, and not to Baptism at all, and both were uttered before either of the Sacraments were instituted by Christ.

s i n t: not "sunt;" "quae—sint" is "which may be," or "to be," as "ut ea sint" would mean. In spite of the aorists in the Greek versions, "instituit" must be a true perfect, else by the rules of sequence of tenses "sint" would be "essent."

Eds. 1685, 1687 also have "sint." Eds. 1696 and 1703 have "sunt." J. W. Parker's "Liber Precum," etc., has "sint:" so has Bagster (1821).

B a p t i s m u m : "in baptisterio praesentibus susceptoribus baptizat," "*christeneth* [baptizeth] *in the font, the Godfathers being present*" (*Janua*).

Duport, Βάπτισμα here, and Nowell also. Petley has Βαπτισμὸν, which masculine form Duport also uses further on.

Quæstio.	*Question.*
Quid intelligis per vocem istam Sacramentum?	What do you understand by that word of yours Sacrament?

Coenam Domini: "sacram coenam," "the Lord's Supper" (*Janua*). Nowell also has "sacram Coenam" in the Large Catechism; "Coenam Domini," in the Small. Further on he has "Coena Dominica" in the Large Catechism, and this occurs also in the Small. Messrs. Bright and Medd use the form "Coena Dominica" throughout the Catechism. In his Vocabulary to the Large Catechism Nowell says, "Coena Domini, vel Dominica, Communio, Eucharistia Graece, Latine gratiarum actio" ["giving of thanks"]. See note on "Quamobrem Sacramentum."

Quid intelligis? "*Quid est Sacramentum?*" Τί ἐστὶ μυστήριον; (Nowell's Small Catechism.)

Τί σοι βούλιται τὸ ῥῆμα τοῦτο, Μυστήριον; (Duport).

"Quid vis per vocem istam Sacramentum" (Harwood, and Parsell previously).

Messrs. Bright and Medd have verbatim the same as Durel.

vocem istam. Bagster has a comma after "istam." τὸ ῥῆμα τοῦτο (Duport); ἡ ῥῆσις (Petley).

The following answer is strictly a definition of the *word* Sacrament; it is a sign (1) external and visible, (2) of a grace, (3) given unto us, (4) instituted by Christ, etc. The next question and answer, which follow this, refer to the *thing:* "Quot sunt partes," etc.? And the answer there is Two, a sign *and* a grace; for the *thing* (as distinguished from the mere name), the true Sacrament, only exists when the recipients duly receive it, and in such cases there is an accompanying grace.

Externum & visibile signum: "*Est externum & aspectabile signum internam arcandmque spiritualem gratiam representans (sic:* and also in 1633), *ab ipso Christo institutum, ad testificandum Diuinam erga nos per eundem Christum Seruatorem, beneuolentiam atque beneficentiam: quo Dei promissiones de remissione peccatorum, & aeterna salute per Christum data, quasi consignantur, & earum veritas in cordibus nostris certiùs, confirmatur*" (Nowell's Small Catechism: Ed. 1633 has no comma after certiùs).

"Τὸ ἔξωθεν καὶ ὁρατὸν σημεῖον, ὃ τὴν ἔνδοθεν καὶ πνευματικὴν χάριν παρίστησιν, ὑπ' αὐτοῦ Χριστοῦ διατεταγμένον πρὸς τὸ (no accent) τεκμήριον εἶναι τῆς τοῦ Θεοῦ πρὸς ἡμᾶς δι' αὐτοῦ Χριστοῦ τοῦ σωτῆρος φιλοδωρίας τε καὶ μεγαλοδωρίας: (sic) ἐν ᾧ αἱ τοῦ Θεοῦ ἐπαγγελίαι περὶ ἀφέσεως ἁμαρτιῶν καὶ ἀϊδίου σωτηρίας διὰ Χριστοῦ δοθείσης οἱονεὶ ἐπισφραγίζονται καὶ ἡ ἀλήθεια αὐτῶν ἐν ταῖς καρδίαις ἡμετέραις ἐνεργέστερον βεβαιοῦται" (Nowell's Small Catechism).

*   *   *   *   *

In both this edition and that of 1633 the ἐν of ἐνεργέστερον is separate from the rest of the word ; in the Middle Catechism the word is ἐμφαντικώτερον.

In his Middle Catechism Nowell has " Sacramentum est externa diuinae erga nos per Christum beneuolentiae beneficentiaéq ; testificatio, signo aspectabili arcanam spiritualémq ; gratiam repraesentans : qua Dei," etc. : continued the same as in the Small Catechism. In the Greek he commences, Μυστήριόν ἐστι τὸ ἔξωθεν τῆς τοῦ Θεοῦ πρὸς ἡμᾶς διὰ Χριστοῦ εὐνοίας καὶ φιλανθρωπίας μαρτύριον, δι' ὁρατοῦ σημείου ἀόρατον καὶ πνευματικὴν χάριν παρεμφαῖνον, κ.τ.λ.

In his Large Catechism Nowell has " Est externa Divinae," etc., continuing the same as the Middle Catechism, with some difference in stops. Norton's Translation of this is, " It is an outward testifying of God's good-will and bountifulness toward us, through Christ by a visible sign representing an invisible and spiritual grace, by which the promises of God touching forgiveness of sins and eternal salvation given through Christ, are, as it were sealed, and the truth of them is more certainly confirmed in our hearts."

This answer in Bagsters first Ed. (1821) is almost the same as Durel's : " Externum et visibile signum intelligo internae ac spiritualis gratiae, quod nobis datur, ab ipso Christo institutum, tanquam medium, quo eam recipimus, et arrhabonem, qui nos de ea certos faciat." But it appears to be rewritten in his edition of 1866, which gives : " Externum volo et aspectabile Signum interna (sic) et spiritualis Gratiae, collatae nobis, ab ipso Christo institutum, tanquam medium quo eam adipiscimur, et pignus certitudinis, nos eam adepturos esse." His later version is the same as Harwood's, who however has " internae," and " adeptos," not " adepturos." Harwood got his version from Parsell's, which is verbatim the same in Ed. 1733 (in Ed. 1713 Parsell had "adepturos;" this he afterwards altered to " adeptos ").

Duport has Ἐννοῶ τὸ ἐκτὸς καὶ ὁρατὸν τῆς ἔσω καὶ πνευματικῆς χάριτος ἡμῖν δοθείσης σημεῖον, τὸ ὑπ' αὐτοῦ τοῦ Χριστοῦ διαταχθὲν, ὡς ὄργανον δι' οὗ ἐπιτυγχάνομεν αὐτῆς, καὶ ἐνέχυρον ἡμῖν αὐτὴν βεβαιῶσαι.

Responsio.	*Answer.*
Externum & visibile signum intelligo, internae ac spiritualis gratiae,	I understand an outward & visible sign, of an inward and spiritual favour,

This is almost wholly taken from Petley; the latter, however, has a comma after ἴσω; he also has ὑπὸ τοῦ Χριστοῦ καταταχθὲν; τὸ μέσον, not ὄργανον; ἐπιτύχωμεν; and for the last clause, ὡς παρακαταβολὴν ἐπὶ τὸ προσκυροῦσθαι ἡμῖν αὐτήν.

Messrs. Bright and Medd give a different version of the answer from that of Durel, though their version of the question is the same. They have, "Intelligo signum externum et visibile gratiae internae et spiritualis nobis collatae, a Christo ipso institutum, tanquam instrumentum per quod eam accipimus, et pignus quod eam nobis confirmet."

E x t e r n u m : or "outer." "*De Sensibus externis*," "Of the outward Senses" (*Janua*).

"*externum*" in Nowell's Small Catechism: "externa" goes with "testificatio" in Large and Middle Catechism. The Greek in Small and Middle is τὸ ἔξωθεν, in the former with σημεῖον, in the latter with μαρτύριον. τὸ ἐκτὸς, Petley and Duport. Note that the Greek has the article.

v i s i b i l e : "visibilia objecta," "anything set before the eye" (*Janua*). "visibile" is a better word than Nowell's "aspectabile," which Harwood follows; for the latter comes too near to the idea of "to be gazed upon," which is condemned by Article xxv.

Nowell's Small Catechism has ὁρατὸν in the Greek, and so Petley and Duport: it is to be remarked that in the Greek we have both "outward" and "visible" under the vinculum of a common article.

s i g n u m : so Nowell's Small Catechism: and in Greek σημεῖον, which is also Petley's and Duport's word here. Further on, in the next answer, both Petley and Duport have σύμβολον.

i n t e r n a e : or "inner." Cf. note on "Quaenam est pars externa." "De Sensibus internis," "Of the inward Senses." (*Janua*).

"*internum arcanumque*," Nowell's Small Catechism; and in Greek, τὴν ἔνδοθεν. τῆς ἴσω, Petley and Duport.

s p i r i t u a l i s : "*spiritualem*," and "πνευματικὴν" (Nowell's Small Catechism): the latter, in the genitive case, is the word in Petley and Duport; here, too, "inward" and "spiritual" are under a common article, as "outward" and "visible" above.

g r a t i a e : Nowell has, as we have seen, "gratiam repraesentans," representing a grace or favour, and in the Greek, ὅ ... χάριν παρίστησιν, which ... sets a favour before the mind, and χάριν παριμφαῖνον, showing or indicating a favour. What he means by "gratiam repraesentans" is clear

quod nobis datur, ab ipso Christo in- | which (sign) is given to us, having

---

from his use of the word a little further on in his Large Catechism: "First, as the uncleannesses of the body are washed away with water, so the spots of the soul are washed away by forgiveness of sins. Secondly, the beginning of regeneration, that is, the mortifying of our nature, is expressed (exprimitur) by dipping in the water, or by sprinkling of it. Finally, when we by and by rise up again out of the water, under which we be for a short time, the new life, which is the other part, and the end of our regeneration, is thereby represented (repraesentatur)."—Norton's Translation. Nowell uses "repraesentatur," therefore, as parallel to "exprimitur."

So "signum . . . gratiae" is a sign of, that is, representing or expressing a grace or favour; and not a sign of, as implying necessarily the existence of, the grace.

Compare Archbishop Secker's Lectures on the Catechism. He calls a Sacrament "the outward and visible sign," which "must denote some Favour freely bestowed on us from Heaven; by which our inward and spiritual condition, the state of our souls, is made better" (vol. ii. p. 209). "A Sacrament expresses on His Part, some Grace or Favour towards us," and "a sacrament is a Sign or Representation of some heavenly Favour" (ibid. p. 212).

quod nobis datur: "which (sign) is given to us." "quod" must refer to "signum," for had the relative referred to "gratiae" we must have had "quae," not "quod." Durel therefore settles the question whether "given" was considered at the time of the Last Revision to refer to "sign" or to "grace," nor could we have weightier evidence than his authoritative enunciation. Eds. 1680, 1685, 1687, 1696, and 1703 all agree with the first Ed. of 1670 in this sentence.

It is this *giving* of the sign which makes the Sacraments to be something other than object lessons from material things. The sign, which signifies the favour, is given to us in accordance with the institution of Christ himself; and by the words of the institution we learn the favour or grace which is denoted by the sign.

Cf. Ezek. xx. 12: "Moreover also, I gave them my sabbaths, to be a sign between me and them, that they might know that I *am* the Lord that sanctify them." Other signs were given to Noah and Abraham: the Rainbow, in Gen. ix. 12, 13; Circumcision, in Gen. xvii. 11. In none of these was the privilege objectively in the sign, but in all cases the favour was denoted by the words of the institution. So when the sacramental signs—which differ from these as ordained by Christ himself—

stitutum, tanquam medium quo eam recipimus, & arrabonem ad nos de eâ certos faciendos.

been appointed by Christ himself, as if a mean by which we receive that (favour), & an earnest to make us sure about that (favour).

are given to us, it is from the words of His Institution that we learn the favour signified by them.

This interpretation of Durel, which makes "given" refer to "sign," and not to "grace" (which latter construction would imply the invariable gift of grace in the Sacraments, irrespective of our "worthily receiving the same"), is supported by the pointing of the Sealed Books and other early editions. They are pointed as follows : " I mean an outward and visible sign of an inward and spiritual grace, given unto us, ordained" etc. Now the word "sign," in the sentence thus pointed, is undoubtedly the principal word on which all the others hinge ; that is to say, the word "sign" is the simple answer to the question, and all the other succeeding words are, grammatically speaking, merely explanatory of that term. Put into the form of question and answer the sentence would stand thus :—

What sign ?
1. An outward and visible
2. of an inward and spiritual grace
3. given unto us
4. ordained by Christ himself { *a.* as a means. *b.* as a pledge.

In other words, "sign" is the principal object; "outward" and "visible" are adjectives attributive to the principal object ; "of an inward," etc., is a prepositional phrase attributive to the principal object ; and "given unto us" and "ordained," etc., are participial phrases attributive to the principal object. No. (1) describes the sign, (2) gives the thing signified, (3) refers to the Form, and (4) specifies the Institution.

As to the evidence for the existence of the comma before "given," it is overwhelming. It is found in the book annexed to the Act of Uniformity of Charles II.; this book was signed by the Convocations of the two Provinces, and is now in the Library of the House of Lords. It is also in the Prayer Book of 1634, printed by Robert Barker, King's Printer, and the Assigns of John Bill, in which Dr. Sancroft copied the suggestions of Bishop Cosin, and which is supposed to have been the copy laid before Convocation : this we have examined in the Bodleian ; it reads, " I meane an outward and visible Signe, of an Inward & Spirituall grace, giuen vnto vs, ordained by Christ himselfe," etc. The comma also occurs in a Prayer Book of 1662, printed by John Field, Printer to the University of Cambridge, and in one of 1663, printed by John Bill and Christopher Barker, King's Printers, both of which books we have examined in the Bodleian. It is also found in Stephens's "Book of Common Prayer, with Notes Legal and Historical," the text of which is from the Sealed Book for the Chancery, and was collated by Stephens with the Sealed Books for the King's Bench, Common Pleas, Exchequer, St. Paul's, Christ Church, Ely, and the Tower. It also occurs in his "MS. Book of Common Prayer for Ireland," the text of which is from the MS. originally annexed to Stat. 17 and 18 Car. II. c. 6 (Ireland), and now in the Rolls' Office, Dublin. It is also in a Prayer Book of 1671 in our own possession, printed by John Bill and Christopher Barker, King's Printers. The comma is also found in "A Comment on the Book of Common Prayer," etc., by William Nicholls, D.D. London, MDCCX. : this book we have inspected in the Bodleian Library. Also in "The Catechism Set forth in the Book of common-Prayer, Briefly explained, by Tho. Marschall, D.D. Oxf. 1679."

This comma is rightly retained by the Rev. W. Keeling, in his "Liturgiæ Britannicæ," and by Messrs. Parker and Co., in their "First Prayer Book of Edward VI.," under "James I. 1604." We are, however, surprised to find that it is omitted by Messrs. S. Bagster and Sons in "The Book of Common Prayer in Eight Languages" (1866), and it is omitted also by Mr. Blunt in his "Annotated Book of Common Prayer." After omitting the comma, Mr. Blunt proceeds to explain the text as follows : "'I mean an outward and visible sign (ordained by Christ Himself) of an inward and spiritual grace given unto us. This outward sign was ordained by Christ, first, as a means whereby we are to receive the inward grace, and, secondly, as a pledge to assure us of that inward grace;' for the grace cannot ordinarily be separated from the sign which Christ has ordained." We cannot but enter our protest against such an alteration in the pointing of the text of that Book, which is sanctioned by the Act of Uniformity ; and still more must we protest against a tacit alteration of the text, accompanied by explanations which teach an entirely different doctrine from that held and maintained by the Church at the period of the Last Review. The Rev. E. Daniel also says that the words "given unto us" are "to be connected with 'grace.'"

The English and Latin Prayer Books of the time of the Last Revision

* * * * * * * *

---

agree in making "given unto us," or "quod nobis datur," refer to "sign," and not to "grace." Let us look briefly at other versions. It is to be regretted that here we have not the assistance of the Prayer Book of Queen Elizabeth and that printed by Vautrollier: of course the part of the Catechism which relates to the Sacraments was not introduced till 1604. In Nowell's Small Catechism, the immediate forerunner of that of 1604, we find simply "*gratiam repraesentans, ab ipso Christo institutum*," and nothing to imply at all that "grace" is inevitably and universally given in the Sacrament. For the passage in full, and also the readings of his Large and Middle Catechisms, and of Norton's Translation of the former, see note on "Externum & visibile signum."

Harwood (1785) indeed has "collatae nobis," and Messrs. Bright and Medd have "nobis collatae;" so too has Bagster in his Ed. of 1866 ("Book of Common Prayer in Eight Languages"), whereas in his first Edition (1821) he here, as almost throughout, follows Durel, and has "quod nobis datur." This change is at all events worthy of attention.

The first place in which we find the version "nobis collatae" is in "DOCTRINA, ET POLITIA ECCLESIAE ANGLICANAE," etc., by Mockett (London, 1617). This book met with an unfortunate fate. It is now exceedingly scarce, but there is a copy, which we have seen, in the Bodleian Library. At the commencement of the book we find these words in manuscript: "This volume was, immediately after its publication, 'publico Edicto flammis consignatus,'" and on turning to Wood's "Athenae Oxonienses," etc., we find that the statement is correct.

J. W. Parker's "Liber Precum," etc., rightly follows Durel.

Turning now to the Greek versions, Whitaker, of course, has not the passage in question. Nowell has simply ὁ . . . χάριν παρίστησιν, "which . . . sets a favour before the mind" (Small Catechism), and χάριν παριμφαῖνον, "showing or indicating a favour" (Middle Catechism), but no reference to the giving of grace. Petley, however, has χάριτος ἡμῖν ἐοθείσης σημεῖον, and this is followed by Duport. This, we admit, shows that Petley and Duport understood "given" to refer to "grace," but it shows equally that they did not think "given" meant "given in the Sacrament;" had they thought so, they would have used the present not the

* * * * * * * *

---

aorist participle passive; ἐσθιήσης implies that the grace is already given before we come to the Sacrament; just as in Nowell's Small Catechism we have αἰτίου σωτηρίας διὰ Χριστοῦ ἐσθιήσης. Nowell's Latin for this is "data," and it is possible that the meaning we can accurately fix upon Petley's Greek was also that intended by Mockett in his "collatae;" only, as there is no present passive participle in "conferre," it would have been advisable to have chosen a less ambiguous term or expression. In any case, however, the private opinion of Petley and Duport cannot be set against the clear expressions of the English and Latin Prayer Books of the reign of Charles II.

One more version must be compared, the Welsh Prayer Book of Charles II., "LLYFR Gweddi Gyffredin," etc. The copy from which we quote is in the Bodleian. The Imprint is, "A Brintiwyd yn *Llundain*, gan *S. Dover*, tros *Edward Ffowks* a *Phetr Bodvel*. MDCLXIV. Cum Privilegio." This has been compared, with reference to important passages, with a copy of 1677 in the Library of the Rev. John Pryce, M.A., Rector of Trefdraeth. In both editions the comma (which is omitted in modern Welsh Prayer Books) is exactly in the same position as in the Sealed Books, thus agreeing also with Durel's version. "Yr Wyfi yn ddeall ["deall in Ed. 1677], Arwydd gweledig oddi allan, o râs ysprydol oddifewn, a roddir i ni; yr hwn a ordeiniodd Crist ei hun, megis modd i ni i [no "i" in Ed. 1677] dderbyn y grâs hwnnw trwyddo, ac i fod yn wystl i'n sicrhau ni o'r grâs hwnnw." This is literally as follows:— "I understand a Sign visible and outward, of spiritual grace within, given to us; which Christ himself ordained, as a means for us to receive grace through it, and to be a pledge to assure us of that grace."

In conclusion we may compare Nowell's Large Catechism, "cujus nunc mysteria nobis traduntur;" "whose mysteries are now delivered us" (Norton's Translation). We may also support Durel's view by the following argument:—The definition as it stands in Durel, and in the English books of 1662, refers to the Sign, the Thing signified, the Form, and the Institution. But, if "given" referred to "grace," the "Form" (a very important factor) would be entirely omitted. See note below on "signum, aut forma." Whereas, we ought to have the "Form" in this general definition of the word "Sacrament," as we have it in the detailed accounts of both Baptism and the Lord's Supper. In the former, the words "quâ quis Baptisatur, *In Nomine*," etc., and in the latter, the words "quae Dominus jussit accipi," both hint at the "Form" or mode of *giving, delivering,* or *appropriating* the Sign.

Cf. "A Practical Exposition of the Church-Catechism, by Matthew Hole B.D. Fellow of Exeter Coll. in Oxford. Dedicated to Sir John Trelawny Bart. Lord Bishop of Winchester, &c., &c., &c. London M.DCC.VIII."

Several things are declared necessary to constitute a Sacrament. As,
" 1. There must be an outward and visible Sign.
" 2. An inward and spiritual Grace represented by it.
" 3. It must be given or apply'd to us.
" 4. It must be ordain'd by Christ himself.
" 5. It must be ordain'd as a Means to convey Grace.
" 6. It must be ordain'd as a Pledg or Earnest to assure us thereof."

Hole explains the 3rd thing thus :—

"'Tis further requir'd to a Sacrament, that it be *given to us;* that is, that it be duly administer'd and apply'd to us. To the due administration of it 'tis necessary that it be done by proper Officers, that is, by Persons duly qualify'd and authoriz'd thereunto ; without which 'tis utterly void and of none effect : and therefore all baptizing by Women or Persons that have no Commission, is no better than ordinary Bathing; and the Lord's Supper, when administer'd by such, is no better than a Common Meal. Again, to make these effectual, they must be duly apply'd as well as administer'd to us ; for as the best medicine is of no use, unless it be apply'd, so neither can a Sacrament be of any avail without a right Use and Application of it."

See also " The Baptisme of Christ : etc. By Master William Cowper, Minister of Gods Word (Bishop of Galloway, and Dean of His Majesty's Chapel Royal). Lond. 1623." A copy of this work is in our possession.

" euen as the Lord Iesus, by consecrating bread and wine which grew in *Canaan,* did thereby sanctifie all bread and wine, in any part of the world, to be a Sacrament of his body and blood, it being vsed according to his institution : so by washing in the water of *Iordan*, he hath sanctified water in any part of the world, to bee a Sacrament of regeneration, and remission of our sinnes, if so be it be vsed according to his institution."

It is this *use according to Christ's institution* to which " quod nobis datur " refers.

   i n s t i t u t u m : διαραχθὶν, Duport. καταταχθὶν, Petley.

   t a n q u a m : (tam quam) "a particle implying comparison ; *as much as, so as, just as, like as, as if, as it were*," etc. (Smith's Dictionary).

   m e d i u m : not classical for " means," nor in *Janua* in that sense. So Petley τὸ μέσον, which Duport alters to ὄργανον. Harwood has "medium." Messrs. Bright and Medd have "instrumentum," as also had Mockett.

In "The Catechism, etc., Briefly explained," 1679, Tho. Marschall, D.D., says : "As a means whereby we receive &c.] The outward Signes do signify, exhibit, and seal the spiritual Graces to the believing receiver."

The Romish Church teaches that the Sacraments *contain* the grace which they signify, and *confer* grace ex opere operato (Council Trent) : the English Church, that a sacrament is a sign ordained by Christ himself as a means whereby we receive grace, and a pledge to assure us of it.

   e a m : *sc.* gratiam.

   r e c i p i m u s : ἐπιτυγχάνομεν, Duport. ἐπιτύχωμεν, Petley.

   a r r a b o n e m : " pledge, gage" (*Janua*). " arrha," or " arrhabo," is from the Hebrew word meaning "to give security." It is an " earnest," or " deposit," rather than a pledge. " The *arræ* were either signs of a bargain having been struck, as, for instance, when the buyer deposited his ring with the seller (D. xix. 1. 11. 6), or consisted of an advance of a portion of the purchase-money. They were also intended as a proof that the purchase had been made " ("Institutes of Justinian," by T. C. Sandars, M.A. Fifth Ed., p. 357).

   παρακαταβολὴν, Petley : ἐνέχυρον, Duport.

Quæstio.	*Question.*
Quot sunt partes in Sacramento?	How many parts are there in a Sacrament?
Responsio.	*Answer.*
Duae, externum visibile signum, & interna spiritualis gratia.	Two, an outward visible sign, & an inward spiritual favour.

Harwood has "pignus," and so have Messrs. Bright and Medd.

Archbishop Secker, referring to Eden. Elem. Jur. Civ. p. 238, Gronov. in Plaut. Rud. 5. 3. 21, says, "Sacramentum was, among the heathens, particularly applied to denote a pledge deposited in a sacred place."

e a : *sc.* "gratia." From Archbishop Secker's "Lectures on the Catechism" we see that this "gratia," or "favour," of which we are assured, was not such as to be objectively in the Sacrament or Sign; he writes, "Our souls are purified from Sin by the Baptism of Repentance; and strengthened in all goodness by partaking of that Mercy, which the wounding of the Body of Christ, and the shedding of his Blood, hath obtained for us."

c e r t o s   f a c i e n d o s : ἡμῖν α'τὴν βιβαιῶσαι, Duport.

Q u o t   s u n t   p a r t e s : "*Sacramentum quot partibus constat?*" (Nowell's Small Catechism).

Πόσα μέρη ἐστὶν ἐν τῷ Μυστηρίῳ, Duport; Petley has ἔνεστι τῷ, κ.τ.λ.

D u a e : Transubstantiation destroys one part, and so "overthroweth the nature of a Sacrament."

"*Duabus: signo externo atque aspectabili, & interna inuisibilique gratia.*" Ἐκ ἐυοῖν: (sic) τοῦ τε ἔξωθεν καὶ ὁρατοῦ σημείου, καὶ τῆς ἐνδοθεν καὶ ἀοράτου χάριτος (Nowell's Small Catechism).

"*Duabus: externo elemento, seu signo aspectabili, et invisibili gratia*" (Nowell's Large Catechism). "Of two parts: the outward element, or visible sign, and invisible grace" (Norton's Translation).

"*Duas: extrarium elementum* [τὸ διὰ τῶν ἔξωθεν στοιχεῖον], *siue rem creatam* [ἡ κτίσμα], *quod est signum aspectabile* [ὅπερ ἐστὶ σημεῖον ὁρατόν]: *& arcanam gratiam, quae conspicua non est* [τὴν ἀπόκρυφον χάριν, τὴν ἀόρατον οὖσαν]."—Nowell's Middle Catechism. We give the Greek in brackets.

Harwood has the same as Durel, but "aspectabile" for "visibile:" so had Parsell, Ed. 1733, who, however, has "spiritualis & interna" in Ed. 1713.

Duport has Δύω· τὸ ἔξω καὶ ὁρατὸν σύμβολον, καὶ ἡ ἔσω καὶ πνευματικὴ χάρις. Petley had Δύω· τὸ ἔξωθεν, καὶ προῦπτον σύμβολον· καὶ τὸ ἔσωθεν καὶ θεόπνευστον χάρισμα.

s p i r i t u a l i s : Bagster, "spiritalis."

THE CATECHISM.

Quæstio.	*Question.*
Quodnam est externum visibile signum, aut forma in Baptismo?	What sign pray is (the) outward visible (sign), or (what is the) form in Baptism?

Quodnam est externum: "Quodnam" goes closely with "signum." "*Quod est in Baptismo signum externum?*" (Nowell's Small Catechism.)

Τί ἐστι τὸ ἔξω, καὶ ὁρατὸν σύμβολον, ἢ εἶδος ἐν τῷ Βαπτισμῷ; (Duport). Petley had Τί δῆτα ἐστι τὸ ἔξω καὶ εὐπρόσοπτον τὸ τεκμήριον, ἢ εἶδος ἐν τῷ Βαπτισμῷ;

signum, aut forma: Bagster has a comma after "forma."
"Matter is of the Essence of a Sacrament; for Words without some material thing, to which they belong, may be of the Nature of Prayers or Vows, but they cannot be Sacraments: Receiving a Sacrament is on our part our Faith plighted to God in the use of some material Substance or other; for in this consists the difference between Sacraments, and other Acts of Worship. The latter are only Acts of the Mind declared by Words or Gesture, whereas Sacraments are the Application of a material Sign, joyned with Acts of the Mind, Words, and Gestures: With the *Matter* there must be a *Form*, that is, such Words joyned with it as do appropriate the Matter to such an use, and separate it from all other uses, at least in the Act of the Sacrament. For in any piece of *Matter* alone, there cannot be a proper suitableness to such an end, as seems to be designed by Sacraments, and therefore a *Form* must determine and apply it; and it is highly suitable to the nature of things, to believe that our Saviour, who has instituted the Sacrament, has also either instituted the Form of it, or given us such hints as to lead us very near it" ("An Exposition of the Thirty-nine Articles of the Church of England," by Gilbert Bishop of Sarum (Bp. Burnet), London, MDCXCIX. p. 269).

From this it will be seen that Durel is perfectly correct in saying "aut forma," not "vel forma:" for the "Form" is something different from the "Sign" or "Matter." And so of Baptism itself Bishop Burnet writes, "In Baptism there is *Matter, Water;* there is a *Form*, the Person *Dipped* or *Washed*, with Words, *I baptize* thee in the Name of the Father, and of the Son, and of the Holy Ghost" (p. 269). Cf. also Private Baptism Service: "With what matter" (Durel, "Quo liquore") "was this child baptized? With what words was this child baptized?"

Harwood, too, has "aut." Messrs. Bright and Medd, however, have "sive," which does not retain the distinction between "sign" and "form:" they also have only "signum externum," thus not expressing the English word "visible" at all.

Responsio.	*Answer.*
Aqua quâ quis Baptisatur, *In Nomine Patris, & Filii, & Spiritus Sancti.*	Water by which any one is Baptized, *In the name of* (the) *Father, & of* (the) *Son, & of* (the) *Holy Ghost.*

Cf. a very important statement in Bp. Stillingfleet's "A Rational Account," p. 560.

"Here is the true form *Hoc est Corpus Meum,* the true matter Wheaten Bread, and he that pronounces the form is a true Priest." The objection being made that something else is requisite to the essence of a true Sacrament, Bishop Stillingfleet answers: "The institution of Christ requiring such a solemnity for the administration of it and such a disposition in the Church for the receiving it and the performance of such acts in order to the administration by the dispenser of it; these do sufficiently distinguish the Lord's Supper from all other actions what matter form or person so ever be there."

Cf. also "The substance standeth of two parts as Augustine saith," Augustine 80 Tract in Joan. "Accedit Verbum ad Elementum, & fit Sacramentum, etiam visibile Verbum."

To the ministration thereof five things are required: the party baptizing, the party baptized, a meaning to do that which Christ commanded, the element of water, and the form of words.

Henricus de Vurima in Quartam Sentent. comprehends them in these two verses:—

"Cum tincto tingens, Intentio, post Aqua, Forma
 Verborum, faciunt, ut sit Baptismatis esse."

(Letter of Archbishop of York [Hutton] to Archbishop of Canterbury [Whitgift], Oct. 9. 1ᵐᵒ Jacobi.)

Aqua quâ. In Ed. 1703 there is a comma after "Aqua," and we have "baptizatur." Bagster has a comma after "Aqua," and has "baptizatur." Eds. 1685, 1687, 1696 have no comma, so agreeing with the first Ed. of 1670.

"Aqua" is the Sign, or *Matter.* See last note.

"*Aqua, in quam Baptizatus intingitur, vel ea aspergitar* (sic; "aspergitur," 1633). In Nomine Patris, & Filij, & Spiritus Sancti" (Nowell's Small Catechism). The Greek commences, Τὸ ὕδωρ, εἰς ὃ, κ.τ.λ. Petley has Τὸ ὕδωρ· ὑφ' οὗ ὁ Βαπτισθεὶς ἐναποκίκλυσται, ἢ ἐρράντισται ἐν ὀνόματι κ.τ.λ. Duport has Ὕδωρ ἐν ᾧ βαπτίζεταί τις εἰς τὸ Ὄνομα, κ.τ.λ.

quâ—Sancti: the *Form* with the accompanying Words.

Before 1662 we find, "wherein the person baptized is dipped, or sprinkled with it," etc. In Sancroft's notes in the book of 1634, "is

Quæstio.	*Question.*
Quaenam est spiritualis & interna gratia ?	What favour pray is (the) spiritual & inward (favour) ?
Responsio.	*Answer.*
Mori peccato, & denuo nasci justitiae : cùm enim simus naturaliter in	To die to sin, & to be born anew to justice : for since we have been

dipped," etc., is struck out, and "is" inserted before "baptized." Compare Nowell's "*in quam,*" etc., and Petley's version.

In Nomine. So Nowell, but in the Greek (Small Catechism), εἰς τὸ ὄνομα. So Duport, but Petley has ἐν ὀνόματι. Beza has rightly "in nomen," and so has Harwood. Messrs. Bright and Medd have the same answer as Durel, with differences of pointing, etc. Matthew xxviii. 19, the foundation passage, has εἰς τὸ ὄνομα, and the article with the Divine names.

Quaenam est spiritualis & interna. The order of the English Version is here changed : it reads "inward and spiritual."

"*Quae est arcana & spiritualis gratia?*" Τίς ἐστιν ἡ ἀόρατος καὶ πνευματικὴ χάρις ; (Nowell's Small Catechism). The Latin of the Large Catechism is the same here.

"*Quae est occulta & coelestis gratia?*" (Nowell's Middle Catechism.) Τίς ἡ ἔσω καὶ πνευματικὴ χάρις ; (Duport). Petley had Τίς ἐστιν ἡ ἔσωθεν, the rest as Duport.

spiritualis : Bagster, "spiritalis."

Mori peccato, & denuo nasci justitiae. Nowell's Small Catechism has "*Remissio peccatorum, & Regeneratio : quae vtraque habemus a morte & resurrectione Christi eorum verò obsignationem atque pignus habemus in hoc Sacramento.*" And in the Greek, Ἄφεσις (*sic*) ἁμαρτιῶν καὶ ἀναγέννησις, ὧν ἀμφοτέρων ἐκ τοῦ θανάτου καὶ ἀναστάσεως τοῦ χριστοῦ (small χ) τυγχάνομεν, τὴν δὲ ἐπισφράγησιν καὶ τὸ ἐνέχυρον α'τῶν ἐν τούτῳ ἔχομεν τῷ μυστηρίῳ.

His Middle Catechism has "Venia criminum, & regeneratio : has ambas per mortem & resurrectionem Christi consequimur, & est hoc sacramentum nobis illarum quasi obsignatio quaedam atque pignus."

In his Large Catechism Nowell gives this description of "arcana et spiritualis gratia :"—"ea duplex est ; remissio videlicet peccatorum, et regeneratio, quae utraque in externo illo signo, solidam et expressam effigiem suam tenent." "It is of two sorts ; that is, forgiveness of sins, and regeneration ; both of which in the same outward sign have their full and express resemblance" (Norton's Translation). He then asks

peccato nati, & irae filii, hâc ratione facti sumus Filii Dei.	naturally born in sin, & sons of wrath, by this method we have been made Sons of God.

"How so?" The answer (given in the note above on "gratiae") shows how three things are "represented" or "expressed" in Baptism. The following is also worth quoting to illustrate the words of his Small and Middle Catechisms. "*M*. Do we not then obtain forgiveness of sins by the outward washing or sprinkling of water? *S*. No. For only Christ hath with his blood washed and clean washed away the spots of our souls. This honour therefore it is not lawful to give to the outward element. But the Holy Ghost, as it were sprinkling our consciences with that holy blood, wiping away all the spots of sin, maketh us clean before God. Of this cleansing of our sins we have a seal and a pledge in the sacrament. *M*. But whence have we regeneration? *S*. None other ways but from the death and resurrection of Christ. For by the force of Christ's death our old man is, after a certain manner crucified and mortified, and the corruptness of our nature is, as it were, buried, that it no more live and be strong in us. And by the beneficial mean of his resurrection he giveth us grace to be newly formed unto a new life, to obey the righteousness of God."

Nowell's Small Catechism then continues, "*Baptismi vim apertius adhuc mihi edissere*" (*ediscere*, 1633). This answer is also worthy of close attention, as the answer in the Catechism of our Prayer Book seems to be a combination of this answer and the one quoted at the beginning of the note. "*Quum natura alieni ab Ecclesia Deique familia, & per peccatum filij irae* (Greek, δι' ἁμαρτίας υἱῶν τῆς ὀργῆς), *dignique aeterna damnatione simus, per Baptismum* (διὰ τοῦ βαπτίσματος) *in Ecclesiam admittimur* (εἰσερχόμεθα εἰς τὴν ἐκκλησίαν), *certiores facti filios Dei iam nos esse* (σαφῶς εἰδότες ὅτι τέκνα Θεοῦ ἤδη ἐσμὲν), *& in Christi corpus insertos, eiúsque membra factos, in vnum cum ipso corpus coalescere.*" That is, "Whereas by nature we are strangers from the Church and household of God, and through sin are the children of wrath, and worthy of eternal damnation, by Baptism we are admitted into the Church, having been assured that we are already the children of God, and that having been grafted into Christ's body, and made his members, we are growing into one body with him."

His Middle Catechism has, "Quum naturaliter filij irae, hoc est, in grauissima apud Deum offensa, & ab eius ecclesia siue familia alienati simus, per baptismum in ecclesiam recipimur, certúmq; habemus nos iam Dei filios esse, & cum Christi corpore copulatos, in illúdq; quasi

* * * * * * * * *

---

insitos esse, eiúsq; membra factos, in eodem cum ipso corpore concrescere."

Similarly in his Large Catechism Nowell writes, "Quum natura Filii irae, id est, alieni ab Ecclesia, quae Dei familia est, simus, baptismus veluti aditus quidam nobis est, per quem in eam admittimur; unde et testimonium etiam amplissimum accipimus, in numero domesticorum, adeoque Filiorum Dei nos jam esse; imo in Christi corpus quasi cooptari, atque inseri, ejusque membra fieri, et in unum cum ipso corpus coalescere."

Turning to the Greek versions, Petley has : Ὁ θάνατος εἰς ἁμαρτίαν, καὶ ἀναβίωσις εἰς δικαιοσύνην· πεφυκότως γὰρ ἐν ἁμαρτίᾳ κυηθέντες, καὶ τῆς ὀργῆς υἱοὶ ὄντες, ἐντεῦθεν τέκνα χάριτος ἐγινόμεθα.

Duport has a slightly different version, reading ἀναγέννησις for ἀναβίωσις, φύσει for πεφυκότως, γεννηθέντες for κυηθέντες, τέκνα for υἱοί, τῆς before χάριτος, and γινόμεθα for ἐγινόμεθα.

Mori peccato. See note on "hâc ratione" below.

denuo: "again," *Janua*, but "anew" is better.

justitiae: "righteousness, justice, upright-dealing" (*Janua*). "Iustitia suum cuique tribuit" (ibid). The first of these senses, corresponding to the Platonic δικαιοσύνη in its widest meaning, is probably the one to be taken here. So Norton translates "justitiae" in Nowell by "righteousness."

irae filii. Duport has the article both with "wrath" and "grace," but it is noticeably absent in Eph. ii. 3.

hâc ratione facti sumus Filii Dei: "by this method we have been made Sons of God." The words "hâc ratione" must refer to "Mori peccato, & denuo nasci justitiae": this is evident if we consider the structure of the sentence; "cùm enim etc., hâc ratione" is equivalent to the more classical form "quâ ratione, cùm" etc. ; this clearly could only refer to "Mori peccato," etc., which immediately precedes. Durel therefore shows that the "hereby" of the English Version refers to "A death unto sin, and a new birth unto righteousness," and in no way to "Baptism": and this is supported by the following considerations. First, the word "Baptism" does not occur at all in the question to which

* * * * * * * * *

---

this is an answer. Secondly, that "hereby" refers to "A death unto sin," etc., is also shown by the parallel question and answer which precede: "Quodnam est externum . . . in Baptismo?" "What is the outward . . . in Baptism?" (English Version) "Aqua quâ," etc. "Water; wherein," etc. "Quaenam est spiritualis," etc.? "What is the inward," etc.? "Mori peccato, . . . hâc ratione," etc. "A death unto sin, . . . hereby," etc. The words "hâc ratione" must refer to "Mori peccato," just as "quâ" refers to "Aqua." Thirdly, being "in peccato nati," what could be the "ratio" whereby we should become Sons of God except "Mori peccato"? The annulment of the Birth in Sin must be the Death unto Sin. (The Rev. E. Daniel makes "hereby" refer to "inward and spiritual grace," but it rather refers to the explanation of that grace; it refers to the commencement of this answer, and not to the Catechist's previous question.)

Dr. Adam Clarke writes, "Now I ask whereby are such persons made the children of grace? Not by the water, but by the death unto sin and the new birth unto righteousness, *i.e.*, through the agency of the Holy Ghost sin is destroyed and the soul filled with holiness."

The Greek versions of Petley and Duport have ἐντεῦθεν, which must refer to Ὁ θάνατος εἰς ἁμαρτίαν, κ.τ.λ. Duport also has the present tense γινόμεθα, "hereby we are becoming," etc., which of course could only refer to a continued process, and not to the single act of Baptism. For ἐντεῦθεν, referring to words immediately preceding, cf. Petley's answer corresponding to "Ad perpetuam," etc., below: there Petley has ἐντεῦθεν, answering to Durel's "indè," and plainly referring (as Duport's δι' αὐτῆς shows) to the "sacrifice of Christ's death" in the first part of the same answer.

The Welsh Prayer Book, indeed, has "Marwolaeth i bechod, a genedigaeth newydd i gyfiawnder. Canys gan ein bod ni wrth naturiaeth wedi ein geni mewn pechod, ac yn blant digofaint, drwy Fedydd y gwneir ni yn blant grâs." That is, "A death unto sin, and a new birth unto righteousness. For since we are by nature born in sin and children of wrath, through Baptism we are made children of grace." Upon this a Welsh clergyman writes to us: "The Substitution of 'through Baptism' (drwy

❊ * ❊ * * * * ❊ ❊

Fedydd) for '*hereby*' is a serious breach of the order to translate '*exactly* into the British tongue.'"

The Editions of Durel of 1670, 1680, 1685, 1687, 1696, and 1703 all have "hâc ratione." So have Parsell's of 1713 and 1716, and G. Bowyer's Editions of 1733 and 1744. So also has Harwood, 1785. So has J. W. Parker's "Liber Precum Publicarum," and Bagster (Ed. 1821).

Messrs. Bright and Medd read : " Mori peccato, et justitiae renasci ; cum enim naturaliter simus in peccato nati, et irae filii, per Baptismum gratiae filii facti sumus." Now we find no authority in the Latin Prayer Books for this substitution of "per Baptismum" for "hâc ratione," or "hereby." The phrase "per Baptismum" does certainly occur in Nowell's Catechisms, but not in this connection. Nowell says, "*per Baptismum in Ecclesiam admittimur, certiores facti filios Dei iam nos esse*" (Small Catechism) ; "through Baptism we are admitted into the Church, having been assured that we are already the children of God (Greek, σαφῶς εἰδότες ὅτι τέκνα Θεοῦ ἤδη ἐσμέν)." So in the Middle Catechism, "per baptismum in ecclesiam recipimur, certúmq ; habemus nos iam Dei filios esse," etc. ; "through baptism we are received into the Church, and have an assurance that we are already the children of God." So too in the Large Catechism, "baptismus veluti aditus quidam nobis est, per quem in eam (*sc*. Ecclesiam) admittimur ; unde et testimonium," etc.

According to Nowell, therefore, we are by Baptism (not made the Sons of God, but) admitted into the Church, and receive a pledge that we are already the Sons of God. Whence then comes the "Mori peccato, & denuo nasci justitiae," by which we are made the Sons of God, and of which Baptism is a Sign and Pledge? Regeneration comes, says Nowell, "*a morte & resurrectione Christi*" (Small Catechism), "per mortem & resurrectionem Christi" (Middle Catechism), "Non aliunde quam a morte et resurrectione Christi" (Large Catechism), "None other ways but from the death and resurrection of Christ" (Norton's Translation).

We may compare *Paraphrasis cum Annotatis ad Difficiliora loca Catechismi Anglicani*, 1674, to show to what "hereby" refers : " *Nam,*

Quæstio.	Question.
Quid ab iis requiritur qui baptizandi sunt?	What is needed by those who must be baptized?
Responsio.	*Answer.*
Resipiscentia, quâ deserant pecca-	Repentance, by which they may

cùm natura nati simus in Peccato, filiique Irae, hinc [id est, non per externum Baptizationis opus, sed per mortem ad Peccatum, & ortum ad Justitiam in Baptismo, etc.] facti sumus Filii Gratiae;" and in the English which follows, " *A death unto sin, and a New Birth unto Righteousness* [that is, a solemn and open Vow (by inward grace) to dye unto Sin, and to live unto Righteousness] *for being by nature born in sin, and the children of wrath, we are hereby* [that is, Not by the outward work of being Baptized, but by the death unto sin, and new birth unto righteousness, as but now these things have been explained; that is by the Vow in Baptism; for the Stipulation or Answere of a good conscience towards God, 1 *Pet.* 3. 21, seems to be nothing else but the Vow in Baptism] *made children of Grace.*"

f a c t i s u m u s : for the tense compare the second answer in the Catechism.

F i l i i D e i : "Sons of God." This Bagster retains. Note here the divergence from the English Version, which has "children of grace." Harwood has "filii Gratiae," as also Parsell (1713, 1716), and G. Bowyer, 1733, 1744. For Durel's version cf. Rom. viii. 13, 14 in Beza's Bible: "sed si Spiritu actiones corporis mortificetis, vivetis. Quotquot etiam Spiritu Dei aguntur, ii sunt filii Dei."

Q u i d a b i i s. See note below on " Quia utrumque" *sub fine.*

"*Quae requiruntur ab ijs, qui ad Baptismum accedunt?*" Τίνα δεῖ προσιέναι τοῖς προσερχομένοις τῷ βαπτίσματι; (Nowell's Small Catechism).

Τί ἔτι ἀπαιτεῖται ὑπὸ τῶν Βεβαπτισομένων; (Petley). Τί ζητεῖται ἐν τοῖς βαπτισθησομένοις; (Duport).

r e q u i r i t u r : or "is required from." In *Janua*, clock dials are said to "*ask* (requirunt) *divers engines or jimmals to make them go true.*" So in Cicero "in hoc bello Asiatico virtutes animi magnae et multae requiruntur" (*i.e.*, are necessary) Manil. 22. 64. So we use such words as "require" and "demand" in the sense of "need."

Bagster has a comma after "requiritur."

b a p t i z a n d i : for the readings of Nowell's Small Catechism see note on "Quid ab iis." "*qui baptismo sunt initiandi*" (Middle Catechism).

Petley has the future perfect; Duport the first future passive.

R e s i p i s c e n t i a, q u â, etc.

tum; & fides, quâ firmiter credant promissionibus Dei sibi factis in eo Sacramento. | forsake sin; & faith, by which they may steadily believe God's promises made to them in that Sacrament.

"*Fides, & poenitentia*" (Greek, Πίστιν καὶ μετάνοιαν). (Nowell's Small Catechism). It then continues: "*Haec planiùs explica.*" The answer to which is: "*Anteactae impiè vitae vehementer primùm poenitere, & certam fiduciam habere debemus, nos Christi sanguine à peccatis purgatos, atque ita Deo gratos esse spiritumque eius in nobis habitare. Et secundum fidem & professionem in Baptismo actam, omni ope enitendum, vt carnem nostram mortificemus, & pia vita declaremus nos Christum induisse, & eius spiritu donatos esse.*"

Cf. his Large Catechism: "*M.* Tell me then briefly in what things the use of baptism consisteth? *S.* In faith and repentance [Latin, "In Fide et Poenitentia"]. For first we must with assured confidence hold it determined in our hearts, that we are cleansed by the blood of Christ from all filthiness of sin, and so be acceptable to God, and that his Spirit dwelleth within us. And then we must continually, with all our power and endeavour, travail in mortifying our flesh, and obeying the righteousness of God (Latin, 'justitiae Divinae'), and must by godly life declare to all men that we have in baptism as it were put on Christ, and have his Spirit given us."

Petley has Μετάνοια, παρ' ἧς τὴν ἀνομίαν ἀπολιμπάνουσι· καὶ Πίστις, παρ' ἧς τοῦ Θεοῦ ἐπαγγελίαις, ταῖς ἐν τούτῳ τῷ Μυστηρίῳ πεποιημέναις, στερρῶς πεποίθασιν.

Duport has Μετάνοια· δι' ἧς τὴν ἁμαρτίαν ἀπολιμπάνουσι καὶ πίστις δι' ἧς, ταῖς τοῦ Θεοῦ ἐπαγγελίαις ταῖς ἐν τούτῳ τῷ Μυστηρίῳ πεποιημέναις, στερρῶς πεποίθασιν.

Resipiscentia: used as an equivalent to "poenitentia" in *Janua*.

"For that one interpreteth somthynge obscurely in one place, the same translateth another (orels he himselfe) more manifestly by a more playne vocable of the same meanyng in another place. Be not thou offended therfore (good Reader) though one cal repentaunce, that another calleth pennaunce or amendment. For yf thou be not deceaued by mens tradicions, thou shalt fynde no more dyuersite betwene these termes then betwene foure pens and a grote. And this maner haue I vsed in my translacyon, calling it in some place pennaunce, that in another place I cal repentaunce. And that not onely because the interpreters haue done so before me, but that the aduersaries of the trueth maye se how that we abhorre not this worde pennaunce (as they vntruly reporte of vs) no more then the interpreters of Latyn abhorre penitere, whan they reade resipiscere. Onely our hartes desyre vnto God is, that his people be not

Quæstio.	*Question.*
Qui fit itáque ut infantes Baptizen-	How does it accordingly come to

blynded in theyr vnderstondyng, lest they belieue pennaunce to be ought saue a very repentaunce, amendment, or conversyon vnto God, and to be an vnfayned newe creature in Christe, and to lyue accordynge to hys lawe. For els shall they fall into the olde blasphemye of Christes bloude, and beliue, that they themselues are able to make satisfaccyon vnto God for theyr own synnes, from the whiche erroure God of hys mercye and plenteous goodnesse preserue all hys" ("A Prologe to the Reader." Myles Couerdale's Bible, pub. Southwark, James Nycolson, 1537).

This shows how "repentance" and "penance" (*i.e.*, penitence), and the Latin "resipiscentia" and "poenitentia" were regarded as the same thing. Cf. Pareus, "Poenitentia est effectus gratiae, fluentis a dilectione Dei, in filio Dei fundata," for the meaning of "poenitentia."

In connection with the word Μετάνοια, which Nowell, Petley, and Duport use in this same context, we may quote the following from Dr. Harrison :—

"Subject: Repentance ($\mu\epsilon\tau\acute{a}\nu o\iota a$, $\mu\epsilon\tau a\nu o\acute{\iota}\omega$) and conversion ($\dot{\epsilon}\pi\iota\sigma\tau\rho o\phi\acute{\eta}$, $\dot{\epsilon}\pi\iota\sigma\tau\rho\acute{\epsilon}\phi\omega$) Biblically considered as used to express or to imply a spiritual change or turning for the better, showing that both designate one and the same thing. Jonah iii. 10 = Matt. xii. 41 ; Luke xi. 32. Ezekiel xiv. 6; and xviii. 30 = Acts iii. 19. In the ancient Peshito Syriac Version, in the first three texts, one and the same verb is used, and in the last three texts one and the same phrase.

"That each alike is required as a condition or prerequisite for the remission of sins, or in order to life. Ezekiel xviii. 32 ; Acts ix. 35 ; xi. 21 ; & xv. 3, 19 = Mark i. 4 ; Luke iii. 3 ; Acts ii. 38 ; xi. 18 ; 2 Cor. vii. 10 ; 2 Peter iii. 9.

"It is not presumed that the righteous, who have been converted, need conversion ; and according to Scripture the righteous do not need repentance. Matt. ix. 13 ; Mark ii. 17 ; Luke v. 32, and xv. 7. In all the above instances, in the Syriac Version the words 'to repent' or 'repentance' do not occur, but either 'to turn' or 'conversion.'

"It is certain then that the 'repentance' of Holy Scripture is one thing, and the 'repentance' of both ancient and modern theology, another and very different thing."

quâ deserant : equivalent to "ut eâ deserant." So "quâ credant" for "ut eâ credant." Note the Greek of Petley and Duport, ἀπολιμπάνουσι and πεποίθασιν, which, like the English Version, are positive and refer to present time.

firmiter : "steadily," applied to ships in *Janua*.

tur, quum ob immaturam aetatem ista praestare non valeant? | pass that babes are Baptized, whereas on account of unripe age they are not able to perform those (things)?

D e i : Bagster has a comma after "Dei."
Qui fit itáque. "Qui fit" is "how cometh it to passe?" in *Janua*.
Nowell's Small Catechism has, "*Qui fit tum vt infantes baptizantur* (*sic*, and in 1633), *qui haec per aetatem hactenus praestare non possunt*. (*sic*, and in 1633). Remark the similarity to Durel's version.
The Greek versions here are remarkable. Πῶς οὖν νιογνὰ τὰ βρέφη (ἐπειδὴ δι' ἁπαλῆς τῆς νηπιότητος οὐχ οἷά τ' ἐστι ταῦτα διαπράττειν) ἐβαπτίσθη ; Petley. Duport has, Διὰ τί οὖν τὰ βρέφη βαπτίζονται, ὅτι διὰ τὴν νηπιότητα, καὶ τὸ ἁπαλὸν τῆς ἡλικίας ταῦτα· ποιεῖν μὴ δυνάμενα ;

Bagster begins, "Cur ergo infantes baptizantur," and has commas after "quum" and "aetatem."

infantes : "infans," "babe," *Janua*. "An infant was properly one *qui fari non potest*, a child not yet old enough to speak with understanding of what he said, *i.e.*, was below the age of seven years" (Sandar's "Institutes of Justinian," p. 341). The term of infancy in English law is thrice as long.

Baptizentur : on p. 160 the word is spelt with an "s." Nowell's Small Catechism has "*vt*" with the indicative ; Durel has rightly the subjunctive, and so has Nowell in his Large Catechism. The word has a small initial in Eds. 1685, 1687, 1696, and 1703.

quum : "quum" may take the subjunctive here as meaning "whereas," "although," or "since ;" or it may simply be "when," and "valeant" be subjunctive as depending upon a dependent sentence.

ob immaturam aetatem : "per aetatem," Nowell's Large and Small Catechisms, and in the Greek, οἱ νιογνοὶ οἱ μὴ δυνάμενοι ὑφ' ἡλικίας ἀποτελεῖν ταῦτα ; His Middle Catechism has "*qui ista propter infirmitatem aetatis efficere nequeunt?*" Note the Greek of Petley and of Duport above, the latter expressing the causes of incapacity by a double phrase.

"propter aetatem immaturam," Harwood.

praestare : Duport has ποιεῖν, for which compare the frequent use of ποιεῖν in the New Testament for "bearing" or "producing," as a tree produces its fruit. Cf. Matthew iii. 8, etc.

"ista praestare" may be "exhibit those [requisites]," or "discharge those [requirements]." "ista," of course, is "which you have named."

Quia utrumque. The Prayer Book of 1604 has "Yes ; they doe performe them by their sueties, who promise and vow them both, in their names : which when they come to age, themselves are bound to

Responsio.	Answer.
Quia utrumque promittunt per	Because they promise both one and

performe" (Ed. of Robert Barker, King's Printer). Nowell's Catechisms here are noteworthy. His Small Catechism has "*Quia ad Ecclesiam Dei pertinent* (Greek τῇ ἐκκλησίᾳ προσήκουσι), *& Dei benedictio, promissióque Ecclesiae facta per Christum, in cuius fide* (εἰς οὗ τὴν πίστιν) *baptizantur, ad eos pertinet* (ἐκείνοις προσήκει): *quae postquam adoleuerint, ipsos intelligere, credere, atque agnoscere oportet: enitique vt Christiani hominis officium, quod in Baptismo polliciti sunt atque professi, moribus & vitae* (*sic*, but "vita" 1633) *praestent.*"

In the Middle Catechism we have "Quia de Dei Ecclesia sunt, diuináque benedictio atque promissio ecclesiae per Christum, in cuius fide baptizantur, facta, ad eos pertinet. In quarum rerum cognitione, & fide, ipsi ineunte pueritia imbuendi sunt, vt agnoscant, quid in baptismo spoponderint atque professi sint," etc.

The answer in his Large Catechism (Norton's Translation) is as follows: "That faith and repentance go before baptism, is required only in persons so grown in years, that by age (Latin, 'per aetatem') they are capable of both. But to infants the promise made to the Church by Christ, in whose faith they are baptized, shall for the present time be sufficient; and then afterward, when they are grown to years (postquam adoleverint), they must needs themselves acknowledge the truth of their baptism, and have the force thereof to be lively in their souls, and to be represented in their life and behaviours."

Then, after comparing baptism with circumcision, Nowell continues: "*M.* Thinkest thou these so like, and that they both have one cause and order? *S.* Altogether. For as Moses and all the prophets do testify that circumcision was a sign of repentance, so doth St. Paul teach that it was a sacrament of faith. Yet the Jews' children, being not yet by age capable of faith and repentance, were nevertheless circumcised;" and further on he writes, "*S.* Sith it is certain that our infants have the force, and as it were the substance of baptism common with us (vim, et quasi substantiam Baptismi communem nobiscum habere), they should have wrong done them if the sign, which is inferior to the truth itself, should be denied them; . . . Therefore most great reason it is that by baptism, as by the print of a seal (impresso quasi sigillo), it be assured to our infants that they be heirs of God's grace, and of the salvation promised to the seed of the faithful" (Norton's Translation).

Dr. Cardwell ("History of Conferences," Third Ed., p. 357) gives the Answer of the Bishops to the Exception of the Ministers to the question, "*What is required*" etc.?—"The effect of children's baptism depends

| sponsores suos, quod promissum te- | the other through their sureties, which |

neither upon their own present actual faith and repentance (which the Catechism says expressly they cannot perform,) nor upon the faith and repentance of their natural parent or pro-parents, or of their godfathers or godmothers; but upon the ordinance and institution of Christ. But it is requisite that when they come to age they should perform these conditions of faith and repentance, for which also their godfathers and godmothers charitably undertook on their behalf."

Petley has Πάνυγε· ταῦτα γὰρ τυγχάνει διανύσαντα παρὰ τῶν κατεγγυητῶν τὰ ἀμφὼ ὑποσχομένων, καὶ ἐν ὀνόματι αὐτῶν εὐχομένων· ἃ ἐκ παίδων εἰς ἡλικίαν προβεβηκότες, ὑπόχρεω κατέχονται βεβαιοῦσθαι.

Duport's version is, Ὅτι ἀμφότερα ὑπιχνοῦνται (sic) διὰ τῶν ἐγγυητῶν αὐτῶν· (ἥν δήπου ὑπόσχεσιν εἰς ἡλικίαν ἥκοντα αὐτὰ ἐπιτελεῖν ὀφείλουσι).

utrumque: i.e., Repentance and Faith. "utrumque" is "each," or "both the one and the other:" "ambo" would have been "both together."

For the close connection between the two, cf. "His duobus summa doctrinae Evangelicae conprehendi solet. Non hic praeponitur poenitentia fidei quasi prior dignitate, vel tempore" (Tossanus). "Fides nisi praeluceat, nulla vera μετάνοια esse potest, licet adsit μεταμέλεια, qualis fuit in Juda" (Tossanus). "Poenitentia ad desperationem trahit, nisi fulciatur verâ fide de remissione peccati, ut est videre in Caino, Iudâ, Saule, etc." (Aretius). "Sine fide omnis poenitentia non solum odiosa est, sed expeditum iter ad desperationem" (Mentzerus). Cf. also "England's sole and Soveraign way of being saved," a preface to which was written by Dr. Manton of the Savoy Conference: here Zanch. in Hos. xiv. 1 is quoted: "Sine fide in Christum nulla vera resipiscentia esse potest."

sponsores: Hebrews vii. 22, "Tanto melioris pacti sponsor factus est Jesus" (Beza). To render the covenant of Baptism valid, the conditions must be fulfilled, and the vows performed which our sureties made.

suos. Bagster has a colon after "suos."

quod—praestare. The whole description of Baptism in the Catechism is based upon an assumption, which is hinted at in these words. The two parts of true Baptism might ordinarily be presumed to exist in the case of Adult Baptism. In early times adults had "before, or rather, at baptism itself" (says Nowell) to "render reason and account of their religion and faith." It is to this Adult Baptism after examination, which obtained in the primitive Church, that our Catechism refers; and accordingly it asks how infants come to be baptized. The answer is that they make through their sureties a promise binding upon themselves; and by

nentur ipsi praestare, postquam adoleverint,	promise themselves are bound to perform, after that they shall have come to youth.

the performance of this promise (which they are assumed to carry out), they fulfil after Baptism those conditions which adults were supposed to fulfil before Baptism, and must fulfil if the Baptism is to be true and effectual.

praestare. Duport's word here is ἐπιτελεῖν, whereas in the question he has ποιεῖν. He puts the clause "which—perform" in a parenthesis. For ἐπιτελεῖν compare the future of that verb used of God in the exposition of the Lord's Prayer in Duport.

postquam adoleverint. The age of "adolescentia" commenced strictly at fifteen years. *Youth* is here shown to be the time for fulfilling baptismal engagements. Nowell has the same words in his Large Catechism, and Norton translates them "when they are grown to years," and below, "after they were grown more in years." *Janua* also has "ubi adoleverint," "*being at full growth*." Harwood, "ut ex ephebis excesserint." At this point, in his Large Catechism, Nowell passes on to consider Confirmation. In explanation of a previous statement "that children, after they were more grown in years, ought to acknowledge the truth of their baptism," he writes: "*S*. Parents and schoolmasters did in old time diligently instruct their children, as soon as by age they were able to perceive and understand, in the first principles of Christian religion, . . . For the which purpose also little short books, which we name Catechisms, were written (breves libri, quos Catechismos nostri appellant, conscribebantur), wherein the same, or very like matters as we now are in hand with, were entreated upon. And after that the children seemed to be sufficiently trained in the principles of our religion, they brought and offered them unto the bishop. *M*. For what purpose did they so? *S*. That children might after baptism do the same which such as were older, who were also called *catechumeni*, that is, scholars of religion, did in old time before, or rather, at baptism itself. For the bishop did require and the children did render reason and account of their religion and faith: and such children as the bishop judged to have sufficiently profited in the understanding of religion he allowed, and laying his hands upon them, and blessing them, let them depart. This allowance and blessing of the bishop our men do call Confirmation." Rev. E. Daniel says the age meant in the Catechism is "so soon as he shall be able to learn what a solemn vow," etc. But that is the time when he is to be TAUGHT. Durel (Paedobaptismus Publicus): "Meminisse vos oportet vestri muneris esse ac officii, providere ut Infans iste doceatur, ubi primum per

Quæstio.	*Question.*
Quamobrem Sacramentum Coenae Domini institutum est ?	Wherefore has (the) Sacrament of (the) Lord's Supper been appointed ?

aetatem doceri potuerit, quam solemne votum," etc., and then follows the mode of instruction. Surely the age referred to is a time *after the Infant is instructed*, as Durel (Paedobaptismus Publicus), "& in Catechismo in eum finem edito, plenius instituatur." Cf. 61st Canon (1603), "Such as can render an account of their faith according to the Catechism in the said Book contained" (in which they have been instructed); and 112th Canon (1603), "Non-Communicants at Easter to be presented"— "all the Parishioners, as well men as women, which being of the age of sixteen years, received not the Communion at Easter before," indicates the age—*sixteen years:* and it shows that it was never intended at the Revision for *little children* to be confirmed, and then taken to the Holy Communion.

Quamobrem Sacramentum: Διὰ τί Μυστήριον τοῦ Κυριακοῦ Δείπνου ἐντέτακτο ; Duport. Petley has ἐγνωσμένον ἦν ; Nowell's Small Catechism commences the subject of the Lord's Supper as follows : "*Quae est Coena* (sic, *Coenae*, 1633) *dominicae ratio* (Greek, τύπος) ? " "*Eadem nimirum, quam Christus dominus instituit:* Qui ea, qua traditus est, nocte, accepit panem, & postquam gratias egisset, fregit, & dedit Discipulis suis, dicens : Accipite, edite, hoc est corpus meum, quod pro vobis datur : hoc facite in mei commemorationem. Ad eundem modum & calicem accepit, (peracta Coena) & gratijs actis, dedit eis, dicens. Bibite ex hoc omnes : Hic est enim Sanguis meus noui Testamenti, qui pro vobis & pro multis effunditur, ad remissionem peccatorum : Hoc facite, quotescunque biberitis, in mei commemorationem. *Hanc formam rationémque* (Greek, τοῦτον τὸν τύπον καὶ ταύτην τὴν διάταξιν) *Coenae Dominicae tenere, donec ipse veniat, & inuiolatè seruare, piéque atque religiose celebrare oportet.*"

The Middle Catechism has, for "*Hanc formam,*" etc., "Hanc praescriptionem atq ; hunc ordinem sequi," etc.

Two things are here worthy of remark. First, that Nowell retains the order of the Greek of Matthew xxvi. 27 (cf. Mark xiv. 24) in "Bibite ex hoc omnes." See note on "quae" in the answer to the next question. Secondly, that he says, "postquam gratias egisset" and "gratijs actis," "after that he had given thanks" and "when thanks had been given," and says nothing of blessing the elements. This is correct : for in Matthew xxvi. 26, 27 we have εὐλογήσας concerning the bread, and εὐχαριστήσας concerning the cup ; here the Authorized Version has "blessed *it*" in the former, and "gave thanks" in the latter case : the

| *Responsio.* | *Answer.* |
| Ad perpetuam memoriam sacrificii | For a continuous remembrance of |

Revised Version rightly has "blessed" simply, and "gave thanks." In Mark xiv. 22, 23, again, we have εὐλογήσας concerning the bread, and εὐχαριστήσας concerning the cup; here the Authorized Version has "blessed" in the former case, and "when he had given thanks" in the latter: the Revised Version has "when he had blessed," and "when he had given thanks." In Luke xxii. 19 we have εὐχαριστήσας concerning the bread, and simply ὡσαύτως [*sc.* εὐχαριστήσας] concerning the cup; here the Authorized Version has "gave thanks:" the Revised Version, "when he had given thanks." In 1 Cor. xi. 24 we have εὐχαριστήσας concerning the bread, and ὡσαύτως concerning the cup; the Authorized Version here has "when he had given thanks," and so too the Revised Version. The Revised Version has removed the liability to error which existed in the Authorized Version of Matthew xxvi. 26; εὐλογήσας is "having blessed" (as the Authorized Version rightly takes it in Mark xiv. 22), not "having blessed it" (*i.e.*, the bread): the object of εὐλογήσας is "God" understood, and in this way the εὐλογήσας of Matthew and Mark is equivalent to the εὐχαριστήσας of Luke and St. Paul. In "giving thanks" or "blessing God" Christ conformed Himself to the Jewish custom of acknowledging God as the author of every good and perfect gift. This they did at their ordinary meals by giving thanks on taking the bread and taking the cup. In fact the Jews were forbidden to eat or drink without rendering thanks to God, and he who transgressed this command was held guilty of sacrilege. The Jewish form of blessing, which in all probability Christ employed upon this occasion, is as follows: on taking the bread, "Baruch atta Elohinoo, Melech, haôlam, ha motse Lechem min haarets," "Blessed be thou, our God, king of the universe, who bringest forth bread out of the earth!" and on taking the cup, "Baruch Elohinoo, Melech, haôlam, Boré perey haggephen,' "Blessed be our God, the king of the universe, the creator of the fruit of the vine." From this it is clear that the *blessing God*, and the *giving thanks* refer to one and the same act. This custom still obtains among the Jews; as one example among many, see the "Sketch of the Life and Journal of the Rev. J. Wolff, Missionary to Palestine and Persia:" "I would not recite the prayer before washing hands because it says that is commanded of God, but performed that they use on breaking the bread! 'Blessed be thou, oh Lord our God, King of the worlds! who hast brought forth the bread from the earth.'" Again, in describing a wedding, Mr. Wolff writes: "Mercado [the high priest] took the cup of wine, saying, 'blessed art thou, O Lord our God, king of the world!'"

mortis Christi, & beneficorum quae | (the) sacrifice of Christ's death, &
indè percipimus. | of (the) benefits which we receive
| thence.

Nowell's Small Catechism then continues "*In quem usum?*" which question corresponds to "Quamobrem—institutum est?" The word "institutum" is the only equivalent in Durel's version for the account of institution in Nowell.

C o e n a e : Ed. 1687 has "Coeni." Eds. 1685, 1696, and 1703 have "Coenae" rightly.

A d p e r p e t u a m : Πρὸς ἀδιάλειπτον ἀνάμνησιν τῆς θυσίας τοῦ θανάτου τοῦ Χριστοῦ, καὶ τῶν εὐεργεσιῶν ὧν δι' αὐτῆς μεταλαμβάνομεν. Duport. Petley's version was the same with a different order of words, and ἐηνεκῆ for ἀδιάλειπτον, no article with θανάτου, ἐντεῦθεν for δι' αὐτῆς, and μετεσχηκότες ὦμεν for μεταλαμβάνομεν.

Nowell's Small Catechism has a longer answer : "*Vt mortis Domini, summique beneficij illius* [beneficijq'; maximi in nos per eam collati, Middle Catechism], *quo per eam affecti sumus, gratam perpetuò memoriam celebremus & retineamus : & sicuti in Baptismo renati sumus, ita Coena Dominica ad vitam spiritualem atq; sempiternam iugiter* (Greek ἀηνικῶς) *alamur atque sustentemur. Ideòque semel baptismo initiari, vt semel nasci, satis est* [vt semel in lucem edi, ita & baptismo semel expiari sat est, Middle Catechism]: *at Coena* (sic) *Dominica* (sic), *perinde atque alimenti, vsus identidem est repetendus.*"

Harwood has "Ut in perpetuum memoriae proderetur sacrificium mortis Christi, et beneficia nobis inde collata."

Messrs. Bright and Medd commence this answer " In perpetuam commemorationem Sacrificii mortis Christi," etc., continuing as Durel.

A d : for "ad" of purpose ; cf. Ter. Heaut. 4. 4. "ad discordiam."

p e r p e t u a m : "perpetuis nexibus," "*by bonds—all along*," *Janua*. Duport's ἀδιάλειπτον is "uninterrupted," "with no gap left."

m e m o r i a m : "The Lord's Supper is rightly said here to be for a *Remembrance* of it, not a Repetition as the Church of *Rome* teaches" ("Secker's Lectures on Catechism," vol. ii. 239).

Rev. E. Daniel says there is a second sense of Remembrance, "as a memorial of. This second sense relates to the sacrificial aspect of this sacrament." He says the " Holy Communion is a memorial sacrifice." Durel's word certainly expresses nothing of that sort. Cf. Homily concerning the Sacrament : " Neither can he be devout, that otherwise doth presume than it was given by the Author. We must then take heed, lest of the memory, it be made a sacrifice."

Quæstio.	*Question.*
Quaenam est pars externa, seu signum Coenae Domini?	What part pray is (the) outward (part), or (the) sign of (the) Lord's Supper?

---

beneficiorum: "*to take in good part a poor present* (munusculum boni consulere), *to acknowledge a good turn* (beneficium)," in *Janua*. "beneficiorum" of course depends upon "memoriam."

indè: *sc.* "per mortem Christi," or, "per sacrificium mortis Christi." Cf. Nowell's Small Catechism above, "*per eam*" (*sc.* mortem), and so his Middle Catechism. So too Duport has δι' αὐτῆς (*sc.* τῆς θυσίας τοῦ θανάτου); the gender of course precludes reference to "sacrament." Petley has ἐντεῦθεν.

percipimus. Eds. 1685, 1687, 1696, and 1703 have "percepimus," the perfect tense. The English Version has the present.

The word might refer to a mental action, "perceive," but more probably it means "receive." It occurs again in the next answer but one, and in the question which follows it. The verb appears to mean literally "to take thoroughly," or perhaps rather, "to take through some medium." Ernesti, in his "Clavis Ciceroniana," quotes from N. D. ii. 59 a passage which well illustrates the sense of mediate taking: "per arteriam (through the windpipe) vox a mente principium ducens (the voice *drawing its beginning from the mind*) percipitur et funditur." It is true that he adds that Davies would read "projicitur" and Buherius, "praecipitatur" there, but he further adds that he himself sees no cause for change: "*Nempe vox*," he writes, "*per arteriam venit in os, ore percipitur*, h. e. *colligitur, excipitur: quo sensu* percipere *dici constat*." So it has an agricultural meaning, in the sense of *gathering in fruits*, and so here we might translate "gather," "harvest," or again, "ingather," or "appropriate:" cf. Cic. de Off. i. 18. 59. and ii. 3. 12. And so, philosophically used, "percipere (says Ernesti) *dicitur de iis rebus, quas certo scimus, quae comprehenduntur, quibusque sine errandi periculo assentimur.*"

Quaenam est pars: Τί ἄρα ἐστὶ τὸ ἔξω μέρος, ἢ τὸ σύμβολον τοῦ Κυριακοῦ Δείπνου; Duport. This is substantially the same as Petley's, who, however, has ἐκτὸς, not ἔξω; and σημεῖον, not τὸ σύμβολον.

Nowell again has a question and answer here, which are not in our Catechism. His Small Catechism reads: "*Quae sunt huius Sacramenti partes, atque materia?*" "*Duplici materia, vel partibus duabus* [Greek, Ἐκ δυοῖν μὲν μεροῖν for both] *hoc sacramentum, perinde atque baptismus constat quarum vna terrena* [Greek, γηΐνον] *est atq; sub sensus cadens* [Greek, αἰσθητόν]: *altera coelestis* [οὐράνιον] *est quae sensibus externis*

THE CATECHISM.

Responsio.	*Answer.*
Panis & Vinum, quae Dominus jussit accipi.	Bread & Wine, which (things) (the) Lord has bidden to be taken to oneself.

percipi non potest [τὰς ἔξωθεν λανθάνον αἰσθήσεις]." He then proceeds with a question corresponding to "Quaenam—Domini?" "*Quae est huius Sacramenti terrena & sensibilis pars?*"

s e u ; rightly used here, as the "pars externa" and "signum" are the same: Harwood also has "seu;" it is quite Ciceronian in this sense of "or," not equivalent to "or if;" and so too in *Jantua*.

s i g n u m : Bagster has a comma after "signum."

C o e n a e. Ed. 1687 again has "Coeni." Eds. 1685, 1696, and 1703 have "Coenae."

P a n i s & V i n u m . In his Large Catechism Nowell has : "*M*. Dost thou say that there are two parts in this sacrament also, as in baptism? *S.* Yea. The one part, the bread and wine, the outward signs, which are seen with our eyes, handled with our hands, and felt with our taste; the other part, Christ himself, with whom our souls, as with their proper food, are inwardly nourished" (Norton's Translation).

Nowell's Small Catechism has "*Panis & vinum* [Greek, Ο ἄρτος, καὶ ὁ οἶνος : *sic*], *quibus vtrisq ; vt omnes peraequè* [Greek, ἐξίσης ἅπαντας] *vterentur, Dominus disertè praecepit.*"

Duport has Ἄρτος καὶ οἶνος, οὕς ληφθῆναι προσέταξεν ὁ Κύριος. The relative clause in Petley is ἄττα κατὰ τὴν τοῦ Κυρίου ἡμῶν διάταξιν ἀποσχόμεθα.

Harwood's answer is the same as Durel's.

P a n i s. "In the Lord's Supper, there is *Bread* and *Wine* for the *Matter*. The giving it to be Eat and Drunk, with the Words that our Saviour used in the first Supper, are the *Form*. 'Do this in remembrance of me' is the Institution." Bishop Burnet, in "Exposition of the Thirty-nine Articles," London, 1699, p. 270. See note on "signum, aut forma." Note also that it is to be "bread," not wafer stamped with similitudes contrary to the second Commandment. Durel says, "Satis erit si modo Panis sit vulgaris usus ; sed lectissimus & ex meliore tritico confectus qui commode parari queat."

q u a e : neuter gender and plural number: not "which bread" only, nor again, "which Christ," but simply "which things," or "which elements."

It implies both the inanimate and material character of the elements, and the necessity for the use of both kinds. Thus Nowell (Small Catechism) "*quibus vtrisq ; vt omnes peraequè vterentur,*" etc, ; and in his Large Catechism : "*M*. And dost thou say that all ought alike to receive

Quæstio.	*Question.*
Quaenam est pars interna seu res significata?	What part pray is (the) inward (part) or (the) thing signified?

both parts of the sacrament? *S.* Yea verily, master. For sith the Lord hath expressly so commanded, it were a most high offence in any part to abridge his commandment" (Norton's Translation).

In "A Rational Account of the grounds of Protestant Religion," by Bishop Stillingfleet, London, 1665, we find the following remark: "it is learnedly proved by *Pet. Picherellus* ['*P. Picherel. de Missâ.* c. 4.' in margin], that the *bread* was appointed to represent not the *body* in its compleat *substance*, but the meer *flesh*, when the *blood* is out of it, according to the division of *Sacrifices* into *flesh* and *blood;* from whence it appears, that the *Sacrifice* of Christs death cannot be represented meerly by *one* kind," etc.

Cf. also Matt. xxvi. 27, Πίετε ἐξ αὐτοῦ πάντες, and Mark xiv. 24, ἔπιον ἐξ αὐτοῦ πάντες, in both of which passages the word "all" occupies an unusual and emphatic position: we might translate the first, "Drink of it all men," or, "Drink of it every man" (for it is not πάντες ὑμεῖς, as in ver. 31, but simply πάντες), and the second, "they drank of it all of them," or, "they drank of it every man."

Note that here is the Communion signified by the bread and wine. The Apostle had said (1 Cor. x. 4), "that Rock was (or signified) Christ," and then (ver. 16) he says, "the cup of blessing which we bless, is (or signifies) it not the communion of the blood of Christ? The bread which we break, is (or signifies) it not the communion of the body of Christ?"

jussit. The command "Do this," etc., is as imperative as the mandates of the Moral Law revealed to Moses.

accipi. Bagster has "sumi jussit." "accipere," as Conington puts it (Index to Georg. of Virgil), is a correlative to "dare." "Accipere," to take to oneself; "recipere," to take back; "percipere," to take thoroughly or through a medium; "sumere" (see below), to take up, lay hold of. "Tenemus quae sunt in nostra potestate; sumimus posita (things stationary); accipimus data (what is offered)." Isidorus, Diff. 1.

Quaenam est pars. Τί τὸ ἔσω, ἢ τὸ σημαινόμενον [*sc.* μέρος]; (Duport). Petley had Τί ἐί τὸ ἔγκατον μέρος, ἢ τὸ αἰνιττόμενον;

Nowell's Small Catechism has "*Coelestis illa pars & remota ab omnibus externis sensibus* (Greek, μὴ αἰσθητὸν) *quaenam est?*"

seu. Eds. 1685, 1687, 1696, 1703 have a comma before "seu." "seu" implies that "pars interna" and "res significata" are equipollent. Cf. the Table of the Sacraments in App. G. Harwood also has "seu."

Responsio.	Answer.
Corpus & sanguis Christi, quae	Christ's body & blood, which

significata: "significare," "*to certifie of*," in *Janua*. Eds. 1685, 1687 have a full stop after "significata." Eds. 1696 and 1703 have a note of interrogation.

Corpus & sanguis Christi: Τὸ σῶμα καὶ τὸ αἷμα τοῦ Χριστοῦ, ἅπερ ἀληθῶς καὶ ὄντως ὑπὸ τῶν πιστῶν ἐν τῷ Κυριακῷ Δείπνῳ λαμβάνονται (sic) καὶ μετέχονται (sic). Duport. Petley had the same with some difference in the order, no article before αἷμα, and κεκόμισται καὶ παρείληπται for the verbs. Harwood has the same as Durel.

Nowell (Small Catechism) has a somewhat longer answer: "*Corpus & sanguis Christi, quae in coena dominica fidelibus dantur* [Greek ἃ οἱ πιστοὶ προσενεχθέντα αὐτοῖς ἐν τῷ κυριακῷ δείπνῳ λαμβάνουσι], *ab illisque accipiuntur, eduntur, & bibuntur, coelesti tantùm spiritualique modo* [οὐρανίῳ μόνον καὶ πνευματικῷ τινι τρόπῳ], *reuera tamen* [ἀληθεῖ δὲ καὶ γνησίῳ], *adeo quidem, vt sicuti panis corpora nutrit: ita & Corpus Christi animas nostras spiritualiter per fidem* [πνευματικῶς διὰ πίστεως] *alat: & sicut vino hominum corda exhilarantur, & roborantur vires: ita Sanguine Christi animae nostrae reficiantur atque recreantur per fidem* [διὰ πίστεως], *qua ratione corpus & sanguis Christi in Coena recipiuntur. Nam Christus sibi fidentes* [τοῖς γε πιστοῖς] *tam certò facit corporis atque sanguinis sui participes, quàm certò se panem atque vinum ore & ventriculo recepisse sciunt.*"

The guarded manner in which Nowell insists upon the necessity of *faith* to a due reception of the Sacrament is worthy of all attention. We subjoin a translation: "The body & blood of Christ, which (things) in the lord's supper are given to the faithful, and by those are taken, eaten, & drunk, in a heavenly and spiritual manner only, yet in truth, so far indeed, that like as the bread nourishes (our) bodies : so also Christ's Body feeds our souls spiritually by faith : & like as by the wine men's hearts are cheered, & (their) strength confirmed : so by Christ's Blood our souls are relieved and refreshed by faith, by which method Christ's body & blood are received in the Supper. For Christ as surely makes them that believe in him partakers of his body and blood, as they surely know that they have received the bread and wine with (their) mouth & stomach." In this translation we have followed, where possible, Norton's language in the Large Catechism.

Nowell's Middle Catechism concludes this answer thus: "*Coena etiam Dominica vitae nobis sempiternae signa communicans. immortalitatis nobis nostrae pignus, atque resurrectionis obses existet.*"

quae. See note on "quae" in last answer.

verè & re ipsa sumuntur, & percipi- | (things) truly & in very deed are
untur à fidelibus in Coena Domini. | taken, & received by (the) faithful
| in (the) Lord's Supper.

---

verè & re ipsa: or "really," "in reality" for "re ipsa." Cf. Cic. Rosc. Am. 15. 44: "ab re ipsa atque a veritate." ἀληθῶς καὶ ὄντως (*i.e.*, truly and essentially), Duport. ὄντως καὶ ἀληθῶς, Petley.

Nowell's Small Catechism, "*reuera tamen*," ἀληθεῖ δὲ καὶ γνησίῳ (τρόπῳ). Middle Catechism, "verè tamen, atque re ipsa," ἀληθῶς δὲ καὶ ὄντως.

In "A Supplement to the Commentary on the Book of Common Prayer," Wm. Nicholls, D.D., A.D. 1711, we find certain "*Puritans objections against the Common-Prayer, answered*." This work is in the Bodleian Library, and the answers are said to be by Tho. Hutton, "*Printed* Anno Dom. 1606," *i.e.*, two years after the portion on the Sacraments was added to the Catechism. "Exception 14" is as follows: "*The Catechism saith further, that the Body and Blood of Christ are* verily and indeed taken and received of the faithful: *which savours too much of Transubstantiation*," etc.' The Answer to this is: "In this Sentence is set down a Difference between *Anabaptists* and *Papists*: The one making them bare and naked Signs; the other the real and corporal Presence. Here one Clause distinguisheth both dangerous Opinions (*the Body and Blood of Christ verily and indeed:*) So then not only bare and naked Signs: (*are taken and received*.) So then not (*are* only) as if there was a Stop or Breath (but *are taken and received*) to shew that they are not if out of use, and out of use if not (*taken, and taken and received of the faithful*) as if no Faith, then *verily* and *indeed* no Body nor Blood of Christ:" etc. We give the original pointing, in accordance with our uniform rule, though the sense here is rather obscured by the punctuation.

"Verily and indeed" means that the communion is true and real in the case of the faithful in the Lord's Supper. Physically, the communicant takes and eats the bread with the hand and mouth of the body. Mentally, he does so in remembrance that Christ died for him; in a spiritual and heavenly manner the body of Christ is given to him and taken and eaten by him by means of faith; he feeds on Christ in his heart by faith with thanksgiving.

sumuntur. Bagster has no comma after this word. In Arnold's Döderlein, under SUMERE, we find the extract from Cic. Phil. xii. 7: "Saga sumpsimus, arma cepimus;" but in Cic. de Off. iii. 1. 2, "sumere" seems to be used of that which a man takes *voluntarily*, as distinguished from that which he is compelled to take. See note on "accipi" above:

THE CATECHISM.

Responsio.	*Answer.*
Corpus & sanguis Christi, quae	Christ's body & blood, which

significata: "significare," "*to certifie of,*" in *Janua*. Eds. 1685, 1687 have a full stop after "significata." Eds. 1696 and 1703 have a note of interrogation.

Corpus & sanguis Christi: Τὸ σῶμα καὶ τὸ αἷμα τοῦ Χριστοῦ, ἅπερ ἀληθῶς καὶ ὄντως ὑπὸ τῶν πιστῶν ἐν τῷ Κυριακῷ Δείπνῳ λαμβάνονται (sic) καὶ μετέχονται (sic). Duport. Petley had the same with some difference in the order, no article before αἷμα, and κεκόμισται καὶ παρείληπται for the verbs. Harwood has the same as Durel.

Nowell (Small Catechism) has a somewhat longer answer: "*Corpus & sanguis Christi, quae in coena dominica fidelibus dantur* [Greek ἃ οἱ πιστοὶ προσενεχθέντα αὐτοῖς ἐν τῷ κυριακῷ δείπνῳ λαμβάνουσι], *ab illisque accipiuntur, eduntur, & bibuntur, coelesti tantùm spiritualique modo* [οὐρανίῳ μόνον καὶ πνευματικῷ τινι τρόπῳ], *reuera tamen* [ἀληθεῖ δὲ καὶ γνησίῳ], *adeò quidem, vt sicuti panis corpora nutrit: ita & Corpus Christi animas nostras spiritualiter per fidem* [πνευματικῶς διὰ πίστεως] *alat: & sicut vino hominum corda exhilarantur, & roborantur vires: ita Sanguine Christi animae nostrae reficiantur atque recreantur per fidem* [διὰ πίστεως], *qua ratione corpus & sanguis Christi in Coena recipiuntur. Nam Christus sibi fidentes* [τοῖς γε πιστοῖς] *tam certò facit corporis atque sanguinis sui participes, quàm certò se panem atque vinum ore & ventriculo recepisse sciunt.*"

The guarded manner in which Nowell insists upon the necessity of *faith* to a due reception of the Sacrament is worthy of all attention. We subjoin a translation: "The body & blood of Christ, which (things) in the lord's supper are given to the faithful, and by those are taken, eaten, & drunk, in a heavenly and spiritual manner only, yet in truth, so far indeed, that like as the bread nourishes (our) bodies: so also Christ's Body feeds our souls spiritually by faith: & like as by the wine men's hearts are cheered, & (their) strength confirmed: so by Christ's Blood our souls are relieved and refreshed by faith, by which method Christ's body & blood are received in the Supper. For Christ as surely makes them that believe in him partakers of his body and blood, as they surely know that they have received the bread and wine with (their) mouth & stomach." In this translation we have followed, where possible, Norton's language in the Large Catechism.

Nowell's Middle Catechism concludes this answer thus: "*Coena etiam Dominica vitae nobis sempiternae signa communicans, immortalitatis nobis nostrae pignus, atque resurrectionis obses existet.*"

quae. See note on "quae" in last answer.

verè & re ipsa sumuntur, & percipiuntur à fidelibus in Coena Domini.	(things) truly & in very deed are taken, & received by (the) faithful in (the) Lord's Supper.

---

verè & re ipsa: or "really," "in reality" for "re ipsa." Cf. Cic. Rosc. Am. 15. 44: "ab re ipsa atque a veritate." ἀληθῶς καὶ ὄντως (*i.e.*, truly and essentially), Duport. ὄντως καὶ ἀληθῶς, Petley.

Nowell's Small Catechism, "*reuera tamen*," ἀληθεῖ δὲ καὶ γνησίῳ (τρόπῳ). Middle Catechism, "verè tamen, atque re ipsa," ἀληθῶς δὲ καὶ ὄντως.

In "A Supplement to the Commentary on the Book of Common Prayer," Wm. Nicholls, D.D., A.D. 1711, we find certain "*Puritans objections against the Common-Prayer, answered.*" This work is in the Bodleian Library, and the answers are said to be by Tho. Hutton, "*Printed* Anno Dom. 1606," *i.e.*, two years after the portion on the Sacraments was added to the Catechism. "Exception 14" is as follows: "*The Catechism saith further, that the Body and Blood of Christ are* verily and indeed taken and received of the faithful: *which savours too much of Transubstantiation*," etc. The Answer to this is: "In this Sentence is set down a Difference between *Anabaptists* and *Papists*: The one making them bare and naked Signs; the other the real and corporal Presence. Here one Clause distinguisheth both dangerous Opinions (*the Body and Blood of Christ verily and indeed*:) So then not only bare and naked Signs: (*are taken and received.*) So then not (*are* only) as if there was a Stop or Breath (but *are taken and received*) to shew that they are not if out of use, and out of use if not (*taken, and taken and received of the faithful*) as if no Faith, then *verily* and *indeed* no Body nor Blood of Christ:" etc. We give the original pointing, in accordance with our uniform rule, though the sense here is rather obscured by the punctuation.

"Verily and indeed" means that the communion is true and real in the case of the faithful in the Lord's Supper. Physically, the communicant takes and eats the bread with the hand and mouth of the body. Mentally, he does so in remembrance that Christ died for him; in a spiritual and heavenly manner the body of Christ is given to him and taken and eaten by him by means of faith; he feeds on Christ in his heart by faith with thanksgiving.

sumuntur. Bagster has no comma after this word. In Arnold's Döderlein, under SUMERE, we find the extract from Cic. Phil. xii. 7: "Saga sumpsimus, arma cepimus;" but in Cic. de Off. iii. 1. 2, "sumere" seems to be used of that which a man takes *voluntarily*, as distinguished from that which he is compelled to take. See note on "accipi" above:

Quæstio.	*Question.*
Quaenam sunt beneficia quae indè percipimus?	What benefits pray are (the benefits) which we receive thence?

"sumere" is "sub-imere (emere)," to take up, lay hold of; cf. N. T. λάβετε φάγετε.

à fidelibus: emphatic as coming after the verb. ὑπὸ τῶν πιστῶν, Petley and Duport.

Nowell's Small Catechism, "*fidelibus,*" οἱ πιστοί, "*per fidem,*" and ἐὰ πίστεως twice, "*sibi fidentes,* τοῖς γε πιστοῖς. Cf. the whole answer, as given in note on "Corpus & sanguis Christi," and also his Large Catechism: "*M.* Are then the only faithful fed with Christ's body and blood? *S.* They only. For to whom he communicateth his body, to them, as I said, he communicateth also everlasting life" (Norton's Translation). In his vocabulary to the Large Catechism Nowell defines "fidelis" as "pro tali fide praedito," standing for one endowed with such faith; this faith he had explained to include "not only knowledge of God, and readiness of belief, but also trust in God."

Tho. Marschall, D.D., in "The Catechism etc. Briefly Explained," 1679, writes : " The Body and Blood of Christ are really received into the heart of the worthy Communicant, by the grace of faith."

Quaenam sunt beneficia. Bagster has a comma after "beneficia."

Ποῖ ἄττα ἐστὶ τὰ εὐεργετήματα ὧν ἐντεῦθεν μέτοχοι ὄντες τυγχάνομεν; Duport. Petley had Τίνα ποτ' ἐστ. τὰ ὠφελήματα, ὧν ἐνταῦθα μέτοχοι τυγχάνομεν ὄντες; There is no question in Nowell corresponding to this, as the subject matter of the answer is included in the last answer, which is given in the note on " Corpus & sanguis Christi."

Harwood has "Quaenam beneficia apud nos inde collata sunt?" Parsell (Ed. 1713) had "collocata;" Ed. 1733, "collata."

indè: *i.e.,* from the Lord's Supper participated in by the faithful. ἐντεῦθεν, Duport; ἐνταῦθα, Petley.

Messrs. Bright and Medd have, for "quae indè percipimus," "quorum per hoc sumus participes?" To what "per hoc" refers is at least not obvious.

percipimus. See note on "percipimus" above.

Animarum nostrarum corroboratio: Ἐπίρρωσις καὶ ἑστίασις τῶν ἡμετέρων ψυχῶν διὰ σώματος καὶ αἵματος τοῦ Χριστοῦ, καθάπερ τὰ σώματα ἡμῶν διὰ τοῦ ἄρτου καὶ οἴνου ἐπιρρώννυνται (sic) τε καὶ ἀνατρέφονται (sic). Duport. Petley had, Ἐπιρρώννυσις καὶ ἀνάπαυλα ἡμετέρων τῶν ψυχῶν . . . (as Duport), μετὰ τοῦ ἄρτου καὶ οἴνου ἐστὶ τεθραμμένα. Harwood has the

Responsio.	Answer.
Animarum nostrarum corroboratio & recreatio per corpus & sanguinem	An invigorating & refreshing of our spirits through Christ's body &

same as Durel, but "confirmatio" and "confirmantur" for "corroboratio" and "corroborantur," and "et" for "ac."

The matter of this answer is included in the fuller answer of Nowell's Small Catechism, which we quote above in the note on "Corpus & sanguis Christi." Nowell then continues with further explanations upon the important subjects of the identity or permanence of the substance of the bread and wine, and of the non-sacrificial character of the ceremony: "*An ergo panis* [ὁ ἄρτος] *& vinum* [ὁ οἶνος] *in substantiam* [τὴν ... οὐσίαν] *corporis & sanguinis Christi mutantur?*" Are then therefore the bread and the wine changed into the substance of the body and blood of Christ? "*Minime: illud enim esset naturam sacramenti, quod è materia coelesti atq; terrena constare oportet, extinguere?*" No: for that would be to extinguish the nature of a sacrament, which (*sc.* sacrament) ought to consist of a heavenly and also an earthly material. "*An instituta fuit a Christo Coena, vt Deo patri sacrificium pro peccatorum remissione offeratur?*" Has then the Supper been ordained by Christ, in order that a sacrifice may be offered to God the father for the remission of sins? "*Nequaquam. Est enim peccati, atque illi debitae damnationis onus tam graue, tam immensum immaneque pondus, vt solus Dei filius Iesus Christus sacrificium, quo nos ab illis liberaret, facere posset. Quum ergò Seruator noster Christus ipse in cruce se morti pro nobis obtulit, vnicum* [*sic*, but "unicam" 1633. The Greek of both is τὴν μίαν (*sic*)] *illam perfectam sempiternámq; hostiam, Deo patri gratissimam, ad peccati expiationem semel in perpetuum immolauit, scelerum nostrorum maculas sanguine suo eluens atq; delens ad nostram in aeternum salutem. Nobis verò nihil reliqui fecit, nisi vt fiduciam atque spem omnem firmissime in illo collocemus, sempiternṭq; illius sacrificii vsum fructum gratis animis capiamus: quod quidem in Coena Dominica maximè facimus.*" By no means. For the burden of sin, and of the damnation due to it is so heavy, the weight so immeasurable and enormous, that only God's son Jesus Christ was able to make a sacrifice which should free us from them. When therefore our Saviour Christ offered himself to death on the cross for us, he made once for ever unto the expiation of sin that only perfect and everlasting sacrifice, most pleasing to God the father, washing away and blotting out with his own blood the spots of our sins unto our eternal salvation. But he made nothing left for us, except to place (our) confidence and all hope most firmly in him, and to take the use and benefit

| Christi; quemadmodum pane & vino corpora nostra corroborantur ac recreantur. | blood; in such wise as our bodies are invigorated and refreshed by (the) bread & (the) wine. |

of that everlasting sacrifice with grateful hearts, which indeed we chiefly do in the Lord's Supper.

This answer, "Animarum," etc., points to the mental and spiritual operation; and "quemadmodum pane & vino," etc., proves that the bread and wine are still bread and wine.

If they are not bread and wine, then what the Lord commanded to be taken (jussit accipi) is not there. And if the body and blood of Christ are under the form of bread and wine, and put into the communicant's hand by a priest, they are not given or taken in a heavenly and spiritual manner, and the means whereby they are received is not faith: for the process is under the eye.

In "The Catechism etc. Briefly Explained," Tho. Marschall, D.D., Rector of Lincoln College, 1679, there is a very clear statement on this answer: "The strengthning and refreshing of our Souls &c.] as the Soul, or inward man, to be here fed, is a Spirit: so the Body and Blood of Christ is a spiritual food, and is to be received after a spiritual manner."

corroboratio. This appears not to be a classical word. Harwood has "confirmatio." Nowell (Small Catechism) uses "*alat*" of the "Corpus," and "*reficiuntur atque recreantur*" of the effect of the "Sanguis" upon our souls "*per fidem.*" With regard to our bodies, he uses "*nutrit*" of the bread, and "*corda exhilarantur*" and "*roborantur vires*" of the action of the wine.

"corroborantia:" "*strengthening*," *Janua*.

recreatio: or, "recruiting," or "reanimation." See last note. Messrs. Bright and Medd have "refectio," and below "reficiuntur."

In *Janua* we have "sopor recreat," "refresheth:" the verb is used classically of both body and mind.

pane & vino: "the bread and wine" probably, not "bread and wine;" for both Petley and Duport have the article. It is also worthy of note that they place both "bread" and "wine" under the vinculum of a common article, τοῦ ἄρτου καὶ οἴνου, the two elements being jointly and indivisibly necessary to the due administration of the Sacrament. See note on "Animarum," etc.

corroborantur: the Latin here supplies the ellipsis which the English leaves.

Quæstio.	*Question.*
Quid ab iis requiritur qui accedunt ad Coenam Domini?	What is needed by those who come to (the) Lord's Supper?

Quid ab iis. Τί ζητεῖται ἐν τοῖς ἐπὶ τὸ Κυριακὸν Δεῖπνον ἐρχομένοις; Duport. Τί ξῆτα εἰσπράττονται οἱ πρὸς Κυριακὸν τὸ Δεῖπνον φοιτῶντες; Petley.

Nowell's Small Catechism has "*Nostrum quod est officium, vt rectè ad Coenam dominicam accedamus?*" [Middle Catechism, "*Quomodo officio nostro satisfaciemus, vt ritè coenam Dominicam celebremus?*] The answer to this is: "*Ut nosipsos exploremus, num vera simus Christi membra.*" He then continues, "*Quibus id notis deprehendemus?*"

requiritur. Bagster has a comma after this word.

Ut probent: "Ut explorent seipsos" (Harwood).

Nowell has a somewhat longer answer in his Small Catechism. It runs thus: "*Primùm si ex animo nos poeniteat peccatorum nostrorum: deinde, si certa spe de Dei per Christum misericordia nitamur, atque nos sustineamus, cum grata redemptionis per mortem eius acquisitae, memoria. Praeterea, si de vita in futurum piè degenda seriam cogitationem & destinatum propositum suscipiamus. Postremò, cum coniunctionis etiam, charitatisque inter homines mutuae Symbolum in Coena dominica contineatur, si proximos, id est mortales omnes, fraterno amore, sine vlla maleuolentia odióue prosequamur.*" With this answer Nowell's Small Catechism concludes.

Ut. All this answer of course depends upon "requiritur" in point of construction. Τὸ ἐοκιμάζειν ἑαυτοὺς, Petley and Duport.

probent: "Lydio lapide probamus metalla an proba sint," "*with a touchstone we try metals, whether they be good*" (*Janua*). Cf. 1 Cor. xi. 28, ἐοκιμαζέτω ἑαυτόν. See last note.

seipsos: the examination is to be self-conducted, not confession to another, much less to a Priest.

num: the correct word for "whether," where there is only one division of a question. The three questions here introduced by "num" are independent of one another. εἰ ἄρα γε, Petley and Duport. "an," Harwood.

praecedentium—poeniteat: literally "it repents them of foregoing sins." Bagster here has "num praeteritorum eos peccatorum vere poeniteat."

propositum: "purpose," *Janua*. βεβαίως προῃρημένοι, Duport. Cf. the Aristotelian προαίρεσις, and such passages as τῷ γὰρ προαιρεῖσθαι τἀγαθὰ ἢ τὰ κακὰ ποιοί τινές ἐσμεν (Eth. iii. 2), etc.

Responsio.	Answer.
Ut probent seipsos, num verè praecedentium peccatorum eos poeniteat, firmum propositum habentes novam	That they may try their very selves, whether they are sorry truly for previous sins, having a steady purpose of

novam vitam: "*Vita nova*, pro innocentia" (Nowell, Vocabulary to Large Catechism). See next note.

instituendi: "of beginning." Cf. note on "*Institutio*" in the heading of the Catechism, and contrast the English Version, "to lead a new life," and the Greek (διάγειν) of Petley and Duport. This divergence is worthy of note. Duport also has τὸν καινὸν βίον, "*the* new," not "*a* new life." "Instituere," in *Janua*, is "*to take in hand*." Cf. also Tert. adv. Herm. c. 12: "horum enim" lapidum, *sc.* viperarum, hominum, "natura, habendo institutionem, habere poterit et cessationem." Harwood agrees with Durel here, though in different language: "firmiter in animo instituentes novam vitae rationem."

num fidem vivam habeant: in other words, "num fideles sint," whether they are of the class who alone can duly receive the Sacrament. See note on "à fidelibus" above. Καί γε ἔχωσι πίστιν ζῶσαν (Duport). Petley has ἔχοντες πίστιν τὴν βιώσιμον.

misericordiam: "misericordia," Bagster. But both Petley and Duport have εἰς τὸ ἔλεος. Harwood has the ablative with "in;" Messrs. Bright and Medd have the dative.

gratâ memoriâ mortem illius recolentes. This points to the memorial character of the Lord's Supper. μετὰ τῆς εὐχαρίστου ἀναμνήσεως τοῦ θανάτου αὐτοῦ (Duport). μετὰ τῆς εὐχαριστικῆς θανάτου αὐτοῦ ἀειμνηστίας (Petley). See 'memoriam,' p. 175.

recolentes. This verb is properly to "till" or "work anew," so to "think over," or "recall to mind." There is no equivalent for this word in the English Version, or in Petley or Duport.

eâ. Bagster has a comma after "eâ" and after "est," but Eds. 1685, 1687, 1696, and 1703 agree with Ed. 1670 in the pointing of this passage.

charitate: "love or charity" (*Janua*). Bagster, "caritate."

Note the divergence from the English Version, which has simply "and be in charity with all men." Duport has, καὶ πρὸς ἅπαντας ἀνθρώπους τὴν ἀγάπην ἐνδεικνύωσι. Petley before him had, Τελευταῖον δὲ, πρὸς ἅπαντας τοὺς ἀνθρώπους ἐν τῇ ἀγάπῃ διακείμενοι. Harwood agrees with Durel, having, however, "complectantur" for "amplectantur." Messrs. Bright and Medd have "denique, utrum ad omnes habeant charitatem."

"But hereto these things that I have spoken of do tend, that every

vitam instituendi; num fidem vivam habeant in misericordiam Dei per Christum, gratâ memoriâ mortem

beginning a new life; whether they have a living faith on God's tenderheartedness through Christ, with

man bring with him to the supper, repentance, faith, and charity [Lat. charitatem], so near as possibly may be, sincere and unfeigned" (Nowell's Large Catechism. Norton's Translation).

The Revised Version of the New Testament substitutes "love" for "charity" in all passages. To such a substitution three objections we think might be offered. First, that there is a great difference between ἀγάπη and ἔρως, or even φιλία, between "charitas" and "amor," between "charity" and "love." Archbishop Trench writes in his "Synonyms of the New Testament," Ed. 7th, pp. 39, 40: "there are aspects in which the 'diligi' is more than the 'amari,' the ἀγαπᾶσθαι than the φιλεῖσθαι. The first expresses a more reasoning attachment, of choice and selection ('*di*ligere'='*de*ligere'), from a seeing in the object upon whom it is bestowed that which is worthy of regard; or else from a sense that such is due toward the person so regarded, as being a benefactor, or the like; while the second, without being necessarily an unreasoning attachment, does yet give less account of itself to itself; is more instinctive, is more of the feelings or natural affections, implies more passion; . . . while men are continually bidden ἀγαπᾶν τὸν Θεόν (Matt. xxii. 37; Luke x. 27; 1 Cor. viii. 3), and good men declared so to do (Rom. viii. 28; 1 Peter i. 8; 1 John iv. 21), the φιλεῖν τὸν Θεόν is commanded to them never."

And again, p. 41: "I observe in conclusion that ἔρως, ἐρᾶν, ἐραστής, never occur in the N. T., . . . Their absence is significant; in part no doubt to be explained from the fact that, by the corrupt use of the world, they had become so steeped in earthly sensual passion, carried such an atmosphere of unholiness about them (see Origen, *Prol. in Cant. Opp.* tom. iii. pp. 28–30), that the truth of God abstained from the defiling contact with them; yea, devised a new word for itself rather than betake itself to one of these."

Upon similar grounds we object to the substitution of "love" for "charity," because the latter is pure of the pure, whereas the former is tainted with the defilements of the world.

The second objection is that as ἀγάπη was a new term coined to express a new idea, so in our English translation of 1611, the translators were right in using a new word which had no worldly connotation attaching to it. Archbishop Trench writes (*loc. cit.* p. 41): "it should not be forgotten that ἀγάπη is a word born within the bosom of revealed religion: it occurs in the Septuagint (2 Sam. xiii. 15; Cant. ii. 4; Jer. ii. 2), and

| illius recolentes; num tandem eâ quâ par est charitate omnes homines amplectantur. | thankful remembrance recalling his death; whether lastly with that charity with which it is fit they embrace all men. |

in the Apocrypha (Wisd. iii. 9); but there is no trace of it in any heathen writer whatever, and as little in Philo or Josephus; . . . But the reason may lie deeper still. Ἔρως, as has been the case with so many other words, might have been consecrated anew, despite of the deep degradation of its past history; and there were tendencies already working for this in the Platonic use of the word, namely, as the longing and yearning desire after that unseen but eternal Beauty, the faint vestiges of which may here be everywhere traced; . . . But in the very fact that ἔρως did express this yearning desire . . . this longing after the unpossessed . . . lay its deeper unfitness to set forth that Christian love, which is not merely the sense of need, of emptiness, of poverty, with the longing after fulness, not the yearning after an unattained and here unattainable Beauty; but a love to God and to man, which is the consequence of God's love already shed abroad in the hearts of his people."

In a similar spirit an able writer in the *Edinburgh Review* says of the word "charity" itself, that readers "would instinctively divine that this venerable and rythmical word was specially consecrated to the use of the Apostle, that he might describe more accurately and more impressively the inexpressible grace of that love which never shone in the eyes of men till God had given them the Son of his Love."

The third objection which we have to make to the change is that the loss of the term "charity" from the New Testament would render unexplained the numerous passages throughout our Liturgy (*e.g.*, in the Litany, two Collects, Baptism private and adult, Commination, Holy Communion, Ordering of Presbyters and Deacons, and Catechism, besides Art. XXXIX.), and the writings of divines in which some form of that word occurs; and would tend to increase its employment in the narrower sense of "alms-giving," and decrease its wider and nobler use. We conclude by subjoining a few out of numberless examples of such an use from early times, in its Latin or English garb: "Charitas semper redditur & semper debetur" (Augustine, Ps. xxxiii. tom. viii. p. 94). Beza has the word throughout the New Testament for ἀγάπη, except in Jude 12: "Hi sunt in agapis vestris maculae, dum vobiscum convivantur securè se ipsos pascentes," etc. In "The Sick mans Salue," a black letter book, dated 1564, in our possession, the author of which was Thos. Beacon (who signed the certificate made by the Cathedral Church of Canterbury to the Archbishop's Commissary in reply to the Queen's Letters to

Parker), we find as follows: "Epaph. Surelie I thinke him no good christean, nor friend unto his country (which if he be able) refuseth to help forward the studies of good wittes, I praie you neighbour Philemon, set in two hundred poundes of monie, one hundred to be given to the Universitie of Cambridge, the other unto Oxford. Phile. This is a godlie and charitable deed. Epaph. The high waies may not be forgotten, whiche in manie places are verie foule & ieopardous. unto the repairing of them, I give fortie poundes. write it. For I think this also to be a deed of charitie, and a commendable worke before GOD, to repaire high waies, that the people may safelie and without danger trauell by the waie." And further on, "give mee Lorde thy grace, that my Faith, and persuasion in thy blood waver not in me, but ever be firme and constant, that the *hope* of thy mercie and life everlasting, never decaie in me, that charity waxe not cold in mee." Then we have Hooker: "concerning charity, the final object whereof is that incomprehensible beauty which shineth in the countenance of Christ, the Son of the living God." And Milton's line :—

> " add faith,
> Add virtue, patience, temperance; add love,
> By name to come called charity, the soul
> Of all the rest."

Again, "*Now walkest thou not charitably*] That is, thou transgressest the law of Charity, which commands the(e) to love thy neighbour as thy self" ("Paraphrase and Commentary upon the Epistle of Saint Paul to the Romans." By W. Day, M.A., Divinity Reader in his Majesties Free Chappel of Saint George within the Castle of Windsor. Lond., 1666)." There is a countless array of such passages, the correct comprehension of which would be much endangered by a suppression of the pure and intelligible term "Charity" in the Sacred Writings.

APPENDIX D.

Archbishop Leighton's Catechism.

It is interesting to compare this contemporary Catechism with Durel's upon points of importance. Robert Leighton, who became Archbishop of Glasgow and was also Principal in the University of Edinburgh, was consecrated Bishop of Dumblane Dec. 12, 1661, by Gilbert Sheldon, then Bishop of London, whose name we have had occasion to mention in connection with the orders of Convocation for the Latin translation of the Prayer Book (see Part I. chap. ii.). Gilbert Sheldon enjoyed many promotions; he was Fellow of All Souls, Chaplain to the Lord Chancellor, and to Charles I., Warden of All Souls, Dean of the Chapel Royal, Bishop of London, and Master of the Savoy in 1661, at the time of the Savoy Conference; he presided at the Session of Convocation in 1662, and as Archbishop of Canterbury at that in 1664, on the occasions of the discussion of the Latin Prayer Book. He held the Archbishopric until 1677, seven years after the publication of the Latin Prayer Book of Durel. He was also Chancellor of the University of Oxford, and Founder of the Sheldonian Theatre. In the consecration of Leighton, Sheldon was assisted by three others, one of whom (Stern, Bishop of Carlisle, afterwards Archbishop of York) was a Reviser.

I. Questions and Answers as to "The Sacraments."

Having stated the Gospel doctrine, John iii. 16, and the Gospel practice, Titus ii. 12, and declared that thus to live is "so absolutely necessary, that they that do not in some good measure, whatsoever they profess, do not really believe in Jesus Christ, nor have any portion in him," Leighton proceeds to explain the Sacraments :—

"*Q.* What visible seals hath our Saviour annexed to that gospel, to confirm our faith, and to convey the grace of it to us?

"*A.* The two sacraments of the New Testament, baptism and the Lord's supper.

"*Q.* What doth baptism signify and seal?

"*A.* Our washing from sin, and our new birth in Jesus Christ.

"*Q.* What doth the Lord's supper signify and seal?

"*A.* Our spiritual nourishment and growth in him, and transforming us more and more into his likeness, by commemorating his death, and feeding on his body and blood, under the figures of bread and wine.

"*Q.* What is required to make fit and worthy communicants of the Lord's supper?

"*A.* Faith in our Lord Jesus Christ, and repentance towards God, and charity towards all men.

"*Q.* What is faith in our Lord Jesus?

"*A.* It is the grace by which we both believe his whole doctrine, and trust in him as the Redeemer and Saviour of the world, and entirely deliver up ourselves to him, to be taught and ruled by him, as our Prophet, Priest, and King.

"*Q.* What is repentance?

"*A.* It is a godly sorrow for sin, and a hearty and real turning from all sin unto God."

II. "A Question for young Persons before their first Admission to the Lord's Supper."

"*Q.* Whereas you were in your infancy baptized into the name of Jesus Christ, do you now, upon distinct knowledge, and with firm belief and pious affection, own that Christian faith of which you have given an account, and withal your baptismal vow of renouncing the service of Satan, and the world, and the lusts of the flesh, and of devoting yourself to God in all holiness of life?

"*A.* I do sincerely and heartily declare my belief of that faith, and own my engagement to that holy vow, and resolve, by the assistance of God's grace, to continue in the careful observance of it all my days."

(From "The Works of Robert Leighton, D.D., Archbishop of Glasgow," p. 506. Ross, Edinburgh. MDCCCXXXIX.)

APPENDIX E.

ON DR. OVERALL'S OPINION OF THE LORD'S SUPPER.

"228. In sec. 222 above, your minister rightly infers from the definition of a sacrament as given in the Catechism that whoever receives the sacrament receives the outward and visible sign and the inward and spiritual grace. But this modern definition of a sacrament, which I have shown in my *Answer to Dr Pusey's Challenge*, vol. I., pp. 358-360, is Zwinglian in its origin, does not teach that the outward visible sign, whether water, bread or wine, contains in it the inward and spiritual grace. According to the Catechism there are two sacraments, but one definition equally applies to both. Now no one pretends that water, the outward visible sign, contains the inward and spiritual grace, that is a death unto sin and a new birth unto righteousness, and no one ought to pretend that the outward visible sign, or the outward part or sign of the Lord's Supper, contains the inward and spiritual grace, or the body and blood of Christ and the benefits received thereby. Hooker has well said, 'although it [the grace of baptism] be neither 'seated in the water, nor the water changed into it, what should induce men to 'think that the grace of the Eucharist must needs be in the Eucharist, before it 'can be in us that receive it? The fruit of the Eucharist is the participation of 'the body and blood of Christ. There is no sentence of Holy Scripture which 'saith that we cannot by this sacrament be made partakers of His body and blood 'except they be first contained in the sacrament, or the sacrament be converted 'into them.'—*Eccles. Pol.*, b. v. 67.

"229. It should be noticed that Hooker died before that part of the Catechism was framed which contains the modern definition of a sacrament; he of course uses the word sacrament as anciently defined by Augustine (sec. 44, 45, above). . . .

"230. The Catechism does not teach such a presence in the consecrated elements, and it is not true that 'it states distinctly the doctrine of the Eucharistic presence,' as believed by your minister. The Catechism states that 'the body and blood are 'verily and indeed taken and received by the faithful in the Lord's Supper;' but this gives no proof that the body and blood are received in the bread and wine. In the above words there is an obvious allusion to the words of our Lord in the sixth chapter of St John where He says, 'Whoso eateth my flesh, and drinketh 'my blood, hath eternal life, and I will raise him up at the last day. For my flesh 'is [verily or] indeed meat, and my blood is [verily or] indeed drink.' (John vi. 54, 55.) According to the plain teaching of our Lord, there must be a reception of His flesh and blood in order to the attainment of eternal life. But we have no evidence whatever in that chapter that the reception must be through the means of a sacrament, much less that the flesh and blood in order to be received must be really present in the sacramental elements. A large amount of evidence has been already given in this letter to show that according to the common teaching of the Fathers, even in the sixth century, the flesh and blood of Christ could be savingly received without the Lord's Supper, and before any could rightly receive the body and blood of Christ in the Lord's Supper, they must first be made that body and blood, and so receive the sacrament or mystery of what they really were (sec. 55, 56, 62, 64, 65, 99, above). The Fathers, and the Reformers, Zwingle not excepted (sec. 72, 73), doubtless believed that although the body and blood of Christ had been, or ought to have been, received, before coming to the Lord's Supper, yet the same body and blood were received in that holy ordinance to confirm the life already received and to confer it more abundantly. But as in the first instance the body and blood could not be received otherwise than by faith, so neither can they be received through any other medium in the Lord's Supper. The 28th Article as noticed in sec. 221 above is very explicit on this point. The consecrated symbols rank with the written or spoken word of God, only the former, according to Augustine, in comparison of the latter, are visible words. The Catechism too limits the reception of the body and blood in the Lord's Supper to the faithful. It is true that your minister has given instances as recorded in sec. 223, 224 above, in which the word faithful as a designation of a body of professed Christians must not be construed too literally, inasmuch as all professing Christians are not always what they profess, or what they ought to be. It would have been more to the purpose if your minister had showed that the word faithful is never used in any other sense than as including the unfaithful. It cannot be questioned that the word is here used in its proper sense not as designating a promiscuous number of Christians among whom there might be many who were unfaithful or unbelieving, but as designating those alone who had the requisite aptitude to receive the body which alone was possessed by the faithful or those who truly believed in Christ."

"232. Your minister instructs you that Bishop Overall compiled the latter part of the Catechism, but he really deceives you, as he probably has been deceived, when he would persuade you that the declaration of its doctrine, as given in sec. 226 ['The body and blood of Christ is really and substantially present, and is so

exhibited and *given* to *all* that receive it;' etc.] above, is from the pen of Overall, for it is simply and absolutely untrue. . . . The passage stands in the 'Additional Notes on the Common Prayer,' appended to Dr Nicholls's *Comment on the Book of Common Prayer*. Dean Goode truly says, 'Respecting this pas-
' sage, though adduced with such confidence, and pressed as having all the
' weight which Overall's name and position could give it, it is only necessary to
' inform the reader that it was no more written by Bishop Overall than by himself
' [Archdeacon Denison], and that the compiler of the Catena [in the *Defence* of
' Archdeacon Denison], unless he took it at second hand, must have been aware
' of this. For, in the first place, the statement prefixed to these Notes by Dr
' Nicholls is, that they are "MSS. Notes, written in an interleaved Common
' Prayer Book, in the Bishop of Durham's Library, printed in the year 1619, SUP-
' POSED to be made *from the Collections of Bishop Overall*, BY A FRIEND OR
' CHAPLAIN OF HIS." And in two of these Notes occur statements showing that
' Bishop Overall was *not* the author of them, and that though they were written by
' some one who was chaplain or other personal attendant on Overall, they do not
' profess to be given from his papers. . . .'"

"234. In the *Defence* of Archdeacon Denison, page 34, the following is quoted as expressing the true teaching of Bishop Overall, 'That in the sacrament of the
' Eucharist, or the Lord's Supper, the body and blood of Christ, and therefore the
' whole of Christ, is verily and indeed present, and is verily partaken by us, and
' verily combined with the sacramental signs, as being not only significative, but
' exhibitory; so that in the bread duly given and received, the body of Christ is
' given and received; in the wine given and received, the blood of Christ is given
' and received; and thus there is a communion of the whole of Christ, in the com-
' munion of the sacrament. . . .' 'Yet not in any bodily, gross, earthly manner,
' as by transubstantiation, or consubstantiation, or any like devices of human
' reason, but in a mystical, heavenly, and spiritual manner, as is rightly laid down
' in our Articles.'—*As quoted and translated in Knox's Remains*, vol. II., p. 168.

"235. In reply to this I shall give you the remarks of Dean Goode, and a correct report of the real sentiments of Bishop Overall. The Dean remarks, 'Unfortun-
' ately Mr Knox gives not the slightest intimation whence his extract is taken. . .
' Whence, therefore, Mr Knox derived the statement on the doctrine of the
' Eucharist which he attributes to Overall, I am not aware. He tells us, however,
' that the occasion on which this statement was made was this: that " having, in
' some public disputation, so expressed himself respecting the Eucharist, as to
' excite jealousy in the minds of the puritanical hearers, he thought it necessary
' explicitly to declare what he believed on the subject." And then he gives the
' words which are quoted in the Catena. Now, I shall not stop to make any
' remark on the interpretation that might be given to these words, because it has
' yet to be proved that Overall was the author, and I have not yet found the least
' trace of them elsewhere. And I am still less disposed to do so, because being
' anxious to ascertain, if possible, what really passed on the occasion alluded to, I
' instituted a search for any notice of it I could find, and fortunately discovered
' among the Harleian MSS. at the British Museum, what I suppose will be
' admitted to be the most authentic account of the matter, namely, *one drawn up*

'by Bishop Overall himself. The matter referred to occurred in the year 1599
'when Dr Overall was complained of to the Vice-Chancellor of Cambridge (where
'he was Regius Professor in Divinity), for having publicly propounded in the
'schools certain unsound positions. In the MS. to which I refer, Dr Overall
'gives an account of the proceedings, and in this paper he thus states the matter,
'so far as our present subject is concerned:—"THEY PRETENDED THAT I SHOULD
'AFFIRM that . . . 5. The body and blood of Christ is really and substantially
'present in the Eucharist. I did not solemnly affirm it;" but thus, "In the
'sacrament of the Eucharist the body and blood of Christ, and thus whole Christ
'is applied to those who receive WORTHILY, not by way of transubstantiation, *nor*
'*by the way of consubstantiation*, but BY THE HOLY SPIRIT WORKING THROUGH
'FAITH," &c. Now here we have Bishop Overall's own account of the matter,
'and he says that he stated his doctrine on the subject thus. Could I wish for a
'more satisfactory statement of his doctrine?'—*Ibid.*, vol. II., pp. 829, 830."

(From *The True Bread of Life, and How to receive it*. By John Harrison, D.D.).

APPENDIX F.

ON AUGUSTINE'S USE OF THE WORD "SACRAMENT."

"It will be necessary here to define the word *sacrament*, and to show how it is used by the Fathers. Augustine, who is the greatest of the Fathers, gives the most ample testimony upon this point,—a portion of it must suffice for our present purpose.

"44. He says, 'Signs, when they appertain to divine things, are called sacra-
'ments.'"—*Epist.* v. *ad Marcel.*, tom. II. p. 9.

"45. 'A sacrament is a sign of a sacred thing.'—*De Civ. Dei* lib. x., c. 1, tom. V., p. 193.

"46. 'They (sacraments) receive, for the most part, the names even of the things
'themselves. As, therefore, *after a certain manner* (*quemdammodo*), the sacrament
'of the body of Christ is the body of Christ, the sacrament of the blood of Christ is
'the blood of Christ . . . As speaking of baptism itself, the Apostle says, "We
'are buried with Christ by baptism into death." He does not say, We signify
'burial; but he says outright, "We are buried." Therefore the sacrament of so
'great a thing he called by no other name than that of the thing itself.'—*Epist.* xxiii. *ad Bonifacium*, tom. II., p. 36.

"47. 'Because all things which represent other things appear in a certain manner
'(*quodammodo*) to sustain the characters of those things which they signify, as it is
'said by the Apostle, "that Rock was Christ," since the rock of which this was
'spoken signified Christ.'—*De Civ. Dei*, lib. xviii., c. 48, tom. V., p. 238.

"48. 'Nor may it be denied that sometimes the thing which signifies, receives the
'name of that thing which it signifies.'—*Epist.* cii., *ad Evodium*, tom. II., p. 173.

"49. Wishing to prove to a Manichæan that the words 'The blood is the life' (Deut. xii. 23), must be interpreted figuratively, and not literally, among other instances, Augustine gave the two following:—'For the Lord hesitated not to say, '"This is my body," when He gave a sign of His body . . . For the blood was 'so life as the Rock was Christ. Thus the Apostle says, "For they drank of that 'Rock which followed them, and that Rock was Christ." But it is known that the children of Israel drank water of the smitten rock in the wilderness, of whom the Apostle spoke when he said these things; he did not, however, say, the rock 'signified Christ, but said the Rock was Christ. Which again, that it might not 'be understood carnally, he calls it spiritual; that is, he teaches that it should be 'understood spiritually.'—*Contra Adiman.*, c. xii., tom. VI., p. 78."

(From *The True Bread of Life*, etc.)

APPENDIX G.

ANALYTICAL TABLE OF THE SACRAMENTS.

I BAPTISMUS ......
  1. *externum visibile signum?* Aqua *aut forma?* quâ quis Baptisatur, *In Nomine*, etc.
     [*pars interna seu res significata?* . . . .]
  2. *spiritualis & interna gratia?* Mori peccato, etc.: cum enim etc., hâc ratione etc.

  a. *Quamobrem* (Sacramentum) *institutum?* . . . .
  b. *Quid requiritur?* Resipiscentia, & Fides (Infantes utrumque promittunt per sponsores suos).

II. COENA DOMINI
  1. *pars externa, seu signum?* Panis & Vinum.
     [*aut forma? . . .*]
     [*pars interna seu res significata?* Corpus & sanguis Christi.]
  2. *beneficia quae inde percipimus?* Animarum nostrarum corroboratio, etc.

  a. *Quamobrem* (Sacramentum) *institutum?* Ad perpetuam memoriam, etc.
  b. *Quid requiritur?* Ut probent seipsos, etc.

Note 1. "Quamobrem institutum?" not answered for Baptism.
  2. "pars interna seu res significata?" not mentioned in Baptism; Christ did not himself explain the thing signified by Water, as he did explain the thing signified by Bread and Wine. He did not say of the water "this is" or "signifies" this or that.

3. There is a confusion possible between "pars interna," *i.e.*, "res significata," and "pars (una Sacramenti)," *i.e.*, "interna spiritualis gratia."
4. The "forma" of the Lord's Supper is not given, but only hinted at in " quae Dominus jussit accipi."
5. "beneficia," etc., in the Lord's Supper stands for "interna spiritualis gratia."

APPENDIX H.

On the Use of the Adverb "generally" and Cognate Words.

I. In Johnson's Dictionary, by Rev. H. J. Todd, M.A., F.S.A., and M.R.S.L., Chaplain in Ordinary to his Majesty, London, 1827, only four meanings are given for "generally:"—"1. In general; without specification or exact limitation." "2. Extensively, though not universally." "3. Commonly; frequently." "4. In the main; without minute detail; in the whole taken together."

II. Illustrations of its use up to the close of the seventeenth century:—

"Flaterie is generally wrongful preising" ("Persones Tale").—*Chaucer*, 1328-1400.

"Generally we would not have those that read this work of Sylva Sylvarum account it strange that we have set down particulars untried" ("Natural History"). —*Francis Bacon*, 1561-1626.

"I've been bold,
For that I knew it the most general way"

("Timon:" this passage is quoted by Johnson for sense of "common; usual").— *Shakespeare*, 1564-1616.

"In like sort amongst Papists, fasting at first was generally proposed as a good thing."—*Robert Burton*, 1576-1640.

"Which is only a wise observation that is generally true and in many respects, but not absolutely and universally" (Works p. 153).—*Archbishop Tillotson*, 1630-1694.

"*Aristotle* observed long since, that moral and proverbial sayings are understood to be true generally and for the most part" (*loc. cit.* p. 113.)—Ibid.

"Religion hath generally this effect, though in some cases, and as to some persons, it may be accidentally hindred" (*loc. cit.* p. 114).—Ibid.

"Things in this world... though they generally happen according to the probability of Second Causes, yet sometimes they fall out quite otherwise" (*loc. cit.* p. 359).—Ibid.

"But the particular occasion of this Canon is generally supposed to be this" ("A Rational Account," etc. : the Imprimatur is 1664).—*Bishop Stillingfleet*, 1635—1699.

"That in a general sense they (the Ten Tribes) were called the people of God, as they were Abraham's seed according to the flesh by reason of the promise made to Abraham, etc.; he never dreamt that the ten Tribes were Abraham's seed according to the Spirit; but only sayes, that there was salvation for those thousands that had not bowed their knees to Baal, which cannot be in the ordinary way where there is no Church" (*loc. cit.*).—Ibid.

"For a *Candle* yields but a dim uncertain light, may be put into a *dark lanthorn* and *snuffed* at pleasure; so would your *church* fain pretend of the *Scripture* that its *light* is very *weak* and *uncertain* that your *church* must open the sides of the *Lanthorn* that it may give light and make use of some *Apostolical Snuffers* of the *Popes* keeping to make it shine the *clearer* though they often endanger the almost extinguishing of it; at least as to the generality of those who should enjoy the benefit of it" (*loc. cit.*).—Ibid.

"Though it (this religion) be as generally professed, and as clearly taught among us, as ever it was in any nation, there are but few that are ever the better for it" ("Private Thoughts").—*Bishop Beveridge*, 1638-1708.

"How comes it to pass that his doctrine and precepts are so generally slighted and neglected as they are in our days" (*loc. cit.*)?—Ibid.

"The love of riches and temporal enjoyments is the great reason why men are guilty of such great and atrocious crimes as generally they are" (*loc. cit.*).—Ibid.

"To consider what it is that he requires of those that follow him, in order to be his disciples; a thing as easily understood, as it is generally disregarded" (*loc. cit.*).—Ibid.

"Generally speaking, they have been gaining ever since, though with frequent interruptions" (quoted by Johnson for the meaning of "In the main").—*Swift*, 1667-1745.

"Generally speaking, they live very quietly" ("Guardian").—*Addison*, 1672-1719.

"Where the author speaks more strictly and particularly on any theme, it will explain the more loose and general expressions" ("Improvement of Mind").—*Watts*, 1674-1748.

"The Sides were generally clos'd about the Ancles with Buttons, which were sometimes of solid Gold, or Silver" ("Antiquities").—*Archbishop Potter*, 1674-1747.

"It is probable, that this Piece of Armour was at first either peculiar to the *Grecians*, or at least more generally used by them than other Nations" (*loc. cit.*).—Ibid

APPENDIX I.

On "Generally Necessary."

"You 'ask me to tell you what the Catechism means of sacraments *generally necessary to salvation, and any reason or reasons for my definition.*' To do justice to this subject would take a volume, but I can offer no more than a few lines. *The English Church by affirming that the two sacraments are* GENERALLY *necessary to salvation ignores the Roman Catholic doctrine of baptism being the divinely appointed means or instrument of spiritual regeneration, and by anticipation the same doctrine as held by a certain class of Churchmen.* Dean Hook in his Church Dictionary, under the heading 'Regeneration,' remarks, '*We believe that it* (*the doctrine of baptismal regeneration*) *is repudiated by all Dissenters, except the Romish, who, amidst their many errors, retain this evangelical truth.*' But this doctrine is also repudiated by all 'Christian and Reformed Churches.' For they teach that baptism is the sacrament or sacred sign of regeneration. Rogers, in the earliest exposition which we have of the Articles, states 'Baptism of St. Paul is called the washing of the new birth, of others the sacrament of the new birth, to signify how they which rightly (as all do not) receive the same, are ingrafted into the body of Christ, as by a seal be assured from God that their sins be pardoned, and forgiven, and themselves adopted for the children of God, confirmed in the faith, and so increase in grace, by virtue of prayer unto God. And this is the constant doctrine of all Churches Protestant and Reformed' (p. 276).

"All these Reformed Churches maintain that man is justified or saved by faith only, which is plainly the doctrine of our Church. Luther and those who follow him, notwithstanding their views of the nature of the sacraments, in no respect differ from Zwingle and the other Reformers as to their use. Dr. Pusey rightly says, 'The Zwinglians, then, rightly urged, "All other places of the Confession wherein the sacraments are treated of, confirm our opinion and manifestly exclude that of the Lutherans or Ubiquitarians." For the thirteenth Article stands thus: 'Of the use of sacraments, they teach, that sacraments were instituted, not only to be tokens of profession between men, but rather to be signs and witnesses of God's will toward us, set forth to excite and confirm faith in those who use them.' This is the doctrine of our twenty-fifth Article. Concerning this doctrine the Council of Trent fulminates its curse. 'If any one saith, that these sacraments were instituted for the sake of nourishing faith alone: let him be accursed.' *On the Sacraments in general.* Can. V.

"Children are baptized as 'in the number of Thy faithful and elect children,' and they are baptized, not *really* 'to wash away their sins,' but 'mystically,' that is, sacramentally or symbolically, 'to wash it away.' So that baptism is a sacrament or sacred sign of regeneration.

"Jewel, in his Treatise on the Sacraments, states, 'Infants have the promise of salvation; why should they not receive the seal whereby it is confirmed unto them? They are of the fellowship of the faithful. Augustine saith: "Where place you young children which are not yet baptized? Verily, in the number of them that believe." Why, then, should they not be partakers of the sacrament together with the faithful?' Vol. i., p. 1104. Calvin, in other words, had expressed the very same views.

"*The English Church plainly teaches that regeneration is absolutely necessary to salvation, infants not excepted; but if it believed that baptism was the divinely appointed means to effect salvation the Catechism ought to have affirmed simply and plainly that baptism was necessary to salvation.*

"JOHN HARRISON, D.D."

INDEX.

Absolution, 48, 56, 57.
Acts of Uniformity. See "Statutes."
Addison, 196.
Adult Baptism, 171.
Aerius, 50.
Age for Confirmation, 172, 173.
Aless's Latin Prayer Book, 40, 56, 65, 76, 77, 96, *passim*.
Alfricus, 33.
Alms and Oblations, 61 *seq.*, 65, 79. See "Oblations."
Analytical Table of Sacraments, 194.
Anne, Queen, 37.
Aristotle, 80, 133, 143, 184.
Articles. See "Thirty-Nine Articles."
Assumption with regard to Baptism, 171.
Augustine, 85, 130, 133, 160, 190, 191, 193, 197.
Authority of Liturgia, 11 *seq.*, 17, 21 *seq.*, 27.
Authorized Version (Bible), 25, 29.

Bacon, 1, 21, 195.
Bagster's Latin Prayer Book, 39, 106; change in, 149, 154; 165; *passim*.
Baptism, 87, 91, 95, 97, 105; necessary in general, not universally, 138 *seq.*, 196; 157, 159 *seq.*; admission into Church, 162, 165, 170; Adult, 171; 189, 193, 194; *passim*.
Barlow, Dr., Copy of Liturgia given to him by Durel, 19, 34.
Belief, The. Clause concerning the church, 101 *seq.*
Beveridge, Bishop, 89, 97, 196.
Bible. Promoted Reformation, 24; 48; *passim*; see "Authorized Version;" Coverdale's, 146, 168.

Blessing, Jewish form of, 174.
Blessing God, or giving thanks, 173.
Blunt's Annotated Book of Common Prayer, 61, 145, 153.
Bodleian copy of Liturgia, 19, 34.
Body and blood, Christ's, 179, 191.
Both kinds, 177.
Bowyer's Latin Prayer Book, 38, 165, *passim*.
Bread, 177, 178, 183.
Briefs, 77, 81.
Bright and Medd's Latin Prayer Book, 40, 56 *seq.*, 60, 150, 154, 165, *passim*.
British Museum, copies of Liturgia, 33, 35 *seq.*
Brock, Rev. M., "Credence or Tasting Tables," 82.
Burnet, Bishop, 138, 159, 177.
Burton, R., 195.

Calvin, 198.
Canon LXI., 173; LXXXIV., 80; CXII. 173.
Capel, Monsignor, 46.
Cardwell, Dr., 11, 13, 170. See also under "Oblations."
Catechism, 85 *seq.*; reason for, 87; 172.
Catechism, Leighton's, 189.
Catechisme, The Common, in foure Languages, 103, 108, 111, 145.
Catechisms, Nowell's. See "Nowell's Catechisms."
Channel Islands, 5. See also "Jersey."
Charity, 185 *seq.*
Charles I., 14, 52, 189.
Charles II. establishes Savoy chapel, 2; Durel chaplain to him, 3; appoints Durel to Deanery of Windsor, 3;

INDEX.

sanctions Durel's French Prayer Book, 5; connection with Welsh Prayer Book, 7; Earle chaplain to him before Durel, 12; injunctions to Savoy conference, 16; dedication of Liturgia, 21; supremacy, 24; Prayer Book, 26; Savoy conference, 27; frontispiece representing him, 35; rubric in Revised Prayer Book, 67, 78.

Chaucer, 195.

Christ's body and blood, 179, 183.

Church, Admission into, 162.

Church, Holy Catholic, 101 *seq.*, 107.

Church Militant, Prayer for, 61 *seq.*, 63, 65, 66, 68, 69, See "Oblations."

Church-rates, 79.

Churchwardens to provide elements, 63.

Circumcision, 170.

Clarke, Dr. Adam, 164.

Comenius, 88.

Comma before "given," 152 *seq.*

Commandments, Ten, 108 *seq.*

Confirmation, 172.

Consecration of elements, 48, 57.

Conversion, 168.

Convocation, appointment of translators of Latin Prayer Book, 11, 13. See also 69, 70, 152.

Corroboratio, 181.

Cosin, Bishop, 27, 29, 56, 69, 152.

Coverdale's Bible, 146, 168.

Cowper, Bishop, 49, 62, 65, 156.

Credence Tables, 80, 82.

Creed, 99 *seq.*

Daniel, Rev. E., "The Prayer Book," &c., 104, 111, 112, 115, 126, 138, 146, 154, 164, 172, 175.

Death unto sin, 161.

Dedication to King, 21.

Devotions, 67, 71, 78.

Dionysius, 50.

Divisions of Catechism, 89.

Dolben, John, 13, 14, 17, 18; Dean of Westminster, 15.

Duport's Greek Prayer Book, 43, 64, 74, 86, 96, 101, 116, 119, 143, 154, *passim.*

Durel, John. Life, 1 *seq.*; ordination, 1, 29; at Savoy Chapel, 2; French Prayer Book, 2, 5 *seq.*; chaplain to Charles II., degree of D.D., Dean of Windsor, &c. 3; religious views, 3; Latin Prayer Book, 9; Durel the editor, 11; its history, 11 *seq.*; its character, 16; Durel's resumption of it, 17; Durel's letter to Archbishop Sancroft, 17; Durel's share in translation, 19; Dr. Barlow's opinion, 19; copy given to him by Durel, 19; authority of Latin Prayer Book, 21 *seq.*; dedication to King, 21; connection of royal supremacy with Latin Prayer Book, 23, 27; Durel's promotions, 3, 28; editions of his Latin Prayer Book, 33 *seq.*; Durel's opinion on "Priest," 46 *seq.*, 56 *seq.*; on "oblations," 64, 69, 70 *seq.*, 77, 78; Catechism, 85 *seq.*; his other works, 4, 17, 18, 73.

Durham. Durel, prebendary of, 3; Brerint, dean of, 29; Cosin library, 69, Sancroft, prebendary of, and chaplain to Bishop Cosin, 69; 192.

Earle, 11, 13, 17, 27; Dean of Westminster, 14.

Edinburgh Review, 187.

Editions of Liturgia, 33 *seq.*

Edward VI., Prayer Books of, 26, 65, 85, 94, 100, 129.

Elements, oblation of, 61 *seq.*; not held by Revisers, 63 *seq.*, 72; nowhere vindicated by Durel, 73; not recognized at revision, 73.

Elements, On Placing the, 82.

Elements, permanence of substance of; 182, 183.

Elements, Use of both kinds, 177.

Elizabeth, Q., English Prayer Book, 26, 66, 103, *passim;* Welsh Bible and Prayer Book, 8.

Elizabeth, Q., Latin Prayer Book, 23, 34, 40, 41, 43, 56 *seq.*, 59, 60, 65, 66, 77, 96, 103, 107, 125, *passim.*

English Liturgy, 22; growth of, under royal supremacy, 25; interprets itself, 139.

Evil, 133.

Faith, 98, 167, 171, 179, 185; faithful, 181, 191.

INDEX.

Favour. See "grace."
Forgiveness of sins, 104, 162.
Form in Sacrament, 155, 159, 160, 177.
Future tense in Commandments, 110.
French Prayer Book, Durel's, 2, 5 *seq.*; authority, 5; date of first use, 6; earlier version, 7; on "Oblations," 65, 71, 77.

Garter, Durel, registrar of, 3.
Generally necessary, *i.e.*, necessary in general, not universally, 138 *seq.*; 195, 197; why "generally" was introduced, 139; opinion of cotemporary writers, 140; cotemporary versions, 142; criticisms of certain statements, 145.
Ghostly, 137.
Given. See "Sign."
Godfathers, 90, 171.
Goode, Dean, 192.
Grace, 97, 129, 150, 158; children of, 166.
Grant, Sir A., 144.
Greek Prayer Books; Petley, 42; Whitaker, 43; Duport, 43.
Guernsey, 5.
Gyffredinol, 143.

Haddon, 41.
Harrison, Dr., 105, 168, 190, 193, 197.
Harwood's Latin Prayer Book, 38, 139, 165, *passim*.
Hell, 100.
Henry VIII. acknowledged supreme head of Church, 23.
"Hereby" referring to "A death unto sin," 163.
Hole, Matthew, B.D., 156.
Holy Catholic Church, 101 *seq.*, 107.
Holy Spirit, The, 164, etc. See "Spiritum Sanctum."
Hooker, 33, 51, 188, 190.

Ignatius, 50.
Institution, 152, 157, 160, 177.
Irenæus, 50.
Irish Prayer Book, 52; MS. Prayer Book, 153.

Jackson's Latin Prayer Book, 41, 42, 86.
James I., Prayer Book of, 26, 66, 137,
169; authorized version of Bible, 25, 29; Irish Prayer Book, 52; comma, 153.
Janua Linguarum, 88, *passim*.
Jerome, 50.
Jersey, Durel born in, 1; le Couteur, 1, 2; French Prayer Book, 5.
Jewel, 197.
Justin Martyr, 49, 62, 65.

La Liturgie. See "French Prayer Book."
Latin Prayer Book, required by 14 Car. II., 9; its history, 11 *seq.*; appointment of Earle and Peirson by Convocation, 11; of Earle and Dolben, 13; cf. 189; reasons for Latin Prayer Book, 15; Durel's resumption of translation, 17; submission of, to Archbishop Sancroft, 17; Durel's share in translation, 19; its authority, 21 *seq.*; dedication to king, 21; connection with supremacy, 28; scarcity of, 33; copies collated, 33 *seq.*; a new translation, 35; demand for, 37; for title-page, see 23, 33, 34, and frontispiece. See also "Durel."
Latin Prayer Books; earlier versions, 40 *seq.*; later, 37 *seq.*
Laud, Archbishop, 42, 43, 51.
Learn and labour, 127.
Le Couteur, dean of Jersey, 1, 2.
Leighton, Archbishop, 189.
Letters of Orders, John Wesley's, 55.
Liber Valorum, 54.
Llyfr Gweddi Gyffredin. See "Welsh Prayer Book."
Lord's Prayer, 129 *seq.*
Lord's Supper. See "Sacrament," 173 *seq.*, 179; remembrance, 175, 185; 189, 190, 193, 194, *passim*.
Luther, 197.

Marschall, Thos., D.D., 97, 100, 153, 157, 181, 183.
Matter, 159, 160, 177.
Merton College, Durel at, 1; Earle at, 13.
Mill, J. S., 144.
Milton, 49, 188.
Mockett's Latin Prayer Book, 42, 154.
Modern Latin Prayer Books, 39; contrasted with Liturgia, 40; see also 60.

Nicholls, Wm., D.D., 47, 97, 103, 141, 153, 180, 192.
Nowell, Alexander, letter of, 81.
Nowell's Catechisms, 44 *seq.*, 85, 96, 101, 103, 107, 115, 116, 119, 124, 137, 148, 154, 162, 165, 170, 172, *passim*.
Norwich copy of Liturgia, 33.

Oblations, 61, *seq.*; devotions, 67; Dr. Cardwell's, Mr. Proctor's, and Mr. Purton's opinions, 68, 76, 79; monetary offerings, 68; Cosin's corrections, 69; Durel's Latin Prayer Book, 70; his French Prayer Book, 71, Welsh Prayer Book, 74; Duport, 74; more exact determination of meaning, 75; oblations are offerings to curate, 77, 78, Durel's Latin Prayer Book, 78.
Offertory, 65, 68, 74, 76, 77. See "Oblations."
Offrymau, 74.
Optatus, 50.
Ordinals, Early, 49, 51.
Ordination, Durel's, 1, 29.
Overall, Bishop, 137, 190, 193.

Paraphrasis cum Annotatis, etc., 91, 141, 165.
Parker's Latin Prayer Book, 39, 96, 154, 165.
Parsell's Latin Prayer Book, 37, 165, *passim*.
Peirson, 11, 12, 27.
Petley's Greek Prayer Book, 42, 86, 96, 101, 116, 119, 143, 154, *passim*.
Poor men's box, 65, 79.
Potter, Archbishop, 196.
Prayer Books. See "Latin Prayer Books," "Greek Prayer Books," etc.
Presbyter, 46 *seq.*; Durel's reasons for use, 47; history of term, 49 *seq.*; clergy of second order are presbyteri, 52; Thirty-nine Articles, 53; testimonium, 54; letters of orders, 55; law forms, 55; only true title, 60; use of, 81.
Priest, 46 *seq.*; retained in pure sense, 48; derivation, 49; represents older presbyter, 49 *seq.*; misuse of, 82.

Regeneration, 161, 162, 165, 196.

Registrar of Garter, Durel, 3.
Remembrance, Lord's Supper a, 175, 185.
Remission of sins, 104, 162.
Renuntiatio Papae, 24.
Repentance, 167, 171.
Revised New Testament, 130, 131, 132, 133, 174, 186.
Roscommon, 11.
Royal supremacy, 23 *seq.*

Sacrament, 98, 137, 148; necessary in general, not universally, 138 *seq.*; distinction between doctrine of Church of England and Romish Church, 140, 157; definition of word, 148, 152; definition of "thing," 158; 156; sign and form, 159, 173, 189, 190, 193, 194, 196, *passim*.
Safety, way of, 96.
St. Helier, Durel born at, 1.
Salesbury, William, 8.
Salisbury, Durel, prebendary of, 3; Peirson, prebendary of, 12; Earle, chancellor of, 13; Earle, bishop of, 14.
Salisbury or Sarum Use partly followed by Durel, 16.
Salvation, state of, 96.
Sancroft, Archbishop; Durel's submission of Liturgia to him, 17 *seq.*; 27, 56; "oblations," 69, 70; comma before "given," 152, 160.
Sandar's Institutes of Justinian, 138, 157, 169.
Savoy chapel, 2, 5.
Savoy conference, 27, 12, 14, 16, 30, 67, 80, 189.
Scotch Prayer Book, 48, 51, 66, 72.
Sealed Books, 152, 153.
Secker, Archbishop, 77, 86, 87, 98, 142, 151, 158, 175.
Selborne, Lord, on Durel's Liturgia, 18.
Septuagint, 110 *seq.*, 116, 119 *seq.*, 145, 146.
Shakespeare, 127, 137, 195.
Sheldon, Archbishop, 6, 11, 13, 15, 43, 189.
Sick mans Salue, The, 187.
Sign, outward and visible, 148 *seq.*; given, 151 *seq.*; comma, 152 *seq.*; representing grace, 149, 151, 154.
Sin, A death unto, 163.
Sion College, 41.

Sons of God, 163.
South, Robert, 61.
State of salvation, 96
Statutes: 22 Hen. VIII. c. 12, 77; 26 Hen. VIII., 23; Act of Uniformity, 1 Eliz., 8, 34; Act of Uniformity, 14 Car. II., 7, 8, 9, 47, 152; 17 and 18 Car. II. c. 6 (Ireland), 153.
Stephen's Book of Common Prayer, 153.
Stillingfleet, Bishop, 24, 126, 140, 160, 178, 196.
Stillingfleet, James, 142.
Supremacy, Royal, 23, 43.
Swift, 196.

Tertullian, 50.
Testimonium, 54.
"Then," Meaning of, 64.
Thirty-nine Articles, 28, 46, 49, 52 seq., 141, 150, 187, 191, 197.
Tillotson, Archbishop, 195.
Transubstantiation, 158, 180, 182.
Trench, Archbishop, 186.

Uniformity, Acts, of. See "Statutes."

Vautrollier's Latin Prayer Book, 41, 42, 56 seq., 59, 60, 86, 96, 107, 110, passim.
Verily and indeed, 180

Watts, 196.
Way of safety, 96
Welsh custom, 74.
Welsh Prayer Book, 7 seq., 43; on "Oblations," 64, 74; on "generally necessary," 143; on "given," 155; on "hereby," 164.
Wesley, John, Letters of orders, 55.
Westminster, Earle, dean of, 14; Dolben, dean of, 15; church at, 81.
Whitaker's Latin Prayer Book, 41, 96, 103; Greek Prayer Book, 43, 57, 86, 96, 101, 103, 107, passim.
Whitgift, Archbishop, 48, 51, 82, 160.
Wilson, Bishop, 55.
Windsor, Durel, prebendary and dean of, 3.
Wine, 177, 180, 183.
Witney, Benefice of, 3.
Wolf's Latin Prayer Book, 41, 86.
Wood's opinion of Durel, 4.

VOCABULA.

abrenunciaturum, 93.
accipi, 178.
addiscere, 87.
adoleverint, 172.
aetatem, 169, 172.
Amulâ, 61, 70.
Animarum nostrarum corroboratio, 181.
animorum, 136, 122.
Aqua, 160.
arrabonem, 157.
articulos, 94.

Baptismum, 147. See " Baptism."

CATECHISMUS, 85.
Catechistes, 98.
charitate, 185.
Coenam Domini, 148. See " Lord's Supper."
Communionem, Sanctorum, 104.
Communium in title, 34.
confirmet, 97.
coram me, 111.
corde, 121.
Corpus & sanguis Christi, 179.
CREDO, 99.
Credo, with " in," and with simple accusative, 94, 102.

dimitte, 131.
discam, 127.
Duo tantùm, 138.

Ecclesiam Catholicam, Sanctam, 101 *seq.*
electos, 108.
Et meo, 127.
Externum & visibile signum, 148 *seq.*

factus sum, 91 ; facti sumus, 163, 166.
fidelibus, 181. See " Faith."
fides. See " Faith."
filius Dei, 91 ; Filii Dei, 163, 166.
forma, 159.

gratiâ, 97 ; gratiae, 150 ; gratiam, 135.

habebis, 110.
hâc ratione, 163.
haeres, 91.
hanc salutis viam, 96.

in genere, 138 *seq.* See " generally necessary."
in millia, 114.
infantes, 169.
inferos, 100.
instituendi, 185 ; instituit, 138 ; *Institutio*, 86 ; institutum, 157.

jumentum, 116.

latrocinio, 127.

maledicentia, 127.
malo, 133.
medium, 157.
memoriâ, 185 ; memoriam, 175.
Mori peccato, &c., 161, 163 *seq.* ; 91.

N. aut M., 90.
nec omnia, 120.
nomen, 115, 123 ; in nomine, 161 ; tuo nomine, 92.
NON concupisces, 119.

oblatam eleemosynam, 66, 78.
oblationes, 61 *seq.*, 65, 66, 70, 71, 77, 78.

VOCABULA. 205

obsequar, 125.
Oeconomis, 78.
offeruntur, 62.

Panis, 177.
partes (Sacramenti), 158.
Pastoribus, 126.
PATER noster, 129.
patrem, 117.
percipimus, 176.
pompis, 93.
praeest, 49, 65.
praestare, 127, 169, 171, 172; praestem, 125; praestiterunt, 92.
Presbyter. See " Presbyter" in Index.

quod nobis datur, 151 *seq*. See "given."
quod . . . praestare, 171.
quotidianum, 131.

recreatio, 183.
Remissionem peccatorum, 104, 162.
requiritur, 166.
Resipiscentia, 166, 167.

Sabbati, 116.

Sacerdos, no such order in Reformed Church, 52; decreasing use of term, 56; reintroduction of obsolete term, 60.
Sacramentum. See "Sacrament."
salutis viam, hanc, 96.
Sanctam Ecclesiam Catholicam, 101 *seq*.
sanctificavit, 108, 117.
Sanctorum Communionem, 104.
Servatorem, 97.
sicut in cœlo, 131.
signum, Externum & visibile, 148 *seq*., 150; distinguished from "forma," 159.
similitudinem quae est, 113.
speciali, 129.
Spiritum Sanctum, 101; Deum, 107.
sponsores, 170.
Susceptores, 90.

tentationem, 132.
tuo nomine, 92.

ut probent, 184.

verè & re ipsa, 180.
Vinum, 177.
vocem istam, 148 *seq*.

Just published, crown 8vo, paper covers, 1s. 6d., *cloth,* 2s.

PLUTARCH'S

LIVES OF THE GRACCHI,

TRANSLATED

FROM THE TEXT OF SINTENIS.

WITH INTRODUCTION, MARGINAL ANALYSIS,

AND APPENDICES.

BY

WILLIAM W. MARSHALL, B.A.

LATE SCHOLAR OF HERTFORD COLLEGE; AND OF
THE INNER TEMPLE.

Oxford:

JAMES THORNTON, HIGH STREET.

London ... { SIMPKIN, MARSHALL, & Co.
{ HAMILTON, ADAMS, & Co.

MDCCCLXXXI.

For some Notices of the Press, see next Page.

OPINIONS OF THE PRESS.

"... We are not sorry to see a taste for the writings of the old Chæronian philosopher springing up again; there is much wisdom and much information to be gathered out of them, as many eminent men have found. Mr. Marshall's translation of the Lives of the Gracchi is neatly executed, and is provided with sufficient apparatus of criticism, &c., to enable students to understand the questions raised in Rome by these eminent men. The publication has, we presume, been called for by University requirements. It will be convenient for those who wish to make some slight acquaintance with Plutarch's writings. His defects as well as his merits are carefully pointed out."—*Record.*

"This is one of a series of translations from the classics which Mr. Thornton of Oxford is now publishing ... It is pleasant to see reproduced in a handy form even a few pages from the philosophical historian of the old world worthies, who has furnished classical anecdotes and moral reflections to eighteen centuries of literary men. The translation is well and carefully done. The foot-notes are admirably few and to the point. ... The introduction states concisely the various matters of historical interest during the lives of the two Gracchi, as the Tribunate and the Agrarian Laws; there are several useful appendices at the end; and the translation is accompanied by a marginal analysis which brings into prominence before the eye the more important facts and dates."—*St. James's Magazine.*

"Mr. Marshall has succeeded in cutting out of Plutarch a very neat piece of biography and presenting it in a pleasant English dress, with a careful introduction and a few useful Appendices. The text is that of Sintenis. The English is the editor's, and is very agreeable reading. The Introduction is a clever account of Plutarch, with a critical notice of his work, his merits, and his inaccuracies, together with a summary sketch of the affairs of Rome when the Gracchi came into notice. The student of Roman history will be glad of this small, but carefully edited, account of the two brethren."—*School Guardian.*

"... A well-written general introduction, giving the ascertained facts in the life of Plutarch, his method of writing, and his excellences and omissions, the leading legislative enactments of the Gracchi; and appendices of the chief laws referring to the tribunate, the land laws, and jury courts, are added. The translation of the text of Plutarch is remarkably close and faithful, and the foot-notes, although few, are pregnant. The marginal analysis of the text is one of the most useful features of the work, and likely to help the reader very considerably. As the price is only eighteen-pence or two shillings, every admirer of Plutarch can, without difficulty, procure a copy. The work is excellently printed, and well got up."—*Oxford and Cambridge Undergraduate's Journal.*

"The work is dedicated to the Rev. W. W. Capes, Fellow of Hertford, and Reader of Ancient History in the University of Oxford. It has a lucidly written introduction; this, the work and appendices include the known facts in the life of Plutarch, his mode of writing, the principal legislative enactments of the Gracchi, the chief laws relating to the tribunate, the land laws, and jury courts. The work, says an able critic, 'is interesting and instructive. Indeed, it might be well if some of our modern political theorists would learn some lessons from it, especially if they would learn them in the light of Christianity.' The translation of the text of Plutarch is strikingly strict and true. . The foot-notes though not numerous are valuable. The reader is much helped by the marginal analysis of the work. Published at eighteen-pence or two shillings, the grammar-school scholar, the undergraduate, the literary man of all grades, and the general admirers of Plutarch, are brought within reach of a work which will well repay thoughtful and studious perusal. The merits of the work prove the cultivated and high talent of the writer, . ."—*Chorley Guardian.*

33 & 41 HIGH STREET, OXFORD.

OCTOBER 1882.

JAMES THORNTON'S
List of Publications

CHIEFLY EDUCATIONAL,

MANY IN USE AT THE HIGHER SCHOOLS AND UNIVERSITIES.

CONTENTS.

	PAGE
CLASS BOOKS	6
CLASSICAL	3
LAW AND POLITICAL ECONOMY	9
MISCELLANEOUS	3
OXFORD STUDY GUIDES	11
PALÆSTRA OXONIENSIS	7
TRANSLATIONS	5

Also Sold by { SIMPKIN, MARSHALL, & CO., London.
{ JOHN MENZIES & SONS, Edinburgh.

A Catalogue of these Publications with fuller descriptions, some notices from the press, and specimen pages, will be issued shortly, and will be forwarded gratis on application.

JAMES THORNTON *desires to direct attention to the accompanying List of* EDUCATIONAL WORKS, *many of which have now attained a wide circulation.*

The Authors and Compilers are mostly scholars of repute, as well as of large experience in teaching.

Any notices of errors or defects in these publications will be gratefully received and acknowledged.

The Books can generally be procured through local Booksellers in town and country; but if at any time difficulty should arise, JAMES THORNTON *will feel obliged by direct communication on the subject.*

MISCELLANEOUS.

THE LATIN PRAYER BOOK OF CHARLES II.; or, an Account of the Liturgia of Dean Durel, together with a Reprint and Translation of the Catechism therein contained, with Collations, Annotations, and Appendices by the Rev. CHARLES MARSHALL, M.A., Chaplain to the Lord Mayor of London, 1849–1850; and WILLIAM W. MARSHALL, B.A., of the Inner Temple, late Scholar of Hertford College, Oxford. Demy 8vo. cloth, 10s. 6d. [*Just published.*

The Authors have been led to the present undertaking by a desire to attract more attention to the Latin Prayer Book of 1670, and they desire this for two reasons. Firstly, on account of the remarkable scarcity of the book itself. (In many of the most notable libraries no copy is to be found.) Secondly, because Durel's 'Liturgia' shows what the Revisers understood to be meant by the words which they retained and the words which they inserted; it shows the thought of the time as expressed by a contemporary and an authorised exponent.

CANONS OF THE SECOND COUNCIL OF ORANGE, A.D. 529. With an Introduction, Translation, and Notes. By the Rev. F. H. WOODS, B.D., Fellow of St. John's College, Oxford. Crown 8vo. 2s. [*Just published.*

An UNDERGRADUATE'S TRIP to ITALY and ATTICA in the WINTER of 1880-1. By J. L. THOMAS, Balliol College, Oxford. Crown 8vo. 5s.

THE LIVES AND LETTERS OF GIFFORD AND BUNYAN. By the Rev. T. A. BLYTH, Queen's College, Oxford. [*In preparation.*

CLASSICAL.

The NICOMACHEAN ETHICS of ARISTOTLE. Books I.–IV. and Book X. Chap. 6 to 9, being the portion required in the Oxford Pass School, with Notes, &c. for the use of Passmen. By E. L. HAWKINS, M.A., late Postmaster of Merton College. Demy 8vo. cloth, 8s. 6d. Interleaved with writing paper, 10s. 6d.

The POETICS of ARISTOTLE. The Text after Vahlen, with an Introduction, a New Translation, Explanatory and Critical Notes, and an Appendix on the Greek Drama. [*In preparation.*

CLASSICAL.—*continued.*

DEMOSTHENES on the CROWN. The Text after BAITER. With an Introduction, a New Translation, Notes, and Indices. By FRANCIS P. SIMPSON, B.A., Balliol College, Craven Scholar, 1877. Demy 8vo. cloth, 10s. 6d. [*Just published.*

FROM THE PREFACE.—Several of the Notes—which I have tried to make as concise as possible—may appear unnecessary to a scholar; but they have been inserted for the practical reason that the obstacles they should remove have been felt by some of the many pupils with whom I have read this speech.

The main difficulty which Demosthenes presents to the student lies in the close logical connection of his arguments; and most commentaries consist largely of translation or paraphrase. Paraphrase is dangerous, as it may lead a novice to a belief that he quite understands a piece of Latin or Greek, when he is some way from doing so. I have, therefore, taken the bull by the horns, and have given a continuous rendering, as close as I could decently make it. Its aim is purely commentatorial—to save its weight in notes. It is intended to show what Demosthenes said, but not how well he said it. And, I may say, I believe that every lecturer and tutor in Oxford will admit that an undergraduate, or sixth-form boy, cannot get full value out of reading the De Corona without such help.

In Introduction I. will be found a sketch of Athenian history, as far as is necessary for the thorough understanding of this Oration. In Introduction II. a precis of the oration of Aeschines, as well as of that of Demosthenes, is prefixed to a brief analysis of the two speeches considered as an attack and a defence.

EXTRACTS FROM LETTERS.

'Accept my best thanks for your presentation copy of Mr. Simpson's edition of the ORATION FOR THE CROWN, which I have no doubt will be gratefully accepted by professional scholars and the educated laity.'—Prof. BLACKIE.

'It seems to me very well done and likely to be of great use. I notice with pleasure that several mistakes of other translations and editions are tacitly corrected. Possibly there might be a little more freedom in the translation without merely paraphrasing; but this is no doubt very difficult to do except at the cost of extra notes, and I believe you are quite right in economising notes, which tend now to overlay and efface the texts of the Classics.'—S. H. BUTCHER, Esq., Fellow of University College, Oxford.

'I have made use of it for the last two of a course of lectures on the speech with profit to myself, and I think it is likely to be appreciated.'
Rev. T. S. PAPILLON, Fellow of New College, Oxford.

'It seems to me likely to be very useful.'
A. SIDGWICK, Esq., Fellow of Corpus Christi College, Oxford.

'I am struck with the scholarly tone of all that I have seen. Some of the notes seem models of good scholarship and exegesis.'
A. T. BARTON, Esq., Fellow of Pembroke College, Oxford.

'Its close aim and accuracy will make it very useful for many students.'
Rev. W. W. MERRY, Lincoln College, Oxford.

'One or two test passages that I have already looked at show that delicate points have been considered and common traps avoided. The abstract of the speech of Aeschines is an especially useful feature, and so is the copious index.'
Rev. J. R. KING, Fellow and Tutor, Oriel College, Oxford.

A SYNOPSIS of LIVY'S HISTORY of the SECOND PUNIC WAR. Books XXI.–XXIV. With Appendices, Notes, Maps, and Plans. By J. B. WORCESTER, M.A. Second Edition. Fcp. 8vo. cloth, 2s. 6d.

A SYNOPSIS and SUMMARY of the ANNALS of TACITUS. Books I.–VI. With Introduction, Notes and Indexes. By G. W. GENT, B.A. Crown 8vo. cloth, 3s. 6d.

A SYNOPSIS and SUMMARY of the REPUBLIC of PLATO. With a Prefatory Excursus upon the Platonic Philosophy, and Short Notes. By GEORGE WILLIAM GENT, B.A. [*Preparing.*

A FEW NOTES on the ANNALS of TACITUS. Books I. to IV. For Passmen. Crown 8vo. [*In the press.*

TRANSLATIONS.

The AGAMEMNON of ÆSCHYLUS. A new Prose Translation. Crown 8vo. cloth limp, 2s.

The NICOMACHEAN ETHICS of ARISTOTLE. A New Translation, with an Introduction, a Marginal Analysis, and Explanatory Notes. By D. P. CHASE, M.A., Fellow of Oriel College, and Principal of St. Mary Hall, Oxford. Fourth Edition, revised. Crown 8vo. cloth, 4s. 6d.

ARISTOTLE'S ORGANON: Translations from the Organon of Aristotle, comprising those Sections of Mr. Magrath's Selections required for Honour Moderations. By WALTER SMITH, New College, and ALLAN G. SUMNER GIBSON, Scholar of Corpus Christi College, Oxford. Crown 8vo. 2s. 6d.

The ELEMENTS of ARISTOTLE'S LOGIC, following the order of Trendelenburg, with Introduction, English Translation, and Notes. By THOMAS CASE, M.A., Tutor of Corpus Christi College, and sometime Fellow of Brasenose College. [*Preparing.*

The PHILIPPIC ORATIONS of CICERO. A New Translation. By the Rev. JOHN RICHARD KING, M.A., Fellow and Tutor of Oriel College, Oxford. Crown 8vo. cloth, 4s. 6d.

The FIRST and SECOND PHILIPPIC ORATIONS of CICERO. A New Translation. By JOHN R. KING, M.A. Second Edition. Crown 8vo. 1s. 6d.

The SPEECH of CICERO for CLUENTIUS. Translated into English, with an Introduction and Notes. By W. PETERSON, M.A., late Scholar of Corpus Christi College, Oxford; Assistant to the Professor of Humanity in the University of Edinburgh. Crown 8vo. cloth, 3s. 6d. [*Just published.*

'We have gone over the translation with some care, and we have found it of uniform excellence. If any young scholar ever takes Niebuhr's advice about translating the speech, he could not do better than compare his own with this version before he began to retranslate it. The translation is not only accurate, but it abounds in neat and scholarly renderings of awkward Latin idioms.'—GLASGOW HERALD, *September* 1, 1882.

LIVY'S HISTORY of ROME. The Fifth, Sixth, and Seventh Books. A Literal Translation from the Text of MADVIG, with Historical Introductions, Summary to each Book, and Explanatory Notes. By a First Classman. Crown 8vo. 4s. 6d.

The MENO of PLATO. A New Translation, with Introduction and Explanatory Notes, for the use of Students. Crown 8vo. cloth limp, 1s. 6d.

PLUTARCH'S LIVES of the GRACCHI. Translated from the Text of Sintenis, with Introduction, Marginal Analysis, and Appendices. By W. W. MARSHALL, B.A., late Scholar of Hertford College. Crown 8vo. paper covers, 1s. 6d., or cloth, 2s.

The ÆNEID of VIRGIL. Books I. to VI. Translated into English Prose. By T. CLAYTON, M.A. Crown 8vo. cloth, 2s.

The ÆNEID of VIRGIL. A new Prose Translation. By THOMAS CLAYTON, M.A., Trinity College, Oxford. [*In preparation.*

CLASS BOOKS.

MELETEMATA; or, SELECT LATIN PASSAGES IN PROSE AND VERSE FOR UNPREPARED TRANSLATION. Arranged by the Rev. P. J. F. Gantillon, M.A., sometime Scholar of St. John's College, Cambridge, Classical Master in Cheltenham College. Crown 8vo. cloth, 4s. 6d.

The object of this volume is to furnish a collection of about 250 passages, graduated in difficulty, and adapted to the various Examinations in which 'Unprepared Translation' finds a place.

'The work is nicely got up, and is altogether the best of the kind with which we are acquainted.'—THE SCHOOLMASTER, *December* 3, 1881.

'We find this collection to be very judiciously made, and think it one of the best which has yet been published.'—EDUCATIONAL TIMES, *April* 1, 1881.

MELETEMATA GRÆCA; being a Selection of Passages, Prose and Verse, for unprepared Translation. By the Rev. P. J. F. Gantillon, M.A. [*In the press.*

Forming a Companion Volume to the above.

SELECTED PIECES for TRANSLATION into LATIN PROSE. Selected and arranged by the Rev. H. C. Ogle, M.A. Head Master of Magdalen College School, and T. Clayton, M.A. Crown 8vo. cloth, 4s. 6d.

This selection is intended for the use of the highest forms in Schools and for University Students for Honour Examinations, for whom it was felt that a small and compact book would be most serviceable.

'The selection has been made with much care and the passages which we have more particularly examined are very appropriate for translation.'
SCHOOL GUARDIAN, *June* 7, 1879.

LATIN and GREEK VERSIONS of some of the SELECTED PIECES for TRANSLATION. Collected and arranged by the Rev. H. C. Ogle, M.A., Head Master of Magdalen College School; and Thomas Clayton, M.A., Trinity College, Oxford. Crown 8vo. 5s. [*Just ready.*

This Key is for the use of Tutors only, and is issued on the understanding that it does not get into the hands of any pupil.

For the convenience of Schoolmasters and Tutors these Versions are also issued in another form, viz. on separate leaves ready for distribution to pupils, thereby saving the necessity of dictating or copying. They are done up in packets of twenty-five each, and not less than twenty-five sets (=75 packets) can be supplied at a time. Price—Thirty-five Shillings net.

DAMON; or, The ART of GREEK IAMBIC MAKING. By the Rev. J. Herbert Williams, M.A., Composition Master in S. Nicholas College, Lancing; late Demy of Magdalen College. Fcp. 8vo. 1s. 6d.

This small treatise claims as its merit that it really teaches Greek Iambic writing on a system, and this system is based on no arbitrary analysis of the Iambic line, but on the way in which the scholar practically regards it in making verses himself.

A Key, for Tutors only. Fcp. 8vo. cloth, 3s. 6d.

CLASS BOOKS—*continued.*

SHORT TABLES and NOTES on GREEK and LATIN GRAMMAR. By W. E. W. COLLINS, M.A., Jesus College. Crown 8vo. cloth, 2s.

ARS SCRIBENDI LATINE; or, Aids to Latin Prose Composition. In the Form of an Analysis of Latin Idioms. By B. A. EDWARDS, B.A., late Scholar of Jesus College, Oxford. Crown 8vo. 1s.

OUTLINES of CHEMICAL THEORY. By FREDERICK FINNIS GRENSTED, B.A., University College. [*In preparation.*

ARITHMETIC FOR SCHOOLS. Based on principles of Cause and Effect. By the Rev. FREDERICK SPARKS, M.A., Mathematical Master, the High School, Plymouth, and late Lecturer of Worcester College, Oxford. [*In preparation.*

ALGEBRAICAL QUESTIONS AND EXERCISES. For the Use of Candidates for Matriculation, Responsions, and First Public Examinations, and the Oxford and Cambridge Local and Certificate Examinations. Crown 8vo. 2s.

ARITHMETICAL QUESTIONS AND EXERCISES. For the Use of Candidates for Matriculation, Responsions, and First Public Examinations, and the Oxford and Cambridge Local and Certificate Examinations. Crown 8vo. 1s. 6d.

QUESTIONS AND EXERCISES IN ADVANCED LOGIC. For the Use of Candidates for the Honour Moderation Schools. Crown 8vo. 1s. 6d.

The RUDIMENTS of LOGIC, with Tables and Examples. By F. E. WEATHERLY, M.A. Fcp. 8vo. cloth limp, 1s. 6d.
  'Here is everything needful for a beginner.'—EDUCATIONAL TIMES.
  'Is a clever condensation of first principles.'—SCHOOL GUARDIAN.

A FEW NOTES on the GOSPELS. By W. E. W. COLLINS, M.A., Jesus College. New Edition. Crown 8vo. paper covers, 1s. 6d.

PALÆSTRA OXONIENSIS.

The object of this Series is to furnish Exercises and Test Papers for Candidates preparing for the various Examinations at our Public Schools and Universities.

QUESTIONS and EXERCISES for MATRICULATION and RESPONSIONS. CONTENTS: (1) Grammatical Questions in Greek and Latin; (2) Materials for Latin Prose; (3) Questions on Authors. Sixth Edition. Crown 8vo. cloth, 3s. 6d.

PALÆSTRA OXONIENSIS—*continued*.

QUESTIONS and EXERCISES for CLASSICAL SCHOLAR-SHIPS. CONTENTS: (1) Critical Grammar Questions in Greek and Latin; (2) Unseen passages for translation. Adapted to the Oxford and Cambridge Schools Certificate and the Oxford First Public Examinations. Second Edition, corrected and enlarged. Crown 8vo. cloth, 3s. 6d.

Elucidations to the Critical Questions, with Key to the Unseen Passages. [*In the press.*

QUESTIONS and EXERCISES for CLASSICAL SCHOLAR-SHIPS. Second Division. CONTENTS: (1) Historical and General Questions; (2) Subjects for English Essays. Crown 8vo. cloth, 3s. 6d.

QUESTIONS and EXERCISES in ELEMENTARY MATHE-MATICS. CONTENTS: (1) Arithmetic; (2) Algebra; (3) Euclid. Third Edition, enlarged. Adapted to Matriculation, Responsions, and First Public Examinations, and the Oxford and Cambridge Local and Certificate Examinations. Crown 8vo. cloth, 3s. 6d. With ANSWERS, 5s. The ANSWERS separately, paper covers, 1s. 6d.

QUESTIONS and EXERCISES in ELEMENTARY LOGIC, DEDUCTIVE and INDUCTIVE; with Index of Logical Terms. Crown 8vo. cloth. (New Edition in the press.)

QUESTIONS and EXERCISES in RUDIMENTARY DI-VINITY. CONTENTS: (1) Old Testament; (2) New Testament; (3) The Thirty-Nine Articles (4) Greek Passages for Translation. Adapted to the Oxford Pass and the Oxford and Cambridge Certificate Examinations. Second Edition. Crown 8vo. cloth, 3s. 6d.

ELEMENTARY QUESTIONS on the LAW of PROPERTY, REAL and PERSONAL. Supplemented by Advanced Questions on the Law of Contracts. With Copious References throughout, and an Index of Legal Terms. Crown 8vo. cloth, 3s. 6d.

QUESTIONS and EXERCISES in POLITICAL ECONOMY, with References to Adam Smith, Ricardo, John Stuart Mill, Fawcett, J. E. Thorold Rogers, Bonamy Price, Twiss, Senior, and others. Crown 8vo. cloth, 3s. 6d.

JAMES THORNTON, 33 & 41 HIGH STREET, OXFORD.

LAW AND POLITICAL ECONOMY.

THOMAS HOBBES, of MALMESBURY, LEVIATHAN; or, the Matter, Forme, and Power of a Commonwealth. A New Reprint. With a facsimile of the original fine engraved Title. Medium 8vo. cloth, 12s. 6d. A small edition of 250 copies only on Dutch hand-made paper, medium 8vo. 18s.

Students' Edition, crown 8vo. cloth 8s. 6d. [*Just published.*

'In matters of reprints, such as this is, it is always well to retain as much as possible the old spelling, and the old form of printing. By this means we are constantly reminded that we are reading a seventeenth century writer and not a nineteenth: and hence students will apply more checks to their process of reasoning than they might be inclined to do if the book were printed in modern form. This is, we are glad to say, applicable to the present excellent reprint, which is issued in old spelling, and contains in the margin the figures of the pagination of the first edition.'

THE ANTIQUARY, *October* 1881.

'We have received from Mr. James Thornton, of Oxford, an excellent reprint of Hobbes's 'Leviathan.' The book is one which is not always easy to obtain; and a satisfactory reprint at a reasonable price may do more to advance the knowledge of Hobbes's philosophy than one of the condensed handbooks which are now extensively popular.'

WESTMINSTER REVIEW, *January* 1882.

REMARKS on the USE and ABUSE of SOME POLITICAL TERMS. By the late Right Hon. Sir GEORGE CORNEWALL LEWIS, Bart., sometime Student of Christ Church, Oxford. A New Edition, with Notes and Appendix. By Sir ROLAND KNYVET WILSON, Bart., M.A., Barrister-at-Law; late Fellow of King's College, Cambridge; Author of 'History of Modern English Law.' Crown 8vo. 6s.

FROM THE EDITOR'S PREFACE.

'The value of the book for educational purposes consists not so much in its positive results, as in the fact that it opens a vein of thought which the student may usefully follow out to any extent for himself, and that it affords an instructive example of a thoughtful, scientific, and in the best sense academical style of treating political questions.

'With regard to my own annotations, the object which I have chiefly kept in view has been to direct attention to such later writings as have expressly undertaken to fix the scientific meaning of the political terms here discussed, and above all "Austin's Lectures on Jurisprudence," to which the present work may be considered as a kind of companion volume.'

QUESTIONS and EXERCISES in POLITICAL ECONOMY, with References to Adam Smith, Ricardo, John Stuart Mill, Fawcett, Thorold Rogers, Bonamy Price, Twiss, Senior, Macleod, and others. Adapted to the Oxford Pass and Honour and the Cambridge Ordinary B.A. Examinations. Arranged and edited by W. P. EMERTON, M.A., B.C.L., Christ Church, Oxford. Crown 8vo. cloth, 3s. 6d.

This volume consists of Questions mainly taken from various Examination Papers with references in the case of the easier questions, and hints, and in some cases formal statements of the arguments *pro* and *con.* to the more difficult questions. There are also two Appendixes on the debated questions—'Is Political Economy a Science?' and 'Is Political Economy Selfish?'

LAW AND POLITICAL ECONOMY—*continued*.

An ABRIDGMENT of ADAM SMITH'S INQUIRY into the NATURE and CAUSES of the WEALTH of NATIONS. By W. P. EMERTON, M.A., B.C.L. Crown 8vo. cloth, 6s.

This work (based on Jeremiah Joyce's Abridgment) originally appeared in two parts and is now republished after careful revision, with Additional Notes, Appendices, and a Complete Index.

The above can be had in two Parts.   Part I. Books I. and II. 3s. 6d.
Part II. Books III., IV. and V. 3s. 6d.

OUTLINES of JURISPRUDENCE. For the Use of Students. By B. R. WISE, late Scholar of Queen's College, Oxford; Oxford Cobden Prizeman, 1878. Crown 8vo. cloth, 5s.

This book is intended to be a critical and explanatory commentary upon the Jurisprudence text-books in common use; and it endeavours to present a precise and coherent view of all the topics upon which these touch.

'The student of jurisprudence will certainly find the work suggestive and helpful.'
THE ATHENÆUM, *July* 15, 1882.

OUTLINES of ENGLISH CONSTITUTIONAL HISTORY. By BRITIFFE CONSTABLE SKOTTOWE, B.A., late Scholar of New College, Oxford. Crown 8vo. cloth, 3s. 6d.

The object of this book is to assist beginners in reading Constitutional History by arranging in order outlines of the growth of the most important Institutions.

An ANALYSIS of the ENGLISH LAW of REAL PROPERTY, chiefly from Blackstone's Commentary, with Tables and Indexes. By GORDON CAMPBELL, M.A., Author of 'An Analysis of Austin's Lectures on Jurisprudence,' and of 'A Compendium of Roman Law.' Crown 8vo. cloth, 3s. 6d.

An ANALYSIS of JUSTINIAN'S INSTITUTES of ROMAN LAW, with Tables. [*In preparation.*

A CHRONOLOGICAL SUMMARY of the CHIEF REAL PROPERTY STATUTES, with their more important Provisions. For the Use of Law Students. By P. F. ALDRED, M.A., B.C.L. Crown 8vo. 2s.

ELEMENTARY QUESTIONS on the LAW of PROPERTY, REAL and PERSONAL. Supplemented by Advanced Questions on the Law of Contracts. With Copious References throughout, and an Index of Legal Terms. Crown 8vo. cloth, 3s. 6d.

The SPECIAL STATUTES required by Candidates for the School of Jurisprudence at Oxford. Fcp. 8vo. sewed, 2s. 6d. With brief Notes and Translations by a B.C.L. Cloth, 5s.

OXFORD STUDY GUIDES.

A SERIES OF HANDBOOKS TO EXAMINATIONS.

Edited by F. S. PULLING, M.A., Exeter College.

THE object of this Series is to guide Students in their reading for the different examinations. The amount of time wasted at present, simply through ignorance of the way to read, is so great that the Editor and Authors feel convinced of the necessity for some such handbooks, and they trust that these Guides will at least do something to prevent in the future the misapplication of so much industry.

Each volume will be confined to one branch of study, and will include an account of the various Scholarships and Prizes offered by the University or the Colleges in its department; and will be undertaken by a writer whose experience qualifies him to speak with authority on the subject.

The books will contain extracts from the University Statutes relating to the Examinations, with an attempt to explain them as they exist, and advice as to what to read and how to read; how to prepare subjects for examination, and how to answer papers; a few specimen questions, extracts from the Regulations of the Board of Studies, and a list of books.

THEOLOGY. By the Rev. F. H. WOODS, B.D., Fellow of St. John's College. Crown 8vo. cloth, 2s. 6d. [*Ready.*

OXFORD STUDY GUIDES—*continued.*

ENTRANCE CLASSICAL SCHOLARSHIPS. By S. H. JEYES, B.A., Classical Lecturer at University College, and late Scholar of Trinity College. Crown 8vo. cloth, 2s. 6d. [*Ready.*

'It is quite refreshing to find a guide to an examination that so thoroughly discourages cram.'—SCHOOL GUARDIAN, *June* 20, 1881.

'This is a smart book, and a useful comment on the present method of awarding scholarships. There is a certain frank cynicism in much of the advice, as when Mr. JEYES remarks, It is no good wearing out your trousers in a study chair, if you do not set your brains to work;" or that it " is quite useless to play at hide-and-seek with examiners who are familiar with every turn and twist in the game ;" and there seems little doubt that a clever boy, coached by him on his method, would get a scholarship.'—SPECTATOR, *Aug.* 27, 1881.

Mr. Jeyes has provided parents and teachers with an excellent manual by which to guide their sons or pupils in preparing for University Scholarships...... He gives directions as to the best way of preparing for the different sorts of papers...... and also for the best way of tackling with the paper when confronted with it in actual examination. The observations are of the most practical kind...... The book is well done, and ought to be useful.'—THE ACADEMY, *June* 18, 1881.

HONOUR CLASSICAL MODERATIONS. By L. R. FARNELL, B.A., Fellow of Exeter College. Crown 8vo. cloth, 2s. 6d. [*Ready.*

'It is full of useful and scholarly suggestions which many hard reading men will be thankful for......With hints as to the line of reading to be adopted, and the books to be taken up so as to make the most of their time, and to read to the best advantage.'
SCHOOL GUARDIAN, *November* 4, 1881.

LITERÆ HUMANIORES. By E. B. IWAN-MÜLLER, B.A., New College. [*Shortly.*

MODERN HISTORY. By F. S. PULLING, M.A., Exeter College. [*Shortly.*

NATURAL SCIENCE. By E. B. POULTON, M.A., Keble College. [*Shortly.*

JURISPRUDENCE and CIVIL LAW. By W. P. EMERTON, M.A., B.C.L., Christ Church. [*In preparation.*

MATHEMATICS.—*To be arranged for.*

www.ingramcontent.com/pod-product-compliance
Lightning Source LLC
Chambersburg PA
CBHW022011220426
43663CB00007B/1040